I0161079

TILOGOS

Books by Sherman P. Bastarache

Tilogos: A Treatise on the Origins and Evolution of Language
2012

Moral Indignation 2017

Idein Publishing

Tilogos is a 2013 book award finalist for non-fiction—Education in the Readers' Favorite Book Award Contest

****

Readers' Favorite Book Review: Five Star

"Tilogos" is a uniquely written book. I have never seen a book covering this topic. I found the topic interesting and comprehensive. Mr. Bastarache, you stimulated my brain and made me think of a totally different concept. Kudos.

Reviewed by Anne B. for Readers' Favorite

****

Feathered Quill Book Review: Four Star

Readers will truly see that this author offers a very investigative look at the evolution of language that explores, identifies and answers the question of how a variety of sounds can be strung together in order to produce words and actions. A unique text, this look into language stimulates the brain and will have many in the linguistics community listening and understanding what this author has to say.

Quill says: An extremely thought-provoking exposition that will open even more lines of communication.

Reviewed by: Amy Lignor, Feathered Quill Book Reviews

****

Self-Publishing Review

I did find myself going deeper than the actual building blocks of sounds to ponder linguistic communication and why it turned out that humans used it so intensely.

Self-Publishing Review: Catherine Tosko

TILOGOS

A TREATISE ON THE ORIGINS
AND EVOLUTION OF LANGUAGE

SHERMAN P. BASTARACHE

Tilogos
A Treatise on the Origins and Evolution of Language

Copyright © 2010 by Sherman P. Bastarache: Canada
1074449
Published in Canada by Idein Publishing 2013
ISBN 978-0-9921594-0-5

Copyright © 2011 by Sherman P. Bastarache
First published in the United States with iUniverse 2012
Library of Congress Control Number: 2012904492
ISBN: 978-1-4697-3461-3

All rights reserved. No part of this book may be used or
reproduced by any means, mechanically, electronically,
or by graphics, including photocopying. No part of this
book may be used in any information storage retrieval
system. Written permission from the publisher must be
obtained in all cases except in brief quotations
embodied in critical articles or reviews.

To my granddaughter,
Hailey Dawn Marie

Tear your world apart and explore.
Remember to put it back together
better than you found it.

All great truths begin as blasphemies.
—George Bernard Shaw

Book cover design by
Tiffany A. Bastarache

A special thank you

Contents

Preface

I was reading a book on a different subject one day, and it happened to mention language. I don't remember which book it was, so I can't quote it directly. I can give you the gist of it, though. I read a statement about it being impossible for a single sound to carry a meaning the same way words do. This became a strong trigger for my first observation on language.

When I was in my eighth-grade science class, my teacher, Mr. Steeves, was talking about evolution. One of the other students made the statement that language could never have evolved. I was looking at the blackboard, and the word *here* just happened to be written on it. Without much reflection, I said aloud, "Just adding a *t* to *here* changes the word to *there*."

I owe this teacher a debt of gratitude. He was also the principal of the school, and he gave me my first real life-altering break and made it possible for me to go on to high school. Due to certain circumstances, I had failed several grades. During my second year in eighth grade, when I made the aforementioned observation, I was given the opportunity to advance to tenth grade, high school, the following year if I passed that year, allowing me to skip ninth grade. All the teachers were very helpful, and I owe them much gratitude for their unselfish aid.

I worked hard in high school, but toward the end, I ran into trouble again. Going into my senior year, I was suddenly out on my own, jobless and moneyless. I was so determined to finish high school that I went to the welfare office and begged them to support me until I graduated. I paid room and board at my sister's, sleeping in her unfinished basement, and I did finish high school. Never give up trying to succeed!

Anyway, I did nothing about these thoughts on words or the evolution of language, and I had a pet name for evolution, being raised Christian: "evilution." The thought stuck with me all these long years, however: all you have to do is add *t* to *here* to get *there*. Even at that, it never quite clicked with me until recently, when I read the above-mentioned statement. I knew from a young age that I would never get to go to university, and I got a job right away, not getting back to this language issue until only a few years ago. I did meditate on it from time to time. I added to the observation above with a stretch of words over the years, and it is now the main body of this work. Even with all the *here* add-ons that I came up with, the light only came on recently, about three years or so ago, and my sound-word was born—and shortly after that, the idea of sound-cliché.

Mostly, I was bent on trying to find flaws in evilution and to show that language could never ever have evolved. With this observation I had already made, however—the *t here* thing—I found it difficult to discredit. Adding *t* to *here* is evolving the word *here* into the word *there*. Don't get me wrong—there are as many misunderstandings among scientists who do not have a proper concept of the possibility of a god as there are believers who don't understand the process of natural selection. As I made these self-arguments for and against evolution and creation—that's right, both sides—I began to see a process in which language very well could have evolved.

In trying to prove that language was created, I had to take certain liberties, and one of them was this: In order for each new generation to possess language in the creation theory, each word would have to have an innate meaning attached—straight from Adam and Eve, by the hand of God. Adam and Eve would have had words innately created, with concepts attached, as God did not or could not have trained them to speak without knowledge of meaning. This much is recorded in the Bible. Adam named things, language ready, from the start. From this observation, astute readers might see where this line of thinking got me from reading the first chapter, which deals in getting sound communication innate within the genome. I am glad I spent time reading the Bible.

As God did not create us from the ground but designed Adam and Eve to propagate the species, language would have to be innate within the genes. Each word would have to have its meaning created innately within us, or at least in the first man and woman. Without a fully innate meaning, or language to explain the meaning, how would you ever teach the first person to talk? As you can see, this loop needs to be opened somewhere, and I have spent considerable time reading many books on psychology, the workings of the brain and evolutionary thinking, and yes, the Bible, to come up with what I believe to be the answer.

Arguing for the evolution side, we see the same problem arise: it must be innate to some degree. I think that the first chapter handles this problem quite well and no further comments are needed. As I read more and more, I started to see things appear and blindly stumbled upon this process for evolving language. That's right—I readily admit it. I blindly stumbled upon a method of going from calls and cries into articulate speech. Actually, I made observations on how to get *noise communication* innate in the first place; how to evolve calls and cries, which is an analog communication system, into a digital word communication system.

Any book on language that I have ever read could not avoid taking into consideration aspects of the brain and how it works. I found myself having to do the same as well. After all, you can't go from an analog *Aaaaaa* into a digital *A* unless you talk about how the brain goes from analog into digital. In addition to all the other factors going into the makeup of conscious speech, I try to show that it is also a learned property.

According to Steven Pinker's *The Language Instinct*, algorithm is defined as an "explicit, step-by-step program or set of instructions for getting the solution to some problem." I use a step-by-step approach to show how communication can become innate, then altered and learned within our species of Homo sapiens, Latin for *wise* or *knowing man*.

I have discovered a type of algorithm that *some* aspects of language use to make a holistic concept divisible into its many separate smaller concepts. This allows meanings to be changed using the same phonemes combined with other phonemes, which have other meanings, into the words we use today.

Even though I use the word math to show how these transitions take place, you don't need to understand math at all. It is not real math, which you use to manipulate quantity or add and subtract numbers. You don't need to know that one plus one equals two. Nor do you need to know that five is a square number embedded in twenty-five somehow. You only need to know the concept of adding, subtracting, dividing, and multiplying without the work or corresponding numbers. It is just a tool to show how I believe words are made. In fact, I avoid any real math just as one avoids the plague.

Finally, I found it impossible to forget the earlier observations I made about language and began to observe how people in general used language naturally.

I was blessed enough to have had two wonderful daughters, who I would not trade for my life, to have observed growing up. Although admittedly they have taught me more about love and life than I have taught them. My daughters have helped me understand one of the biggest problems of language. If children don't learn to speak unless taught, who was the first to teach language? As my beloved granddaughter teaches me to love anew, she has reinforced this notion and strengthened my resolve.

Chapter One

The Innateness of Language

The most tender care and anxious solicitude for their infant offspring is an innate idea throughout the wide extent of animal nature, much more strongly imprinted on the minds of females than of males. A wise institution of providence, for which various reasons will easily occur to the intelligent reader, and which we need not therefore take the trouble of pointing out.

—William Alexander
The History of Women

It is one thing to say that something is innate and quite another to prove it to be. Innate is the term used for any property, action, or response that you are born "knowing" or "having" without having learned it; instincts are innate. The instinct to suckle as a baby is innate even though practice is required to perfect it or hardwire it into the brain. The innateness of an instinct is what gets the creature in question to perform the necessary task, which fires the synapses used for the task, causing them to become hardwired into permanent, precise functions within the brain. Most if not all of the literature I have read on language acquisition makes the assumption that language is an innate property of the human species. Some authors push that many species of animals have some form of language, while other authors refute this. This argument is outside the scope of this work, and I won't enter into the topic here. I only attempt to show throughout this work what can be innate and what cannot be. This chapter deals with getting noise communication into the genome of the various species as we climb the tree of descent to higher forms.

If we are to believe that the line of descent, beginning with the first creature formed in the steamy waters of our cooling planet, up through placental divergence until this very day, is one continuous, uninterrupted chain, then we must admit that both these terms as true. All animals have some form of innate communication and other forms of communication that are learned. The innate form is passed on to the offspring in the direct form or in a divergent form. The divergent form, of course, would be a slightly different call or cry—as we are dealing in language—like going from the bark of a wolf to the bark of a fox, which differ enough to serve a different niche. Some forms of communication are silent and could not lead to verbal communication but would serve as body language. The ones that are not silent are the ones I will mainly contend with throughout this work, while not ignoring the silent ones completely.

In the simplest terms I can think of to sum up the scientific literature, there are two different ways of thinking about language, one which says that there is actually enough time to learn language without anything being innate except the propensity to learn. This strongly suggests that language was invented and learned, which I will reasonably show to be impossible. The second way of thinking says that grammar is innate, but languages differ in word or tongue but not structure. I have spent the better part of my life contemplating the whole issue, while making any observations I could and researching what information I could find within my means. I believe that I have gathered enough information and ideas to finally write this book. This would be just another book on language speculation if I did not show sufficiently how language could have become innate and passed on through the divergence of the species.

I want to have some contrast and choice to offer you, the reader, on how it could ever be possible to have language become innate. Truly, I have only recently thought of a more reasonable way of getting to the position of having neurons assigned meaningful sounds innately, and I was going to fall, as it were, on this first explanation as the most reasonable one, if not the most probable one, to have happened. This shows that at least there is more than one way to have the innate propensity of language occur in the diversified species of animals. I will use my originally intended idea here as the first example of getting language innate within the genome, but I plan to work throughout the rest of this book using my own original example, as I feel it to be closer to the truth.

The first example is the Baldwin effect, which is now accepted as evolutionarily possible by some but not all scientists. The Baldwin effect predicts that a single sound representing a concept could become innately transferred to offspring. For instance, the sound *o* becomes innate in the adult brain as the concept for "predator" or "leopard," and it is passed on genetically to the unborn offspring. To show the possibility of this, I compare it to and contend it to be no less probable than in the shape recognition system hypothesized as "geons." Pinker does a good job of describing the ability of seeing shapes innately using a hypothesis first put forth by Marr and then expanded upon by

Biederman. Pinker also contrasts the Baldwin effect with genetic assimilation learning, a slightly better alteration of the Baldwin effect as described in *How the Mind Works*, by Steven Pinker.

In the simplest terms I can think of, the Baldwin effect predicts that any species that has the tendency to perform a nonbiological *learned* act can pass the learning tendency toward that act—promoted by better survival—into the next generation. If the next generation of species holds the tendency toward this learned act, eventually it will become a selected trait, not tendency, making it an inheritable characteristic, the same as better vision or hearing is selected for. This gives us the geons as a comparison for selecting the innateness of language, and I shall quickly go over the details, for they hold value in seeing why combinations of sounds containing information are both possible and needed.

Geons are shapes that have become represented in the brain as a particular hardwired neural shape: examples by Pinker are "a cone, a megaphone, a football, a tube, a cube, and a piece of elbow macaroni." They are innately recognized by the neurons of the brain, so they don't have to be learned with each new generation. To put it clearly in context, a brain will automatically be grown with the neuron knowing the shape when seen. A small set of shapes, they go into making up every other shape possible. I wondered why sounds going into words would be any different—that is, calls and cries. If the brain had a tendency to fire the same neurons for the same shape all the time, then it would be possible to pass these shape-firing neurons on through the germ line—discussed below—which is separate from the passed on genes that go into your phenotype makeup. You would pass on the neurological tendency to fire the same shape recognition in the same brain area, thus crossing the germ line boundary. Why is it that we would not think of the same thing happening to sounds representing concepts?

Geons, according to Pinker, takes its name from a term used in physics. I am not quite sure of the word used but believe it to be "gluons." It is intended to relay shape recognition into physics terms. Marr, whose idea it was originally, might have intended it to make the analogy of protons and electrons going into the makeup of atoms and different atoms making up different molecules the same as smaller shapes make bigger shapes by combination. It is an analogy fitting for my purpose in this work, so I will elaborate a little, at the same time going even smaller, as it makes the perfect tool for language innateness.

It takes quarks—smaller particles—to make up the neuron (one up quark and two down quarks) or the proton (two up quarks and one down quark) of atomic nuclei. These are physics terms, and I am not going to go deeply into physics or chemistry, only summarize them, for we only need to see the comparison to use the analogy. These protons and neutrons form the center of the atom, and the electrons orbit—actually, electrons are probability clouds—the nucleus of the atom. Atoms combine into molecules and comprise the different substances. The idea for the comparison is that smaller shapes (geons) go into making up slightly bigger ones, which combine into, say, mountains or trees, the same way that up and down quarks make protons, neutrons, and electrons, combining into atoms. Atoms then combine into molecules, which make up everything else. Therefore, if the smallest shapes—geons—were innate, only the combination would need to be learned: innate curve shapes add up to learned circles. My question would be this: why would language be any different? You need different frequencies of vibrations to make different sounds. You need phonemes—smallest intelligible sounds—added to make syllables, which get added to make words. The real problem of language is how to get sound to mean anything.

Genetic assimilation learning theory differs slightly, as it has some synaptic connections preset and some that are ready to be set with prompting from the environment. The brain is set to innately code a triangle, let's say, as soon as one is seen, instead of having to take the time to learn about a triangle with each new generation. I wondered why hearing some sounds, set to fault state, the same way would be any different. For a better description of how these geons in shape recognition and genetic assimilation work, I will refer the reader to *How the Mind Works* by Steven Pinker. However, I will relate these to language becoming innate within the many species of animals.

Is it possible that there are a finite number of concepts that could attach themselves to single or multiple vibration sounds, eventually leading to a consonant/vowel combination? It would work the same as the purposed geons: a sound, any sound, could thus become innate with any concept attached to it. I will make a statement here, leaving it without comment until a later chapter. The brain is neither wired in series nor parallel, but in series-parallel (technically all three) redundantly. Priority is given to survival, then necessities, and then pleasures, with attention sometimes overriding them. Therefore, if the brain is wired this way, by default, then "thought" must also be series-parallel—riding on the back of the neurological wiring—redundant in structure, with priority given to survival. We are less likely to forget the word "help" if we fall into a pit, which is an innate concept and appears without reflection, naturally, verses forgetting the name of this machine I am typing on. This machine is not, nor could it ever be, an innate concept, which is just a name placed on acquired knowledge or objects—in this case, a computer keyboard. This is the importance of having actions, words, and shapes completely innate and not having to learn them with each new generation of the same species. Learning takes precious time and effort and does

TILOGOS

not guarantee that the next generation will even learn it. If there is even such a thing as being extremely important to evolution, this is one of the more important factors: accumulation of traits.

We may have an innateness to name things in order to communicate about them, and such names would have to be learned and recalled, as opposed to names that could be considered innate, such as calls and cries. These are two different things, and I will here exclude the possible innateness to name things, as doing so requires an "I get it" and places the naming process into the realm of learning, which I will expound fully in a future chapter. If one falls and hurts himself, an automatic innate cry for assistance appears without reflection: *Help!* Anyone who cried for help and got it right would likely pass on his genes. I have yet to have to sit there and think, *Now, what do you call the request for aid again? Oh yeah: help!* On the other hand, quite often—actually, quite regularly—I have to think hard to recall a person's name or the name of an object. If we had an innate concept/word system, the same as an innate shape system, speaking would be as natural as seeing.

These theories—the Baldwin effect and genetic assimilation—have one thing in common: they must cross a barrier. When you were conceived, your DNA was actually divided. A duplicate set of the recombined DNA from both your parents—the DNA in the mother's egg and the DNA in the father's sperm—was separated into two distinct but identical entities. One became you, and the other one became known as your germ line. The germ line makes the eggs of the female and the sperm of the male. The one that became the germ line was in itself renewed.

I won't get into how this renewal was done, but it is important that it was done. After all, it does have to be passed down from generation to generation, without growing old as our genotype/phenotypes do. (The genotype being the combined genes

7

collectively, which are the instructions for making a phenotype. The phenotype is the actual result or body of the creature in question.) This is one of the reasons that germ line is separate and does not change with your body and cannot inherit your learned behaviors. Learned behaviors being, in this case, language, behaviors leaned by your phenotype throughout your life to aid in your survival. I have thought of a way in which this boundary between the germ line and your genotype/phenotype would not even need to be crossed at all. This is the second version that I mentioned. The need to not relearn with each new generation still holds, as do some of the other comments I have already made.

I like the second version better because it is a lineal explanation, and I believe it is a more accurate picture of what has actually transpired, if not the actual transpiration itself. We have all heard "Go big or go home," but I think that when it comes to language, we should go small or not at all: let's try to go reductio ad absurdum. Because I got this idea handed to me on a silver platter while reading something on single-cell communication via chemical signaling, we shall start there. No chemistry, please!

Let us start from the beginning and remotest point in the earth's history, that of the single-celled life form. Any single-celled life form that could sense where food was would be more likely to survive and leave more descendants. All foods are made of molecules, and all molecules have the chemical structure of a specific makeup. It is no problem having chemicals attracted to chemical receptacles for recognition; no one disputes this.

Simply stated, it lies in the way negative and positive charges attract or repel. In the case of proteins, it depends on the way they are folded. Some proteins will or will not fit a specific fold in another protein. The ones that fit the fold would be recognized as such *due to no other reason than their fitting*: no knowledge required at this level. Molecules work the same in "thought" as proteins do. Either they fit together or they do not. Think of water. It is made up from two hydrogen atoms and one oxygen atom. They stop being atoms and become molecules when they become joined together and form water. You can't smell oxygen because it is always present, and you do not need to find it to survive. Animals can smell water sometimes for miles because it is necessary for survival.

In order to avoid losing you, I will not go any deeper into chemistry. I will instead place both of them into another analogy—that of a jigsaw puzzle. Every individual piece of a jigsaw puzzle will only "fit" a certain way into another piece of the same puzzle. If jigsaw puzzles were separate species, the same species would have the same "fit" and other species would have a different "fit," the same way as two different sceneries of jigsaw puzzles.

All life forms—in fact, everything with a chemical makeup—emit chemicals that will "fit" a chemical receptor in some way differently than other chemicals do. Amoebas are different from E. coli and have some different chemical structures that could come to be recognized as different from or the same as the fit of the chemical signature, if nothing else. You can't even go on the Internet without seeing some sexual headline for mate attraction claiming that we are attracted to our mates due to pheromones. The reason is that different DNA structures smell different from others. We are more attracted to potential mates with different DNA structure for the sake of our offspring's survival advantage, but that will not get us to the topic of language.

Single-celled life forms don't smell "proper" but sense chemically: receptors recognize chemicals from their chemical makeup. By proper, it is meant that they don't have brains to say the smell is this or that. It is the starting point of smell, though. Therefore, on the same grounds as food recognition mentioned above, any single-celled life forms that could chemically sense where their enemies were, and could thus avoid them, would also prosper. So through chemical sensation, the survivors would prosper and subsequently pass on their genetic traits to the next generation: that of chemical sensation and *completely innate by default*.

As much as I can remember, all single-celled life forms are asexually reproduced (meaning that because they self-multiply, two individual specimens don't trade DNA through the act of sex), so the drive for food and the avoidance of enemies would be the only true requirements for survival. On average, the surviving offspring would inherit a mean average of these traits, which is the most important requirement for us to remember—actually, it would be natural due to the properties of chemical makeup. Innately, if they could chemically sense food, they could eat food; and if they could chemically sense their enemies, they could avoid them. Those that could not sense food or their enemies would quickly perish, or at least be replaced by those who could. Truly, to go any smaller than this, I would have to enter too deeply into the realm of chemistry and physics: not!

On the other hand, sexual life forms have an additional requirement: finding a member of the opposite sex and of the same species. They would have this innate characteristic included naturally when they evolved from asexual into the sexually reproductive stage. I believe that Fere Charles was the first to observe that chemical attraction was the driving factor in homosexual attraction in insects, which is well commented on in his book *The Evolution and Dissolution of the Sexual Instinct*.

It is known that sexual odours are perceived at considerable distances by insects, and it is these odours which seem to play the most important part in sexual excitement. A male cockchafer which has just indulged in copulation is naturally tainted with odours well-calculated to attract another male, and, moreover, he is half-dead from exhaustion, and quite incapable of resistance; he cannot do otherwise than submit to the mistaken conduct of his brother male, even as the males of other species which have been emasculated by a parasite.

He also writes:

Some time ago I made reservations about M. deKerville's assertion, believing that the odour of the females with which the male may be impregnated is able to cause anomalous sexual conduct.

Both of these examples have one thing in common: *all the life forms know innately*, albeit not necessarily consciously, that these chemical odors are emitted for the purpose of sexual reproduction. Of course, today we don't call them odors. We call them pheromones, representing small units of smell. Phonemes are small units of sound, which I will be discussing later. In the case of sexual species, if a female emits a chemical, *all males of that species sense and respond with sexual interest, instead of the interest in food or flight from enemies, which they also know.* This is a species-wide innate concept of mating by chemical attraction. This also leaves us with three different concepts, and it's not even lunchtime yet: food, enemies, and sexual attraction. In fact, as we climb the scale to higher species of animals, we know that each individual male knows what the other males all know. The most-used example within literature is likely the cockfights in competition for the right to mate with hens in most species of fowls.

Now we can write about everyone's favorite topic: sex. If a call is specific to sex, the whole concept would be much like what follows. Sound triggers the nerve, which triggers the other nerve, which in turn triggers the other nerve. In plain English, the sex call says to the male, "I feel a tingle, and this tingle means that I am supposed to relieve the tingle." We get within this sound the combined concepts of everything needed for sexual reproduction and more: both male and female genitals, relief, opposite sex, reproduction, lucky three Saturday nights in a row—yahoo! Everything needed in one complete sound concept, or "call."

Also worth noting before moving on is the fact that these creatures mentioned above do not recognize male/female differences except for the odors themselves. The chemical attraction from the female odors and the male receptors for those chemicals blindly do the work of sexual reproduction.

A few years ago, I read a book that had within its pages one of the best ideas I have ever read. The author wrote about the widowbirds and their long tails. I have read experiments on testing for the male widowbirds long tail selection in books both before and after reading this book, but the female genes are never mentioned, just her attraction to long tails.

It is one thing to say that females or males have a quality that attracts the opposite sex and is innately recognized by both, but the reason for it must be answered. Richard Dawkins's description nailed it perfectly. I will hit the highlights. If the female is sexually attracted to the males with the longest tails, then there must be a reason. It's one thing for a tail gene to mutate and grow a longer tail, but beauty will not of necessity ensue. The male birds are the only ones with the longer tails, by the way, so it's not a two-way selection. However, Dawkins points out that the genes are in both the male and female genome in different forms and could have different consequences within each genome. The gene for long tails being produced in the males is also in the female genome. The attraction for longer tails gene is also carried within the male genome. Brilliant! I quote:

The general conclusion is this. Any individual, of either sex, is likely to contain *both* genes for making males *have* a certain quality, *and* genes for making females *prefer* that selfsame quality, whatever that quality might be. (Dawkins, *The Blind Watchmaker*, 202)

Of course, this would work both ways, and I will alter the above quote to show the reverse is true: Any individual, of either sex, is likely to contain *both* genes for making females *have* a certain quality *and* genes for making males *prefer* that selfsame quality, whatever that quality might be.

The long-tail gene is also carried with the attraction-to-the-long-tail gene, and it solves my problem as well. It will work for the odors that females produce for sexual attraction, which males do not produce, but are attracted to, just as well as it does for long tails selection.

You are probably wondering what this has to do with language. Let's add some language and see! Languages are just sounds, and the problem with sexually useful sounds is that both genders do not make the same sounds. In some species, the males make the mating calls, and in some species, the females do. The same gene for the sexual call or cry can now be the same gene for the attraction to the sexual call, cry, or better yet, noise. Any noise produced for sexual attraction innate within the genome will also be the gene corresponding in the opposite sex for attraction to the sound for mating.

If we should add some language into the mix, we see that the action, whatever it is, and the name placed on the action now become innate and inseparable in complete concept. Complete concept will be discussed below it more detail, but for now, I want to establish sounds in general so we have something to evolve. It matters not one iota what the word is—from a tweet to a growl to a squeal—as long as it meets the already set requirements just mentioned. All members of the same species innately know what the sound refers to, in the same manner as chemical sensation. (Not restricted to the same species, as we recognize many different species from the noises they make.) Surely the reader can see how a cricket sound could become a mating sound for the same species (crickets) and a food sound for predators: eat that sound. Is it harder to believe noise selection over chemical selection? If you are capable of making any noise, then all the other members of your species are capable of making the same noise or recognizing it.

It could be said that the entire bird family produces songs during mating season. Frogs croak all night long in their marshes and swamps for the purpose of attracting mates. Even insects have mating calls, but they are produced by limbs vibrating or being rubbed together, or other similar methods, and they still qualify for noises produced for sexual purposes.

Now, language is not worth a darn thing it you can't hear anything. (I will omit until later the complications of the deaf and sign languages, as they do not concern us at this early stage.) Since I am looking for innate sounds, I must start small, and this leaves me having to add my own commentary on hearing, as I have little other information. I am not a biologist. If I had to look up the names for everything, I would forget the names as soon as I closed the book anyway. I will therefore use common language that can be readily understood.

The rubbing together of appendages makes vibrating sounds, the noise in most of the noise-producing insects. They have no mouths or voice boxes. Voice boxes would have to become manifested by whatever means has transpired and been selected for. Technically, our voice boxes are our appendages. That said, what good are they? None! We need a means of hearing them. Getting hearing from nothing is just as difficult a problem as getting sight from nothing at all. Sight at least had photosensitive cells to start with. The literature is also infested with the evolution of vision.

Remember, I am still working toward an entry point of making language, or more properly at this point, calls and cries. No, we must start smaller than calls and cries! Reductio ad absurdum and calls and cries are not that, for we can go smaller and still be intelligible. Remember, I started out with chemical selection within single-celled animals. I negated the chemistry. Vibrations are as small as I can go, I think, unless I want to get into physics and talk about the properties of space, atoms, and particles, which I will also negate.

All sounds are made up of vibrations in different frequencies, just as all light is made up of waves, or wavelengths. We see different colors of the world as these wavelengths are reflected from the different objects as they absorb some frequencies and reflect others. We hear sound wave lengths from the different frequencies of the vibrations produced. Vibrations occur or can be made naturally by the environment, such as from earthquakes or tremor, falling stones, or thunder from lightning strikes. These naturally occurring vibrations mean little in selecting for innate speech, however.

I started with insects for this very reason; they are small, older forms of life. Some have been replaced with new varieties, and some varieties are still quite ancient. Any insect, and I won't pick a specific one, that had rough appendages for the selected purpose of grinding down harder materials would make vibrations in the grinding process. These vibrations could be *felt* by nearby organisms of the same species or by predators, the same way one feels the bass in the pit of his stomach while listening to Deep Purple's "Smoke on the Water." The ability could be adapted to the rubbing of the two appendages together for, say, cleaning small particles of dirt from their bodies. This could also be used to make noise. If one member of the unsaid species had the ability to make the noise, and the noise in itself made a survival advantage—such as for cleaning, as I proposed—then every member of the species would have the same ability or at least be susceptible to the recognition of the noise. No one would hear the noise in the beginning.

By the way, air vibration has been known since at least Aristotle's time, as he wrote on it from other earlier sources, however inaccurate they thought it. Since the ancient Greeks, it is understood and well established that the air carries these vibrations, but it need not even be invoked at first. If the vibrations were to travel through dead tree stumps, for instance, they could be felt by other insects. I use the term "felt" literally, as everything is actually felt by the senses and cognizant by the brain in all higher animals possessing brains.

I must interrupt the flow here and define my meaning of the word cognizant for clarity sake. "Cognizant" stems from the words cognate, or cognition. Cognition is understood to mean the *first time the knowledge is presented.* By adding *re* to the word cognition, it becomes the word recognition and understood to be the second, third, fourth … time that the knowledge is represented. My use of cognizant here would be closer to the act of cognition: recognize. So these feelings would become cognized as meaning something unconsciously, of course, within the nerves of lower animals. In the beginning, there would only be vibrations felt, no cognition proper of the feelings past blind responses to the stimuli. Brains are needed for the purpose of cognition in knowledge form. These vibrations would allow all other species of insects to have the possibility of feeling them too. This is probably the most important thing: whatever vibrations each species of insect made would be felt as its own. Another type of vibration would be either food or predator. There would be selective pressure to differentiate vibrations from other species as well as one's own.

Dawkins also has a sound explanation of sonar hearing in bats in place of vision in *The Blind Watchmaker*, which is worth reading, and I will quote him on "feeling" in general:

> Experiments showed that, in fact, "facial vision" is nothing to do with touch or the front of the face, although the sensation may be *referred* to the front of the face, like the referred pain in phantom (severed) limb. The sensation of "facial vision," it turns out, really goes in through the ears.

A few comments on feelings are in order here. It is conceivable that any nerve-bearing animal could have a different nerve or synaptic firing—dealt with better later—specific to a certain vibration. The vibration causing nervation—the activation of nerves—would mean something. Combined vibrations would mean something else. Chemical sensation, as I said, would involve chemical receptors for recognition, and these nervations with vibrations would act the same as chemical receptors—that is, as the same purpose of recognition: the silver platter.

As we leave insects and climb higher in the tree of life, we see nervous systems and then brains develop and start the cognition process completely unconscious at first. Then it begins to become conscious as we enter into the early stages of the Homo species. I will stop here with these statements, as I don't yet want to be at this stage of the work on hearing. I will stay with insects or a slight advancement in species selection for now, returning to brains and higher hearing later.

The next advancement for a better system would be any species of insect that had a better way of feeling these vibrations. I am not a biologist, so I won't foolishly try to explain how it could be done and will leave it for a slightly higher-level animal. A slightly more complex animal with the ability to make a vibration noise, and also having any mechanism that could amplify the sound wave vibration, would do. I will pick a system and evolve it. Any bone surrounded by flesh of some kind and having nervation around that flesh/bone area, with the bone freed from any other use by the species in question, would do.

A loose, freed bone would vibrate slightly more and amplify the sound waves better. It would do this by moving on the nerves at different frequencies—firing the nerves at faster or slower intervals—and some vibration frequencies could come to mean pain, while others would come to mean pleasure, without the cognition. The movement would either be good and calming or poor and alarming. The whole idea of different sounds or vibrations becoming recognized by neurons assigned to them rests on this little fact somewhat, although if it is wrong in the details, I am close enough in theory that it will not be all that destructive to me.

You make a vibrating noise, as do all other members of your species, or at least you can form attraction to the noise by the feel. If they felt these vibrations, they would "know" (feel) that they were the *same* vibrations they themselves, or their kind, produced. There is comfort in numbers, and these sounds would provide comfort. They would convey that it is one's own species, offering safety. Or they could signal that a member of the species is ready to mate. We have a vibration for mating now, *a concept even if it is not conscious.*

If a female of any species of animal had a biological reason or biological urge to make any movement in preparation for the act of sexual intercourse, and that movement produced any sound, it would become a mating call. Since the reason is biological and all members of the same species "know" the noise innately, it can become part of the genotype.

We have crossed the germ line barrier for sounds without crossing it at all. Now selection is free to act on the first source of "hearing" and push for improvements. It now stands on the same ground as the eye, starting from a photosensitive cell. I will evolve it somewhat more, but not in any great detail. Any animal that had freer vibration space around this bone had more unrestricted space to vibrate in, and a slightly more complex form of nervation—better nervous system—would be more discreet in feeling sound vibrations better. She would be able to find her prey easier and be better at avoiding her vibrating predators. Selection!

A better air gap between the bones and flesh would serve better, as they would pick up vibrations from the air: an ear proper has an air space. As it turns out, a bone became disused from another process and was adapted into sound use. The bone in question was believed to be from a jaw, which underwent change, leaving an isolated bone free to be used for another purpose. This freed jaw bone is the current starting point for hearing in most accounts on the evolution of hearing and how it works.

This is far enough for me to go, as I just need to show how it would cross the great genetic germ line barrier and lead to speech. From here, we could have the use of more, different sounds from the same species, thus expanding our sound concepts and evolving calls and cries, which is where I want to be—at least on getting hearing established.

Now back to appendages. Feeling these appendages vibrate through the body leads to feeling them vibrate through the air. We can still hear cricket vibrations, but we can also hear air vibrating as a higher selected form of hearing. We can go to just making the air vibrate, without any rubbing together of appendages felt though solids—or liquids, for that matter. Both you and I can hear simple breathing, heavy breathing, and the holding of our breath when silence is needed to avoid detection. We can make the air in our lungs do the work of rubbing two appendages together. If you blow air across elastic, it will vibrate and make a sound; different tensions applied to the elastic will make different sounds. The same holds true of your voice box, which is the term I'm using generically rather than trying to recall all the separate parts. Our appendages are our soft tissue voice boxes vibrating with air. Incidentally, for the interested reader, in his book *The Language Instinct*, Steven Pinker has a good description of how the voice box and its constituting parts work in producing our sounds and language in general.

To make sure these previous pages are perfectly understood, I will recap in the simplest terms I can think of. Bananas smell different from garlic. They each have a distinct smell because they each have a distinctly different chemical makeup. The chemical makeup has receptors in our noses that "fit" the chemical makeup of the banana differently than the garlic. These have been selected for match, with each new generation acquiring them for food, as opposed to toxins. Actually, taste is chemically based as well and uses the same system of selection. That is, smell is what gives taste to foods. The tongue only tastes sweet, salty, and two or three other differences. Within this paragraph, you should be able to see how chemicals lead to food selection. *The Scent of Desire* by Rachel Herz has a great description of smell, taste, and some surprises, and I would refer you to her work.

Analogous to this is noise. Noise is made up of different tones, frequencies, pitch, notes, decibels, and whatever else has been used from time to time to describe sound. Not that much different from chemical makeup, is it? Different combined sounds, or sounds in general, distinguish different things in general. The receptors of sounds are not chemically recognized, but they are vibration recognized, the vibration receptors being the nervous system in general, feeling these vibrations and growing into a sound-specific system, with the matching receptors of the different sounds as feelings. This has become known as hearing but has evolved from the sounds or vibrations being recognized and making use of them. Just like with chemicals, then, we can say that these vibrations "fit" vibration receptors. Chemical smell receptors would prevent you from eating toxic foods; vibration receptors would recognize predator vibrations and help you avoid being eaten by them. Think of the common supposition, that insects hear with antennae instead of ears.

As the mix of chemicals makes substances and gives these substances their odors, the mix of vibrations gives calls and cries their different complete sounds. This is the geons comparison from the start of the chapter. This is also true of words; think of the alphabet. This presents a problem, though: getting enough calls into words, which is impossible. I will at length deal with the problem in the following chapters, but for now I will ignore it and concentrate on other feelings. All things that we perceive are perceived by feeling of some sort. Sight feels light waves in the different frequencies; touch has the feelings of hard, soft, rough, smooth ... Anything we can't feel by some means, we can't recognize to exist in any form. The biggest problem is getting learned behavior through the germ line with all of the senses of feelings, and I believe this thesis to be a sound enough explanation.

This is not all-new science, by the way. Studies were and are preformed on hearing disabilities almost continually, and many of the points I have been making have been derived from these studies. *The Mind and the Brain* by Jeffrey M. Schwartz MD talks about phonemes not having neurons assigned to them, and children often don't learn words because they miss these sounds. If it is a defect in physiology and can be discovered as unassigned neurons, then it shows that neurons are "assigned sounds," at least close to how I have described the process in the first place. *The Mind and the Brain* will be reintroduced in a later chapter.

With this, the barrier is now broken between vibrating solid things for sound transfer into making air vibrate at different decibels, frequencies, or tones for sound transfer. The germ line barrier is broken without magic. Life is good! We have the ability to produce more innate sounds. These sounds become calls and cries, making more complete innate concepts. We now hear these vibrations as "hearing proper" the same way I use "speech proper" for speaking the vibrations with the same end result: what we currently have in use as opposed to proto-sound or protolanguage. That we need all our species to have the same sounds, meaning the same things, in total concept form is the whole basis of communication. I will discuss total concept form in detail below.

For now, it's back to our search for language, sounds, and concepts. The yelp of a dog in pain is an automatic response, such as when someone steps on its tail. All dogs can yelp, and yelp equals the word for pain, which was carried over from wolves in this case. We don't actually call them words—and neither do wolves. If a wolf did not innately know that her pups' yelps were from pain, possibly from an enemy attack, then she would not know to defend them from whatever enemy was attacking, thus losing all her pups instead of one. Her pups would not survive to leave descendants; she would be the end of her lineage.

I am not what one would call a pet lover by any stretch of the imagination. I would gladly live my life without pets at all. My children wanted a dog, and I was out numbered. One day, I made an observation. Every time the dog would get hurt, it would yelp. I would automatically think to myself, *What did that dog do to get hurt this time?* Sometimes ignorance dawns slowly. I automatically associated this yelp with pain. Since we already had the dog, I began to observe the other noises it made and tried to establish its vocabulary.

All pet lovers will tell you that their pets really do communicate with them. We recognize from dogs that they have different barks, and being a different species, we know what these barks mean without reflection. The dog barks and we automatically go to the door to see who is walking up the driveway. It barks another way and we check his or her water or food supply without thinking twice. Late at night, if the dog jumps up and growls, we automatically have the feeling of fear well up inside of us.

I read about the noises, or "language," of animals from all kinds of sources but did not think much about it. Most of the scientific literature was in conflict anyway. Some authors said that they were not really "words" or "language" per se. Some other unnamed sources argued that they were words but had no real content. They claimed that the animal noises were more subtle and maybe had a huge concept that was too varied to be of any use in communication at all. Examining the vervet monkeys, I will look at this argument in more detail to elaborate on this confusion. For now, I will say that I have no problem with this, and it will not stop my method from evolving language at all, so long as these noises are *innately recognized species-wide* for the same purpose as I have tried to contend so far.

We see from this other examples that hit the mark, in dogs at least. If one dog barks (specific bark), any other dog will automatically start barking the same bark even if it has not heard the same noise, from, let's say, a visitor. They innately know that this particular bark is the noise (sound-word) for the concept of intruder. All dogs—and wolves from whence dogs were bred—have a vicious growl. Moreover, they all innately know that this growl means that every other dog/wolf is ready to defend or do battle. I read somewhere that the word growl came from the *grrrrr* sound in describing the noise wolves make.

Dogs yawn, as do cats and many, if not all, other animals, which is, according to the latest theory, a means to stimulate the brain and body into attention, at least in humans. It is a form of communication signaling, often accompanied with a sigh noise. The value of this could be to put your offspring into synchronization with you as the best survival advantage, thus explaining its contagion to others; this is all completely innate and "total concept present" in all survivors of the past. Dogs also have barks for play and to get your attention. They have whining noises and moans and groans that express pleasure they might receive from relief from an itch, perhaps what they feel when they receive a good belly rub.

As far as humans go, we do have some innate noises that manifest themselves immediately after birth, even before our brains are wired for perfect tongue control:

> Furthermore, mothers have an innate ability that makes them very sensitive to the babies' cries. There are four identifiable types of crying—pain, hunger, boredom, and discomfort—which are apparently distinguishable by the mother by the end of the second week, and by the third day, a mother can distinguish her baby's cry from that of other newborns. (*The Interactional Instinct:* Namhee Lee et al.)

I might add here that babies also employ a fake cry for attention or other purposes. What is language if not communication?

The crying of a baby at times sounds just like crying, but when it's exaggerated, the sound leaves off at being a noise and becomes a *whaaa* in the form of an almost perfectly articulated word, complete with exaggerated vowel-sound proper. It is easy to make out the difference in one- to two-month-old babies. It is not a fake cry; it just sounds more like a word being said than actual crying—a very well pronounced word to my ear.

> The groundbreaking research of Saffran, Aslin, and Newport (1996) demonstrated that eight-month-old infants can extract wordlike strings of phonemes from the statistical properties of the input after only two minutes of exposure. Specifically, the researchers provide evidence that infants can distinguish syllables that regularly appear together from those that are randomly juxtaposed.
>
> (Namhee Lee, *The Interactional Instinct*)

This shows the real importance of random sounds from the world versus actual sounds that have or will come to have meaning being as innate as possible for a genome to acquire. If this is the case—and it seems sound enough—it would eliminate any need to call upon voodoo, newts, or toad bodily parts, and make stiff competition for the Baldwin effect, at least in the case of language acquisition. From what I have written above in this chapter, or at least what I understand of my thinking, I see no problem with evolving language from these last two quotes in *The Interactional Instinct*. One shows differences in cries and the other in syllables. I must at least show how in practical terms sounds could become meaningful, or as meaningful as brain power will allow without cognition of cognition. This is the task of the last few pages.

In the previous few pages, I have used terms without attaching meanings or defining their scope of usage, and I would like to do so before moving on. When I use the term *sound*, I am strictly referring to any sound whatsoever that could be innately used as a form of communication, not restricting it to the magic sounds in the letters of the alphabet. This could include sounds that other species of animals (inclusive sense) make and noises occurring naturally, such as thunder. The term sound-word will be well defined and dealt with in a later chapter.

When I use the term *concept* in some cases, and in all cases the term *total concept*, or *total complete concept*, I am referring to any and every aspect involved with said concept: generally called *holistic*. An example would be water, which would have the total concept of wet, thirst, drown, swim, rain, snow, ice, wash, clouds ...

Like us, the Amazon natives name animals from their sounds: João corta pao is the name of a Brazilian bird that makes that sound. Tanana is the name of an insect that produces the sound *ta-na-na*. I don't consider myself to be a great observer of nature, but I have, however, taken the time to make one observation that did stick with me.

Poecile atricapillus, or black-capped chickadee, does not really say *chick-a-dee-dee-dee* but produces that sound in more of a *buzzing* form. To place a name on the buzzing sounds, we name them *chick-a-dee-dee-dee*, or just a chickadee. The sound *chick-a-dee-dee-dee* is made up of several notes that combine into that sound at different frequencies. These different notes at different frequencies fire the vibration receptors in recognition of these sounds in the analogous way that chemical receptors for smell do. *Chick-a-dee-dee-dee* is a long call as far as calls go. If no other content is to be found in this call, it says to its fellows, "I am here and of the same species," giving it meaning or concept. The concept to us is the name of the bird that makes that sound. So we get bird, flying, and feathers from that, but we also understand that as long as there is noise, it is at least safe from its predators. If we had a mutual predator, recognizing safety when the bird sang and being aware of when it stopped would become a survival advantage and a concept.

Also, these chickadees have a different call for mating. How do we know that this first call is not in fact just a call that says, "The location I am at is safe." When the call stops, that area is no longer safe, and the woods suddenly become silent. We don't know anything of this nature, only that these calls are innate.

Vervet monkeys are the most commonly used example throughout the scientific literature that I have read. If you pick up a book on language or evolution, it is almost guaranteed to have some commentary on vervet monkeys. The most common statements made about them are their distinct calls for different predators. As I will later be using some material from *Adam's Tongue* by Derek Bickerton for other purposes, I will refer the reader to the comments on vervet monkeys made by this author.

In this first chapter, we have covered how it came to pass that calls and cries could become innate, complete with the total concept. There is some dispute as to what these calls actually mean to the vervets:

> Take the vervet alarm call for eagles that we looked at in chapter two. As we saw, this could equally well be translated in at least three different ways: "Look out, an eagle is coming!"; "Danger from the air!"; "Quick, find the nearest bush and hide in it!" Suppose that the call could indeed be broken down into two or more segments. Unless our holistic hominids somehow already knew the equivalent for the call in English (or some other human language), how could they assign an unambiguous reference to those segments? Would the segments be taken to mean "eagle" and "coming," or "danger" and "air," or "bush" and "hide"? (Derek Bickerton, *Adam's Tongue*)

It could be an if-then situation with no real "meaning" behind it. Does it matter? Just as long as you hear a call (specific to situation) and respond (specific to situation), you will pass on your "specific to situation" if-then genes. With the process I suggest, I will have all three meanings forming the same sound shown to be possible, later in the book.

In *The Third Chimpanzee,* Jared Diamond mentions the vervet monkeys on page 54, and again on page 143, where he even asserts that these monkeys actually have ten recognizable calls, which are stated as more of a pro to the theory than a con. The evolution of these calls as survival benefits and more is well discussed. I could give several titles for reference, as vervets are so commonly talked about.

There was an experiment done with monkeys and snakes. Monkeys have a call for snakes that places the fear of hellfire within them. The same fear of snakes is within man and in fact all primates. When the baby monkeys are exposed to the cry alone, without the snake being visibly present, they do not fear snakes upon seeing them. The experimenters in one study used toy snakes and reptiles and, for controls, toy flowers with the recorded screaming of wild monkeys in contact with snakes. Video feed was used in the cages of domestic monkeys who learned to fear snakes with the sight and calls combined, but not with flowers in the presence of the monkeys using the same snake call. The call only triggered the concept of snake with the snake present (Cook and Mineka, 1990–91). These are also mentioned in *Dragons of Eden,* by Carl Sagan, in dealing with fear.

At first blush, this might seem to be a problem for my innate-sound-as-concept theory, but it isn't really. Hearing any sound that is learned after the fact would need to be triggered as the sound for the concept. This differs from the yelp of a dog from pain. It also differs from the cry or scream of a baby in pain. These are noises that they innately make without external stimulus. I will remind the reader that "fear" is innate within every genome and is there from other selective processes not touched on by myself in this work. I only offer a few ways in which sounds can become innate or innately triggered, as sound is the backbone of language.

I have read that pigs make a horrific sound when wounded or in pain, which petrifies the soul within man. The reason given by most of the literature is that some tribes of man had taboos against eating pork. Any cry that could scare the life out of you would do as a cry for signaling of the presence of a snake within the primate family. A fear call or cry could easily have gone through the germ line and been passed directly on to the next generation for the simple reason, by the way, that they would be sounds produced, which would be uncomfortable to your emotional feeling. This is no different from the predator sounds, your own sounds, mating sounds, or any other sounds I mentioned earlier on innateness. They are just a way of learning additional sounds for survival and do not negate my hypothesis.

Applying this back to the vervets and the concept of one bark, say, might include the whole thing: leopard, danger, present now, move quickly, look where you are going, find where the leopard is while moving to avoid it, get to the trees. Actually, while I was rereading this, it occurred to me that this is what we actually experience with speech proper. We say a word and the meaning appears, but also we tend to think of how it is now used, is going to be used, or was used in the application of the person speaking to us. That is what I mean by the whole complete concept represented by one sound. This will be what I work with to evolve speech proper.

We can communicate much without speech, but not everything. For some things, communication is a must! If you grabbed a spear, your tribe members might think that you were going hunting or getting ready to defend yourself from danger and, like the vervets—discussed below—a quick look around might satisfy which hypothesis you are following. To relate to the family that you will be home before dark is another thing. Maybe a few more: Where are the kids? Do you know these people? Do you trust them? There are many must communicate reasons, which can only be communicated through speech as a driving factor for the rise of language. Because one can't have knowledge of everything around you, but many might come to know and that would lead to even higher survival rates. This we call niche change: change one thing in your environment and it alters the environment, causing change to adapt to the now changed environment. We must also be mindful that laziness is the mother of invention—it's easier to tell than to do. That was not really a joke: laziness to a point lets us save our energy for other purposes.

We should not be alarmed at my pointing out that even the cock crows at daybreak, so it should not be hard to conceive of a starting point for time to come into being. Sunrise marks the start of the day and any form of noise in general, indicating the start of day would lead to a time reference. If there were to be an ancient call, innate, as a signal for all our species to awaken, which is the case with most noise producing animals, we would have a base. Since it is impossible to conjure and actually write down such calls, I will take the higher level and step out front to work with that. That is, I will separate one of the sounds from a call or cry and work with it.

If this call, whatever it was, just happened to have a vibrating sound to it, say *vvvvv*, the sound *vvvvv* and not the letter *v* would carry with it the innate concept of time to get up and moving, find food, find water, and watch for predators, get on with life … As per this hypothesis, our entire species would innately "know" this sound to carry this meaning—in a totally complete conception form—of whatever the included meaning entailed. Not to get ahead of myself, but to place a name on the sound is to call it *v* and place it as a phoneme proper solving part of the above problem. Calls need to be separated into individual sounds and then combined into words.

As time and space would by far give the highest survival value of any other concept, save predation itself, in the form of directions, I will start with that. After these first three chapters, I will quickly get to the main thesis of the book: the origins of language. Then I will examine in as much detail as I can how language could have come from calls and cries, the evolution of language, and what was needed to have it happen. Before we continue our journey to words, we will need to consider one more innate basis to language first: grammar, the topic of the next chapter.

Chapter Two

Grammar and Order

Such is the imperfection of our nature, that to chance and neceffity we owe the far greater part of our ufeful difcoveries, as alfo the further improvement of fuch as are already imperfectly known.

—William Alexander
The History of Women

This quote I have used looks misspelled because ƒ is used in place of the usual *s*, but if you look closely, you will see that they also use the letter *s* in some words. I did not correct the spelling for this quote, deciding to leave it as an example. The reason I left it is that if they had these letters, then they had these letters representing different sounds—long and short S—and sounds could evolve as well as language. I have corrected any quotes of the same style in the rest of the book.

We need to dispel one more myth: that we need some type of special brain tools especially selected for by a language instinct to speak properly in grammar form and the innateness of these brain

Sherman P. Bastarache

tools as language specific incorporated into the genome. We need to have emphasis in speaking; we need to have mental holders to remember subjects and objects; we need to have word order, but these could all come from a natural way to express nature and not be genetically learned specifically for language. That is, language did not have to evolve them—only use what was always there for different purposes.

We do not, however, need to have any magic way of ordering our speech, which cannot be satisfied with slow, small steps, selected for naturally, in the exact manner I used to describe sound-words in the previous chapter. Sound-words in that chapter were considered to be calls, cries, and noises in general. I will use sound-words in another form in chapter 3. For now, we need to establish how communication could be in any way innately represented as anything close to grammar.

> Story one: Eat women cold side morning side today past hot side walk huge today past tiger cold see side look past fell cave stone safe deer deer bring today split stone beyond tree giant water fell

The preceding paragraph was actually a complete story, which in fact would have given a survival advantage. The following paragraph has the same story in its proper order. Both stories are in broken English, but the second should be sensible to the reader with a little effort. I will continue to refer to them as story one and story two when mentioned later in the book.

> Story two: Cold side giant tree beyond split water morning side walk. Huge stone hot side fell deer. See tiger cold side stone today past, today past, today past look safe. Fell deer bring cave women eat.

What advantage does the second story have over the first? The second has a natural order to it so that even in this crude form, one can still make out what is being communicated. As there seems to be two different schools of speech—the Chomsky school and the one-word-placed-after-another school—we must examine both. Noam Chomsky was the first theorist to hit upon the idea of grammar being an innate property of humans within all languages. In brief, he believed that we are born knowing the proper form and order of sentence structure, and only have to learn our words, language specific, from our parents' tongue. The different word order used by different tongues set out grammar specifically for that tongue, i.e., French grammar, English grammar ... The one word placed after the other school, or "beads on a string," suggests that language is how you read it. This sentence is just one word added to another, and there is plenty of time to learn all the grammar rules without being innate. In any technical sense, both of these schools fall short. My first example of a story, story one, was in fact one word added to another and is quite unintelligible. Chomsky also need not be invoked here, as story one could never be accurately discovered by learning innate rules of grammar after the fact. The only time you would need any rules for sentence structure would be to refine language and for purposes of teaching these refinements to students, and I will make more comments on the defense of this statement later in the work.

The second story actually fits both schools of thought. As coarse as it is, it does have proper syntax structure, and we can get away with saying that it does just have one word placed after the other. However, it does not have to be the case that anything was actually selected for as far as language goes. When we place the story in a more modern version—that is, remove the coarseness from it—we see where selection would have to be made: going from coarse to refined, at least in the later stages. The better communicators would on average have more descendants. By communicators, I mean more "descriptive words," not better-sounding sentences. Past the calls and cries theory I have established, descriptive words would need to be selected for or more calls and cries, which I will show to be less possible later.

> Story two: Cold side giant tree, beyond split water, morning side walk. Huge stone hot side, fell deer. See tiger, cold side stone, today past, today past, today past, look safe. Fell deer bring cave, women eat

> Second story: On the north side of the giant oak tree, beyond the split in the river, following the east side of the split in the river, you will find a fell deer on the south side of the huge round stone. I saw a tiger there the last three days so be on the watch and be safe. Take the deer back to the cave so the women can cook and eat it.

The major reason that this second story works at all is the fact that it has an order in the events, step-by-step instructions, and/ or directions for how to get to your game. Since language does not predate life, we need to examine life as the starting point in syntax. Anyone who got up with the sun, caught food, and ate it would naturally have an order to life. You don't eat your game before you catch it, and you don't catch your game before you get up. In fact, anything you do has, from necessity, an order to it, and all completely without language—or communication, for that matter. If you had the same hunting grounds as every other member of your tribe and were familiar with that ground, we could reduce the second story, but not the first story, by a number of words and still produce a survival advantage.

In reality, I am only a science hobbyist, not a professional. I love to read about the many different aspects of it—and from early sources as far back as Plato. I read about physics, psychology, chemistry, language, evolution, sociology, biology, and just about all the sciences, as well as religion and mythology. This does not make me an expert, of course, but many great ideas were discovered by nonexperts in many fields of the sciences and other subjects as well. Reading has been my main hobby for a few years now, and I have always been curious about language in general as noted in the preface. Some observations I have made while reading have led me to draw my own conclusions. I admit that I could be a thousand miles left of the target and would not even know any better. When I think through them, I can find no fault with these ideas, nor have I found any books that condemn my thinking. These observations were in fact made on the order of words that Chomsky himself made. In English and other languages, we do allow for some variation of word order, and word order is not perfect. The variations will be discussed deeper below, but they are space/time related.

One day I was doing a renovation to our house and had a wall removed. I remember it perfectly. I was thinking about how best to remove the window, board it in, and install a garden door over slightly to the left of where the window was. I started in my mind to actually install these two-by-fours, one after the other, rearranging them in the proper place to see if they would fit. It then dawned on me that I was doing this without saying to myself, *If I placed a two-by-four here and another one there, it would work.* In short, I did this without any language at all, just manipulating the actual two-by-fours in my brain, or lack thereof. I could not place any object where another object was without removing it first in my mind. I also had some leeway in which I could manipulate the objects as long as they fit the whole of the actions and task I was performing.

We speak grammatically correct because we think grammatically correct and this is the usual order in which the world around us happens. I was looking for a mathematical theory that I could adapt to express conceptual change, and among other books, I was lucky enough to read *The Math Gene* by Keith Devlin. He does not actually come right out and say anything about order involvement relating to either "syntax" or "beads on a string," but the commentary could be construed in that direction. Even though it is not where I got the idea, he did comment a bit more technically than I would have.

> The brain had to be able to represent, internally, a sufficiently rich world *structure*. The "skeletal structure" of the world that the brain simulated in order to think about the world off-line is what we now call syntactic structure or syntax.
>
> When you add syntax to protolanguage, you get language.

I think that if he had said "a sufficiently rich space/time world-ordered structure," he would have come closer than anyone to the truth. The reason both "syntax"—the same as grammar—and "beads on a string" work is because they are not random but ordered. Therefore, protolanguage would have had syntax, or ordered structure, also, but in calls and cries. To have a rich world structure is needed, but we live in this structure directionally, and this directional life predicts ordered life, which predicts when language arises, and it too will be ordered.

When I say that I was lucky enough to read this book, it was not for this idea but for another idea that I will use later in this book for another purpose altogether. Language must follow on the back of what is actually happening in nature and being named, as it is actually happening. That is receiving names in the order, both time and space, that things are happening and being named. If we have no word for a concept, we are silent. We may, however, still have those concepts, as there is no real or imagined law against such. This topic will be covered later. The back on which it follows is not being created by language but is ever present in the order we live our lives. Naming what we are doing, as we are doing it, subject and object, flows naturally from all of life. Every *improvement* in language relays communication *better, but only if in the proper order.* The best order relays the best information more accurately.

We think objectively and subjectively (read: object and subject) in a proper order, so why would we not speak in the same order or proper syntax/grammar in which we think? We speak grammatically correct because we think grammatically correct because this is the usual order in which the world around us happens. No, it is both the order in which we live in the world and the order of the world. If anything about syntax or grammar could be said to be innate, it would be that the brain is programmed as the body acts within its environment, or what the environment causes the body to act upon: ordered. I will attempt to show that words follow the same process as the sounds or letters that go into making them up and, more importantly, why they do. To do this, I must start with what we have at hand, and in our remote ancestry, all we would have had were calls and cries. With new eyes, we should look again at the vervet monkeys.

Nearly all the higher animals have some form of communication, which usually consists of just single sounds or slight combinations of sounds. In thinking of the vervet monkeys of Africa, which have a different call or cry for different predators—eagles, leopards, and snakes—one call gets these monkeys to look up for eagles, another to look down for leopards and snakes. I don't know firsthand what these sounds are like, as I have never witnessed them, but they say they are bark sounds. I have, however, heard from various television shows and movies what noises chimps produce. Chimps all seem to make the vowel sounds, especially *e*, *o*, and *a*. Start small by using two complete calls, or three as a base: *e*, *o*, and *a*, for example. If, over time, the call *o* came to mean predator, and the call *e* came to mean down, and again the *a* call came to mean up, then sounding them one after the other would give a survival benefit.

It will become clear later why I do not believe that words are derived from calls and cries combined together. Going back to the vervets, if *o* meant leopard, whichever monkeys got it right and fled to the trees would survive, but whichever monkeys fled to ground cover would become food. We are neither monkeys nor apes, and we have shaped our niche first into one for the acquisition of language and then into a niche of language.

Will the combining of calls hold up to syntax? We have noun phrases and verb phrases represented as NPs VPs = S, the *S* being sentence. Both nouns and verbs can be descriptive. In the above example, I used *o* as predator and *e* as down, so let's make the predator a noun (leopard) and the down a verb (coming). We now have a first-level NP VP = S: the calls "OE" carrying the concept of "leopard coming." We could add to this by combining more calls and cries: "OEA" could become "Leopard coming—run." Humans have the capacity for consonants above animals, thus putting vowel-consonants/consonant-vowel to use. We see from this untrue scenario, though, that even these alleged calls and cries automatically fall into syntax structure.

We are partway there in getting ordered grammar or syntax structure into calls or cries, but alas, this will not quite work: we cannot say that all these words you are reading are just combined calls and cries. That would be too many concepts to become innate; actually, too many part concepts; in my opinion, that is the real problem. If we only had one hundred concepts, we would only need one hundred calls, and it would work. We can produce about 140 sounds. This, of course, would have to include naming all the other species of animals. In one sense, true enough, we can and likely did combine some calls and cries ordered into sentences. We could grunt (for time to get up), yelp (for we are hungry), and mimic another animal sound (for the food we want). This would become the sentence: grunt, yelp, quack. Perfect in syntax but just enough communicated and no more. The major problem here is that they are additions of complete total concepts.

Actually, there is no real reason to think that a protolanguage was not set up in this manner. Grunt, yelp, moo could be the communication among tribal members that there are cows for food and to follow me. Mimicking any animal sounds would automatically bring up the concept of that animal. Remember chapter 1, when I wrote that these noise concepts would not be restricted to the same species? If you're the predator, you need to recognize the prey. At any rate, if true, and combining calls were possible, it would further aid in making up words as a habit-forming protocol.

Back to the jigsaw puzzle analogy of the first chapter, we can see what the world actually means to the brain. I used the jigsaw puzzle to show how chemicals and chemical receptors work and then compared them to vibrations or sounds. Now I will use it for world structure.

Picture in your mind a busy jigsaw puzzle. Every piece of it only fits a certain way to form the scenery. Combined, it is a whole picture of something. You can remove one piece of the puzzle use it to point out a specific object of the scenery. For instance, if you want to show a flower in a puzzle, you could remove the flower from the whole puzzle and present the piece with the flower separately. In a certain sense, the individual pieces could represent the individual pieces of our world. A flower can be singled out by the brain from our natural surroundings and spoken about. It would be very natural to say about the puzzle and our world that they are ordered. The yellow flower in the middle of the puzzle, just in front of the red flower, left of the orange flower, is the one I want to single out for conversation. Does this not also apply to our world? Note: they are spoken about in directions of time or space. To point out the same yellow flower in your backyard, you would also say that it is the yellow flower in the middle of the backyard, just in front of the red flower, left of the orange flower. Ordered!

ABCDEFGHIJKLMNOPQRSTUVWXYZ is a call, or cry in this case. Three things make you remember things more easily: humor and tragedy are important, and the third is familiarity from redundancy. This being our call or cry is analog in nature. They are all stored in perfect order—the order of the world, if you will. Imagine them to be your surroundings: trees, water, rocks, and the like, for instance. I will deal with the letters as an actual call or cry. If this call represents our natural surroundings, say the call for "picture," "scenery," or "vision," it is analog—one continuous stream—and the scenery is analog because it is how the world appears—one continuous ordered stream. Even if the brain stores it digitally, it will be stored in *analog order* or it will be of no use to us or others, and their possessors will not survive.

I will go over these terms in more detail in a later chapter, but for now an example is needed. If the message got mixed up and you, thinking you were diving into water, dove into a stone, you would not live. I can only spend so much time on this fact becoming selected for, as it is more important how it works. Ordered would be selected for, but only by elimination of cross-wired brains and not a mean average of "better at" per se, as the brain only copies what it sees from vision, sound, or any other facet of life. These would be selected for in better form—vision, sound, and so forth—as they relay world structure better. Evolving creatures cannot change the laws of nature to enhance their survival benefit. This is different from niche change!

The advantage of using the alphabet is that we can now use the digital form to remove separate letters (sounds) from the call or cry. Pictures of our surroundings being digitalized, just like pieces of a jigsaw puzzle in the analogy, does not need to be selected for separately. Everything we name or otherwise describe would automatically be in order: name every piece of a twenty-six-piece jigsaw puzzle with the letters of the alphabet and they will still only fit one way. Name every sound of the alphabet, and they will still only fit one way in the puzzle: the order of the picture or scenery. It would be completely natural to name things in the order they are within this scenery because they are names being placed upon each object of the scenery.

That said, we have a little leeway. We can also say from the above description:

"The yellow flower in the middle of the backyard, left of the orange flower, just in front of the red flower."

The above was:

"The yellow flower in the middle of the backyard, just in front of the red flower, left of the orange flower."

Both are ordered! This is what I referred to above when I wrote that word order is not perfect, and variations are permitted. If grammar were in fact that strict, we would, in every language, have to say it a certain way or be incorrect, as it would have evolved one way. The biggest problem plaguing innate grammar theories is that different languages pick up on these different permissive orders as "preferable selection" from one main source but are not treated as if they were. If I prefer to say white and black but you prefer to say black and white, then a different but grammatically correct "other language" would arise.

I have been using only sight in my explanation so far, but object and subject thought includes all the senses: sight, sound, smell, taste, touch, and collective thought. Here is an example: the smell of a rose might bring up in the "mind's eye" a collective representation of its appearance, the feel of its soft petals, and the buzzing sound of bees as they partake of the nectar. All of this is completely possible without having to place a name on anything. A language instinct is not the same as a grammar or syntax instinct. One is needed for thought, and the other is needed for communication, more properly called speech. I can't help but notice, within my own brain, that I can think in concept form without any symbolic naming, but I also notice that when I talk things out in my brain, I talk to myself in speech. Both of these self-communication properties are in the order of my brain, realizing them and working with them from their natural states in nature.

From this rose example, we might put it in grammatical order as smell, rose, eat honey, bees. Or we might say smell, rose, bee, eat honey, as both would be proper sentences. We would never say rose, eat honey, bee, smell as a sentence, because smell becomes removed from the rose and attached to the bee, leading to the need for it to be referred to again as rose, eat honey, bee, smell rose. Otherwise, it is displaced in time or place. This is what we see in every language as grammar. If you are new to the problems of language, I will refer you to read *Language and Problems of Knowledge* by Noam Chomsky or any other of Chomsky's books, and *The Language Instinct* by Steven Pinker, who was the first to refute Chomsky, to learn about the two arguments. They both have some pros and cons, but I think that language can only evolve so far and syntax can only be so innate. I will discuss these conflicts in a little more detail in different places throughout the book. Now comes the time to tie this chapter in with the last chapter. I hope that I convinced you of the ease in getting grammar-ordered language innate, without special "stuff" being selected. Grammar is a completely natural interaction with the natural world.

All people see the physical world the same way—the physical world being spoken of here as literal and concrete, not in the form of some philosophical ideologist perspective of the natural world. If you see a stone, that means others can see that same stone, and if you don't avoid it, you walk into it. Language added, everyone who sees the stone says "Look out" in all languages. Why would calls and cries complete with their total concepts be any different than words? Words have meanings, so calls, cries, or sounds in general would have meaning also. The meaning of them would in every case have a relationship to the physical world, which is ordered. Therefore, words would also have this order naturally inherent.

In the first chapter, we saw how noises innately came to have meaning. In this chapter, we see that grammar, or syntax, has become innate of words by riding the back of life in the natural order we live it. We saw how calls and cries (sounds)—*wrongly, albeit*—could be combined into words. We also saw how calls and cries could be combined into proper-ordered sentences. These are the basis for the rest of the book. I will be attempting to show how these total concepts became separated into smaller concepts, more precise units of communication. I will also attempt to show how these words as we know them could evolve from calls or cries. First, I attempt to go from sounds to words as a starting point. After all, we need to start somewhere. This next chapter is the whole basis of my book, as it shows how words came into being. It is what I started out with in my thinking. The rest of the book will deal with how this process came about—and what was needed to be in place for it to have happened.

Chapter Three

From Sounds to Words

Turning to words, as distinct from grammar, it's probably reasonable to assume that a given sound will ricochet around a related set of meanings over time. The assumption raises the chances of spotting a relationship between language families, but also of picking up accidental similarities. No single group of cognate words is conclusive, but large numbers can begin to make a case.

—Nicholas Wade
Before the Dawn

The brain deals in concepts, which is the only way language could have begun and risen to higher levels. In our search of the first word, we forgot to start small enough; in fact, we neglected to start at the smallest possible place: the phoneme or sound. I start with the oldest resource I have at my disposal and precede the best I can with my idea—from the Greek word *idein*: to see more. I will begin working with the *vibrating sound vvvvvv*, from the first chapter of this work, rather than the letter *v*.

> Then Adam and Eve entered the cave, and stood praying, in their tongue, unknown to us, but which they knew well. (The book of Adam and Eve chapter 5:1)

If we take words from the Bible, such as Eve, being the first woman's name, and derive a meaning, which was also given—And Adam called his wife's name Eve; *because she was the mother of all living* (Gen. 3:20; emphasis mine; King James version used throughout)—we obtain something to work with. The mother or starting point of Homo sapiens, in one word, carried a meaning.

It could be argued that morn and mourn were derived from the same root source: meaning the ending point or conclusion, one of time and one of life. The Hebrew word translated into day, I understand, carried with it no quantity of time. So epoch would be a better fit than the word day, which carries a twenty-four-hour quantity of time. Because she was the beginning of the human race, using Eve as a starting point and adding to it *ning*, we get evening and gain some insight and a better understanding of what the writer of Genesis was saying. *The evening and the morning were the first day* (as if God worked the night shift) would now become *The starting point and the ending point were the first epoch.*

Actually, the words even and morn were both used in older English to represent the concepts of day and night, without adding the *ing* to them, but they were in the quote above with the *ing* added. We commonly use the word eve for other purposes: Christmas Eve, New Year's Eve, and the eve of destruction.

The word Eve or the sound *v* carried a mental conception of beginnings: the first human starting point, the starting of an event or time. As this book deals in language and not writing, we must remember to drop the *e*s in Eve, so we just have *v*, but I will use the correct spelling for fewer complications. Using it as a place in space/time is now possible. To make it infinite, we would add the sound *r* at the end, giving us ever, or nullify it by adding the *n* sound at the beginning, giving us *never*.

There is something to be said about clarity. Eve (concept of a starting time) and *r* (concept of ad infinitum) give the different concept of starting and continuing forever, in a proper syntax form—that is, the *r* being placed at the end of the word Eve, giving rise to the meaning time ad infinitum—ordered. Now, adding to the front of the word the sound n (concept of not taking place) we get *never* in proper syntax form with a new combined concept of this event could not have started and lasted forever. Note in the following words the position of the add-on sound-words and grammar or syntax.

Eve	starting point
Ever	infinite
Every	all-inclusive matter/space/time
Never	infinitely nullified
Even	the constant of the event
Evening	beginning of an event in space/time
Event	the actual thing or totality of the happening in matter/space/time
Sever	to cut off from matter/space/time

My Greek is nonexistent, but I could easily make up even a poor word to describe what I am suggesting. I used sound-word in the first chapter, promising to deal with it later. Sound-word with the hyphen becomes promoted as one word: soundword, the same as adding a hyphen to any word combination, such as non-chicken. As the words become more commonly used, the hyphen is dropped, as in the word inasmuch, or nonissue. I chose to make up a Greek word for a better combination: *tilogos.* This means the complete word or meaning in one digital sound. It is also where I derived the title of the book. I feel a little history of the word is in order here. To me, the word *tiyol* is just the Greek word for sound, and I took the first two letters of it for the combination. On the other hand, *logos,* commonly translated into English as word, has greater meaning for me.

According to Heraclitus, who brought together the several meanings associated with the word logos, from all the sources before him, its earlier verb meanings included *to say, to count, to gather,* which points to completeness. It also has the sense of logical separation, which I noticed is spelled with the *log* from *logoi*— singular of logos. We here have *word* in Greek, which is made up of combining *to say* and *logic,* which is the art of separating and analyzing information. This will come in handy later.

Cliché was used by the French to speed up printing a phrase that was commonly used. They would permanently cast a phrase for printing purposes to save the time of placing the letters repeatedly throughout the printed material. An example might be the words *in the year of our Lord*—in French, of course. You can imagine only having to add the number twenty-three to *in the year of our Lord*—June 23, 2009, for example—one number at a time, as the date changed daily. You can permanently cast the phrase *in the year of our lord* once and reuse it as one insert. Once a month, change the month; yearly, the last number, such as 2009, 2010 … Clichés have come to represent phrases that are commonly stated. Phonemes are the sounds that distinguish the different letters. If we made phonemes into whole words, combining them would make sound-clichés: roots, syllables, words, or phrases. The phonemes would be the same as sound-words, or *tilogoi.* Combining the sound-word or tilogoi E, with the sound-word V, and the sound-word E, makes phrases, which become sound-clichés, leading to words.

Note below that the same cliché rule applies from the date mentioned above: letters can be changed or added to a base cliché. Complete word language would be very hard, if not impossible, to have evolved innately, but sound-words or sound concepts are easier. If you will please excuse my English examples, I will demonstrate:

H meaning or complete sound-word concept
E meaning or complete sound-word concept
R meaning or complete sound-word concept

In three words would state the location of a place in space/time. Properly, as writing arose, the last vowel was added to define the middle vowel sound, which sounds out the word here instead of the word her or, more to the point, sound-cliché here and sound-cliché her, the better starting point being *her* and *hr*. As we shall see, even these statements aren't entirely accurate, but they're close enough to convey the general idea.

When used often enough, the sounds would flow together, and adding more sound-words like T would add to the length of the sentence, changing the space/time of the sentence. The new sentence or new sound-cliché would now become *there*. In sound-cliché form, *here* and *there* would take less time to speak, and less time equals greater survival. Let's be clear before proceeding. To say the word T pause, then the word H pause, and then the word R pause would take longer than saying *there* all in one smooth sound-cliché. (We will deal with the vowels later.) The question would be addressed as *where* when one did not understand the location from *there* and asked it to be repeated, adding the sound-word or tilogoi W instead of the sound-word T to the sound-cliché *here*.

As these words (phonemes or sounds) became more innately representative of concepts, they also became more easily communicated: faster, smoother, and more accurately. The four phonemes—H, E, R, E—would now become one smooth sentence or sound-cliché because of the continued use of them together for the same meaning. With time, the four sounds would become degraded from a four-word sentence into a smooth one-word set of phonemes proper. At one point, with rapidity, whole sentences would sound like a word, and as larger words grew, the smaller ones would be degraded to syllables. T pause O would become *to*; likewise, *to get here* would become *togethere*, or *together*, a whole sentence, or sound-cliché meaning: for all to gather at a given place. We could parallel this with *gather*. Again, for clarity sake, the sentence H pause, E pause, R pause, E pause would change from sentence into a sound-cliché as soon as it was said without the pauses, thus becoming words. Of course, the words I use are only examples in English and of no real resource for proof of the theory. Older languages would have to be analyzed for proof. I will use a few more examples before proceeding, which will also clarify this example.

In the two examples above, I changed the sound V from eve into the sound, or rather sound-word, R, giving rise to the word *ere*, which in older English meant *before*, so future and somewhere. Adding the H sound-word makes it present and positioned which is where I came to use the word *here* above. By adding the T sound-word, it makes it elsewhere, present, and positioned, and adding the W sound-word to *here* asks for the position *where*. From this, removing the RE and adding the sound-word N to the end of the word or sound-cliché asks for the position in time.

Ere   before now

Are   present tense, continuum

Were	past tenses—in the question capacity: when before now?
Here	present and positioned
There	elsewhere, present and positioned
Where	questioning position
Their	other than I—elsewhere, present and positioned
When	questioning time/future/past/present
Then	answering time/question/future/past/present
The	answering object/singling out portion
Other	changing object
Who	questioning personage
Why	questioning reason
What	questioning object

Take note that at this early stage, all the questions start with the W sound, or more to the point, the W sound-word, which I have called tilogoi. The question *how* is an exception to the standard W5 questions: *who, what, where, when* and *why*, as it does not start with the W. However, it does have the W at the end. I can't help but notice that asking how is transformed into requesting a demonstration by adding S to the front of it, becoming show (s-how). The same observation was noted by Joseph Greenberg, to whom Nicholas Wade in *Before the Dawn* comments on going from *kw* to *w* for questions in English:

In many Indo-European languages, questions are expressed with words starting with "k" or "kw" sounds, though the "kw" has become a "w" in English.

That said, I want to expand on show. We can continue building on the sound-cliché *how*, going to the sound-cliché *show*, adding the sound-cliché ER at the end, giving us *shower*, which relates free flow of knowledge: for example, they showered me with knowledge, with kindness, and so forth. By adding the tilogoi sound-word N to the end of *show*, we get a tense change: *shown*. The one letter, or for us the tilogoi N, also alters in the negative the sound-clichés, now called words. Adding the tilogoi N to *or* gives us the word *nor* and to *either* gives us the word *neither*. It also negated the word *ever* to the word *never* above and was used to smooth in the word *even* above. Before proceeding, it is noteworthy that we still do this same thing. *Hitherto* is a word made up of the two words: *hither* and *to*. *Notwithstanding* is made up of three words, as is *inasmuch* and *nonetheless*. They became one word when they started being said frequently enough to be accepted as one word (cliché) and lost the pauses proper, becoming syllables.

I have so far used two letters to convey these base thoughts and will use one more before entering into how this could be possible.

Older words have two meanings, literal and their common usage, such as expedient: freed feet. Expanding on expedient as my last example of a run on words, we find EX used three times in this sentence alone, and by coincidence only.

Expounded	free description
Exit	passage to freedom
Excuse	freeing reason
Exist	freed entity
Example	freely shown
Explain	freely reason
Expedient	freed feet

When we look at the phoneme X being added to so many other words, we find that it makes all their combined meanings a source of freedom in one form or another. Freedom is a concept represented by Ex in this example, but by saying it, it becomes the phoneme X, one phoneme representing the concept of freedom. Connexion: with the X in the middle, this could be taken as the freeing point *between* two ideas. Expanse: breaks into ex and pan— free and all in Greek. One more example with the X in the middle: flexible means freedom to bend. I should also include one with the X on the end: complex, which means free to be complicated. It could also mean the loss of freedom, as in excommunicate, or being prevented from freely taking communion. If adding word concepts together makes larger word concepts, then why wouldn't adding sound concepts together not make the lesser word concepts the starting point of language?

The reader might think that this is just as big of an impossibility as the example of adding calls and cries together seemed in the last chapter. The title of this chapter is "From Sounds to Words," and we must now examine a way in which a sound could have become transformed into a tilogoi: sound-word or phoneme with a meaning. Let us now take a look at how a simple buzzing or other such noise could have a meaning recognized as a word, but first a brief word on cognates, which are words that resist change. The inventor of the term, Morris Swadesh, has a list of one hundred words, like body parts or items, common to all people, which should resist change when compared to other languages. Sounds that are the same or close in the pronunciation should be a comparable concept, ideally anyway.

The click languages of the !Kung were a problem to my thinking for a considerable time, as I was, for months on end, thinking in letter sounds only, but I decided to treat it as the rest of this thesis, one step at a time. A *click* proper does not sound the same as saying *click*; it is a roll of the tongue. If you were to place a name on that particular roll or flick of the tongue, you would come up with more than one sound: the beginning of a K or hard C sound and a beginning of an L sound. I will leave that one alone. I will instead work with a *tik* sound, as I have found a nice source for my purpose in the book *Before the Dawn* by Nicholas Wade (Wade covers a lot of language material), which I quote:

> One of the most interesting concerns a set of meanings based on the putative Eurasiatic word for finger, which Greenberg thinks was *tik*. Raise your first or index *tik* and you make a universally understood sign for the number one. Point it horizontally and you are drawing attention to something ... Linguists have reconstructed a proto-Indo-European root **deik*, meaning to show, from which comes the Latin word *digitus* for finger, and the English words digit and digital. In the Altaic family, the Turkish word for sole or only is *tek*. In the Korean-Japanese-Ainu group, there is Ainu's *tek* and Japanese's *te,* both meaning hand. As for Eskimo-Aleut, Greenlandic has *tikiq* for index finger, Sirenik and Central Alaskan Yupik have *tekeq*.

A *tik* sound could have easily turned into a sound-word concept. One, eventually you would name the sound *tik*, and in so doing, you would go from making the noise to actually speaking the noise: a huge difference. Two, it would become the word for point, index finger, hand, quantity, or some combination, the total conceptual meaning that we were entertaining earlier. The association made by mirror neurons (neurons that copy actions) and the dissociation from the actual hand gestures made by super mirror neurons (neurons that hold the sound but stop the action) are both shown to be probable, but I won't get into that here. I will stick to the establishment of the total concept for now. We have the word *tik*, now used for relaying any topic related to it: point to something or universally understood to be the sign for one, as quoted above. It also singles out, and gives direction, so we can pull different meanings from the same *tik* word.

I could not help but notice, while reading Plato's great work *Cratylus*, as translated by Benjamin Jowett, that Plato stated that the Greek language originated from Attic. This reminded me of the !Kung click languages, as there is a *tic* in the name Attic. We also have tribes in Africa that go by the names of Aka and Efe. The !Kung are widely stated to be the oldest source of language, and they are in Africa, which is commonly referred to as our place of origin in all the literature. A quick note here: there would be less pressure for selection to act on in the original starting place of language, and clicks would remain a constant without the pressure of divergence. This gives us a main source of clicks, and we find enough to support vibrating sounds from other areas of life all just waiting to receive names. It is into names that we now go.

I came across this myth while reading *Philebus* by Plato as translated by Benjamin Jowett.

Some god or divine man, who in the Egyptian legend is said to have been Theuth, observing that the human voice was infinite, first distinguished in this infinity a certain number of vowels, and then other letters which had sound, but were not pure vowels (i.e. the semivowels); these too exist in a definite number; and lastly, he distinguished a third class of letter which we now call mutes, without voice and without sound, and divided these, and likewise the two other classes of vowels and semivowels, into the individual sounds, and told the number of them, and gave to each and all of them the name of letters; and observing that none of us could learn any one of them and not learn them all, and consideration of this common bond which in a manner united them, he assigned to them all a single art of grammar or letters.

All humans make more noises than any other animals and have the capability of mimicking all, or almost all, other animals. In the case of our own noises, they would be just as innate, complete with total concept, as any other example I have used. From this myth, we can conclude it to be reasonably true as a first step in language formation. The myth says that he, Theuth, called them letters, but a better statement would be that he named the sounds. When I do the elucidation later, I hope this will become clearer. We start by naming the vowel *a* and notice that it does not change the sound by being named but is only altered when silent or shortened. These are only tools I am using to go from sounding into naming the sound and it is a lot more complicated. My examples from necessity are in English and not in the original alleged protolanguage.

The name for the *b* sound is altered, though; it carries another sound with it. That other sound is the vowel *e* added to the end to give us the name *bee* for that innate sound that occurs naturally without the *e* sound. This I call naming. The *e* is also a vowel, and it is not altered by naming it, but it does change when silent or shortened. The same applies to these letters: *dee, pee, tee, vee, zee.* I left out *g* because it is a special case, I think, and should be treated with *j*. The sounds start out the same in both cases, or so close to the same that I believe it to be twice altered. The best way to show this is to write it both ways and ask what the difference is: *jaa* and *gaa* or *jee* and *gee*, as they both have the same consonant sound altered by different vowel sounds.

This now brings us to naming sounds with letters that are vowel altered with the sound A, which does not need to be elaborated on further. *Kaa* has the vowel at the end of the consonant, if you will. On the other hand, *aah* has the vowel sound in front. Possibly the same vowel sound of an altered *e* is in front of the letters *f, r, u,* and *x*. If you sound out the *letters* slowly, you can tell that these letters are made up of sometimes many sounds. Another special case is with *cee*; long *e* and *ees*, with a short *e* in front but carrying the same sound in both cases. The name *l* has the same vowel-altering sound in front. The last vowel that holds its own sound is *o* again, unless silent or short. This does not apply to the vowels *i* spoken as *iee* and *u*, spoken as *eeu*, which do have their sounds altered by naming them, and they all seem to be unique to themselves as vowels, along with the last letters to be named, barring M and N.

On to what is said as *eeu* or the letter *u*, and what is said as *double eeu* or the letter *w*, which seem to be the same sounds, but in a different octave. An octave is known as a doubling of the same sound. Starting with the *double eeu* sound and adding the *i* sound, we get what is said as *wwi* or the letter *y*, and both can be used as vowels. Add to the mix the name of the sound *kku*, or *q*, and we only need be concerned about the hardening and softening of letters, which are true names for sounds. As I deal a lot with the sound *v*, I will use it to point out that when the sounds are added together, they lose their added named sound and take on the different sounds applied: *vaa, voo, vii*—not *veeaa, veeoo, veeii*, and the like.

I don't want anyone to be confused here with the sounds of the letters; I am talking about naming the sounds. To be clear, each sound is known as a phoneme and has a different sound proper. The names placed on the sounds proper are considered the alphabet. We are naming them in English and in fact most languages, with the names of Rome, or New Roman, as the font is called on my Microsoft Word document. If we were naming them in Greek, we would be on par with Plato's thinking when he wrote:

You are aware that our forefathers loved the sounds iota and delta, especially the women, who are most conservative of the ancient language, but now they changed iota into eta or epsilon, and delta into zeta; this is supposed to increase the grandeur of the sound.

I might point out that Greek is not the only language to alter sound for the grandeur. Consider this quote from *The Treatise of the Figures at the End of the Rules of Construction in the Latin Grammar*, by John Stockwood:

In the third example in the word Induperatorem for imperatorem, the syllable _ is put between in the middle, and it is not set down Imduperatorem, but Induperatorem (n for m) for a better sound sake, that is Euphoniae gratia, as they used to say.

I managed to find several sources where the sounds were changed for the sake of Euphoniae gratia, but I will not quote anymore, as I must get back to my Greek.

I might point out here that *iota* means small in Greek. It is part of their alphabet, and it would not be much different from saying *double eeu*, represented by the symbol *w*. Why would we accept *iota* as meaning small but not accept the letter *vee* as meaning, say, time/space? The second point is even more important, for the sound changed with time to sound better: to increase the grandeur of the sound.

To clarify: I don't believe that *vvvvvv* was necessarily the or one of the first sounds, as it could have evolved from another sound, but it makes a good candidate for one. I also pointed out that some words could have arisen from other means, but that would not stop them from evolving along with the sound concepts that I have proposed. Since I don't know any other tongue but English, I will be restricted to that, so the examples used throughout the rest of the book are not to be taken literally. In some cases, it might be true as being the real words origin, but I only use them as tools in place of the true, original sounds.

Before moving along, I have found some support for these conclusions, and they are not just figments of my imagination. I read somewhere, I don't quite remember where now, that there were mostly negative words starting with the letters *sl,* so the idea is not original with me. I checked the *Webster's New Collegiate Dictionary* to see how true it was and came up with this number: fifty-eight words in total, root based only. That is, slap counted as one, ignoring slap shot, slap happy, and so on. Slack counted as one, ignoring slacker and so forth. Of those fifty-eight words, I counted forty-six words with negative connotations, but admittedly, it was as quick of a word count as I could do. Still, it was an approximation of about 80 percent of the words, such as slut, slap, slime, and slip, so they were right.

Now for the *gl* words as mentioned on page 113 of Daniel Tammet's *Embracing the Wide Sky*: glance, glisten, glow, glacé, glad (one meaning shining), glair, glamour (illusory attractiveness), glare, glass, glaucoma, glaze, gleam, glean, gleg, gley, glim, glimmer, glimpse, glint, glitter, gloam, gloat, gloom, glorify (shed radiance or splendor on), gloss, glaze, glum. Again leaving out redundancies, it is very close to the 80 percent mark—or higher, actually—for words dealing with light or shiny. If two examples can be found in English, then examples should be able to be found in a "protolanguage."

What are the odds in favor of having two groups of words beginning with two letters that have a high correlation in one meaning? *Sl* and *gl* both have a high correlation in their respective meanings. For the sake of calling attention to an amount, I used 80 percent. That percentage was in relation to the amount of words and did not take other factors into consideration—such as the fact that we used two of the same letters for one concept, out of a possible twenty-six. I would work out the odds better, but I promised you, the reader, no math. A promise is a promise. See, I'll use any excuse to get out of doing math too.

As I have said, I won't actually do the math, but I will point out its complexity in simple terms. On average, a coin toss has a 50 percent chance of landing on heads and a 50 percent chance of landing on tails. In one hundred coin tosses, you would accept having forty-eight to fifty-two and not think much about it. If in one thousand tosses you had between four hundred and six hundred, you would start to check the coin. If you got between two hundred and eight hundred, you would call the coin magic and head to Vegas. When someone says she got an average of 58 percent on a random event, which should always produce about fifty-fifty average, it means something. When the average is 80 percent, there is something amiss. In high-volume controlled conditions, a sampling of data at 51 percent correlation means something. In fact, it is claimed as empirical evidence.

The coin toss has only two possible outcomes, which is not the case with the alphabet. To get two letters out of twenty-six to mean the same thing also has to be factored into the equation; I believe there are 325 possible combinations. Then to find two examples of it written in the literature screams that something is amiss. Here I add one more example for the literature.

I checked out *ev* while I was at it: evacuate, evade, evagination, evaluate, evanesce (to dissipate), evangel (bring good news), evanish, evaporate, evasion, evection, evert, evict, evidence, evil (arising from bad behavior), evince, eviscerate, evitable, evoke, evolute, evolution, ev-zone (a member of a Greek infantry unit) ... Again, I found that all but two words, which I left out, did not quite fit, excluding again redundancies, for a higher percentage of around 99 percent. I left out the words that I mentioned above (Eve, even ...), and this does not reconcile the likes of vert, pervert, introvert, and extrovert. This dictionary is over fifteen hundred pages long, not a pocket-size one. It's hard not to claim all of these letter combinations as empirical evidence, especially since two of the observations are not mine. For a pair of letters representing small sounds or slight combination of sounds to carry with them a larger meaning has some merit. In adding my *v* to the *sl* and *gl* example, it makes a third example appear in the literature.

For reasons I will never know, I checked the V words and found in the *va* combination a high correlation of words like vacate and vagile (free to move about). The *ve* combination gave many actual names, but when they were not names, it did have a fair correlation such as venison (to pursue), vent, and so forth. In the last two letter combinations of *vi*: violate, and *vo*: vocation, vocal, I found about the same high correlation, but again with lots of names. I can't count names—which are nouns—as meaning anything under the direct topic of this chapter. So without doing the actual math, I guessed—without considering the names—at about a 50 percent occurrence of correlation in meanings, but I think that it is a lot higher. I get a decent correlation with words starting with the combination *av*, which has only two root based words. With the letter combination of *iv*, I find both to be names, ivory, the name for the material of tusk and ivy the name of a creeping plant. The letter combination of *ov* is almost exclusively over and oval, as in dealing with eggs, and finally, the last combination of *uv* has only four words total, three of them dealing in color or pigmentation. All the words have some form of time, out of, or into air about them, like ivy, which is a plant that spreads out or climbs. Even the pigmentation meanings could be reconciled with the right thought process and a little work, which I will not attempt.

I don't use much of the accepted terminology regularly used in describing language. That is, terms like the following: clause, utterance, discourse, pidgins, creoles, gapping, NSL (Nicaraguan sign language), lexical, holistic, or the many more technical terms. The reason is that I am not writing a manual, which I am not qualified to do anyway. I also tend to use the word *word* generically and not as a suffix or prefix—or one of the many other terms used to describe add-on terms. If we are to get words from adding words together, then I shall call them all words. I am aware of the terms and find them too technical for everyone to understand without leaving long definitions when using them. I often found myself looking in dictionaries or other sources while reading some books. As I personally find it easer to think of these terms by examples used, I have chosen this method. This is why most of the following quotes are from older sources and not newer ones: fewer technical terms. The same applies to any biological terminology in the next chapters.

I think picking apart some of these quotes, which have not been answered adequately in the literature, might be in order. I feel that they add some form of evidence to my theory.

I don't have the proper symbols on my computer, so I used blanks in place of the symbols. This was done with all the quotes from *A Comparative Grammar* by Franz Bopp, reprinted by Cambridge University Press, 2009.

> Otherwise _ *s* usually falls back into the sound from which
> it appears to have originated, namely, *k*." (19)

This might be the need to change the state of a whole word or sound-word phoneme into another form: let *k* mean big and the new sound *s* mean bigger yet, while remembering that these are examples only and are *not to be taken literally.*

The Sanscrit could not endure *r* before *t*. The Latin protects the *s* usually at the end of words; but in the classical period generally sacrifices it, when between two vowels, to the *r*. (Bopp, 21–22).

Why? We could think in terms of grammar or order, as per the second chapter: if *r* meant a whole concept and *t* meant a whole concept, it would be like saying, while out hunting, "Shoot me (*rt*)," as opposed to saying, "Me shoot (*tr*)." You would not survive long enough to pass on your genes. This is what I referred to as world-ordered structure. Why is it that we cannot have a word spelled *squortul* as opposed to *squotrul*? It's against the rules! Whose rules? They're all letters! Unless they actually at some point in time meant something and the grammar rule was carried over into spelling rules—even for our new words.

Referring to the same quote, why does the *s* need protecting but will sacrifice it to the *r* if between two vowels? Do grammar rules really apply to words, or are they something we made up? The application of tilogos into sound-clichés as whole words is beginning to make more sense as we add real-life examples.

… or where u had vowelized itself into v or o. (Bopp, 62)

Vowelized itself? Why? At some point, we said, "Let's create letters for each sound so we can write our words down." Fine! It's not as though one day an ape, as is believed by some, said to its brethren, "Let's create sounds so that we can combine them and make up names for everything, to the end that we can communicate." Impossible! I shall look deeper into this invention of language later. For now, why would we soften the letters into vowels and not make new letters to represent those sounds? Unless of course, this softening of consonants into vowels was conceived of as sound alteration for another purpose altogether originally. To slightly vary the meaning of the sound-word—e.g., *go* versus *went*, soft *u* versus hard *u*—proposed a sense or state change with the hardening or softening of different letters. I will return to vowelized as a real property later in the book.

On the same page, we have this:

… in the absence of the letter which protects *o*. (Bopp, 62)

Why would *o* need to be protected, unless at some point it would have completely changed the meaning or concept of the utterance? For example, consider an imaginary word, *"abcdefg,"* which has a meaning of *a* = dead, *b* = elephant, *c* = cold (north), *d* = side, *e* = of, *f* = round, *g* = stone. You could remove the letter *d* and/or the letter *e* without changing the concept of there being food located at the familiar round stone, but if unprotected *f* or *g* were removed, you would not be able to determine, based on the meaning of these words, where to find the food. If it's designed, then why any need to protect anything at all, if any symbol can, in fact, represent any object or thought? This brings into question the origins of rules for language.

Back to that lowly *v,* which I have assaulted so much.

It is surprising, therefore, that the Greek, in this respect, shews no agreement with its sisters; and in its *v* stems, according to the measure of the preceding vowel, abandons either merely the nominative sign, or the *v* alone, never both together … which do not permit the remembrance of the *v* to be lost … (Bopp, 155)

If the word is the all-important part of speech, then throw some letters on a piece of paper, pronounce it however you'd like, and attach an object for meaning. Who would care if the letter *v* disappeared from the face of the earth, unless we lost the most precious meaning with it!

From the monosyllabic roots proceed nouns, substantive and adjective, by the annexation of the syllables, which we should not, without examination, regard as not, *per se,* significative and, as it were, supernatural mystic beings; to a passive belief in whose undiscoverable nature we are not willing to surrender ourselves. It is more natural to suppose that they have or had meaning, and that the organism of language connects that which has a meaning with what is likewise significative. Why should not language denote accessory ideas, by accessory words appended to the root? (Bopp, 121)

Why should the same statement not also apply to a phoneme if it had a meaning? From phoneme, to root, to combination, actually the phoneme would be the root of the root word.

I like the idea of a "sentence within a sentence," as suggested by Douglas Hofstadter in *I Am a Strange Loop* as a method of regulating the combination of (mathematical) concepts within concepts. I can relate a sentence within a sentence to the theory of sound-cliché. If each word we use is a sound-cliché, a sentence making up the word, then a sentence of words in itself would be made up of sentences combined into those sentences. As each sentence normally tells a different aspect of a story, combined into a paragraph, then each sound-cliché would tell a different story, combined into a sentence. In technical terms, I quote:

Although the clauses we have been considering are subordinate to some part of the principal clause, yet two or more of them may become coordinate with each other, and thus form a compound element of the third class ... Either of the principal or of the subordinate elements, when of the third class, may, like the single word or phrase, become compound. (Samuel Stillman Greene, *A Treatise on the Structure of the English Language*)

Take note that he recognizes compound in the single word or phrase as well as in the sentence.

Starting with *Cratylus* by Plato, who was the first philosopher to analyze words (that I know of anyway), we see the combination and alteration of said words. I will include one quote on the soul and deal with this topic later.

SOCRATES: If I am to say what occurs to me at the moment, I should imagine that those who first used the name psuche meant to express that the soul when in the body is the source of life, and gives the power of breath and revival (anapsuchon), and when this reviving power fails then the body perishes and dies, and this, if I am not mistaken, they called psyche. But please stay a moment; I fancy that I can discover something which will be more acceptable to the disciples of Euthyphro, for I am afraid that they will scorn this explanation. What do you say to another?

HERMOGENES: Let me hear.

SOCRATES: What is that which holds and carries and gives life and motion to the entire nature of the body? What else but the soul?

HERMOGENES: Just that.

SOCRATES: And do you not believe with Anaxagoras, that mind or soul is the ordering and containing principle of all things?

HERMOGENES: Yes; I do.

SOCRATES: Then you may well call that power phuseche which carries and holds nature (e phusin okei, kai ekei), and this may be refined away into psuche.

In the brackets are all the words used to make the word *psuche*, as per Plato's thinking. So the word psuche was made up of other names that mean to carry and hold nature. In fact, Plato was on the right track but did not actually go small enough.

Greek myth has many examples that the Greeks named their people and heroes with meaning. Hera was one of the gods, and Herakles, now spelled Heracles or Hercules, was the name given to one of the Greek's greatest heroes; the name means Hera's namesake. I understand that words such as panic were taken from Homer and the poets (pan meaning all) as great fear was struck in the hearts of men from the shriek of this creature that the gods named Pan.

The Hebrew Bible is filled with the same such name meanings: Lucifer (the morning star), Emanuel (God with us), and many more. If arranging names together to get other names was the norm, then why not arrange smaller sounds into words? Actually, this is a list on man in general:

Man
Human
Woman
Eman (adding uel) = God with us
Ahman = spirit

Atman = soul
Naman = name
Imen = name – different language
Adam means man in Hebrew
Manti meaning "spirit" or to "think" (Bopp page 330 #261)

There seems to be a lot of altering to the word man in many languages, and most definitions for man are to think. Just using the words Adam and Eve together is making this statement: the start of thinking man, a base I will use later.

Latin uses names that have their meaning attached in many cases. For instance, the word lavender is named after *lavare*, meaning to wash. Lavender was a plant that gave clothes a nice smell when washed with it, so lavender became the name of the plant as an easy way to remember what was done with it and what it was used for. There are many other examples of this, but I only need to mention one in order to have a basis for the thought.

Arabic does not allow a word to start with a vowel but instead places a mental holder, as in the case of, say, Allah. Not to forget that causative and permissive, and words used both as nouns and verbs, were used in biblical Hebrew, which did not use vowels originally. It is highly possible that all words that were not direct names for objects started out as verbs, as we would be in a constant state of interaction with the world. Interaction is a state of verb when naming. Later, some of these verbs would have become nouns and all the other terms we have placed on them, such as pronoun, to name just one.

As I have already dealt with how grammar works in the second chapter, the next topic requiring attention is to see if words actually fit grammar. As I searched for a word to use for the next purpose, I found this one as an example which seems to fit nicely.

Luluwa, in *The Book of Adam and Eve*, means beautiful: "Because she was more beautiful than her mother" (74:8). There seems to be a problem with some words for my process, so I will deal with the problem of Luluwa from the above example. When I say problem, I mean the double LU, LU in the word. Since we are dealing in concept, let us just assume that Lu is the concept of sight, which can be expressed as either a verb or a noun. NPs, VPs, and a descriptive noun do combine in this word. Let the first Lu stand for the noun sight, the second Lu stand for the verb looking, and the Wa stand for the concept pleasant. We now have a complete sentence: the sight I am beholding is pleasant. It uses proper syntax in a sound-cliché.

This would also be degraded to the word or noun, becoming the name of their daughter, Luluwa, or beautiful by concept. It is an *example* and not necessarily true of that or any other word, but compare it with Lucifer. Think of using illumination or enlightenment, luminosity or light, comparing it with sight: light to see by, look, saw ... a complete concept. The problem with a concept is that it would need to be taken in context, providing need for a better, more precise meaning. The topic of beauty will resurface later.

Listed below are some words taken from tribes from the Americas. I use them to show how they are grouped but will steal this one in advance for another example here on grammar.

I will take the word Zarabatana from below and analyze it, with the reminder that it is just a tool and not the real meaning of the word. In fact, I have no idea whatsoever what the real meaning of the word is, and I need not bother finding out. If I knew the real meaning, I would not be able to work it into another use. Ignorance is sometimes a good thing. Pay attention to the ordered grammar.

Zarabatana is riddled with the vowel *a* and no other vowels. We should be using the proper terminology of sound-word, so this sound-word *a* has a concept in totality and we want to keep this total concept throughout the sound-cliché while changing the meaning. The other sound-words adapt the *a* sound-word throughout the sound-cliché and we get the *Z* sound-word added to the *a* sound-word, giving us the altered sound-word *Za* plus the altered sound-word *ra* and so on.

This is one way of altering a huge concept into smaller ones, or at least refining the total concept for a more precise understanding. I want to keep things uncomplicated here, so I will use an overly simple example of an apple pie. If the sound-word *a* was for the concept of apple, we could get Za = peel apple + ra = cut apple + ba = season apple, and so on, the total of the combined words meaning apple pie. With rapidity, the continued use of them together would produce a sound-cliché. All these words fit what I will call consonant altered and vowel altered, that is, a consonant-vowel combination.

As obtuse as that example was, we need to start sometimes with poor thinking to get at the higher thinking processes. The apple example is admittedly poor; however, it is useful for thinking how to alter sounds and words into their separation and recombination of whole words with meaning. Don't take it literally. We can see that grammar is correct within this word as it is ordered; it has nouns and verbs ... This leads me to show some words that are considered even more ancient.

From *The Naturalist on the River Amazons* by Henry Walter Bates, whom I will not quote here, are some of the words of the aboriginals: Araman-I, Jeronymo, Cafuzo, Mamelucos, Farina, Jacare, Pini, Trabalhadores, Motuca, Manacapuru, Cucama, Arauana-I, Cotopaxi, Jabuti-puhe, Uiki, Wajuru, Zarabatana, Siriri, Aramassa, Mapiri.

Take note that the words are either all consonant-vowel, consonant-vowel, or they are vowel-consonant, vowel-consonant—

and in two or three letter groupings. Sucuruju is the name for anaconda. The names of two different berries but close in their nature: Puruma and Puruma-I. Bates also thought that the natives of the Amazon had a poor vocabulary. From Peru, we have words like Titicaca, and the word Kalasasaya is from Central America.

In the same way that the native words were grouped above, we see them grouped in a like manner in the *Myths from Mesopotamia*. Here I will list a few of these words:

Hehe
Zababa
Dumu-duku
Zulum-ummu
Ubshu-ukkinakku
Igigi
Lahamu
Huwawa

Both of these groupings are considered more ancient in their languages than European, for example. As this chapter is just to show how I arrived at my idea and thought processes, I will continue to take as many proofs as I can find.

Leaving the subject of grammar, we find another source to show single-sound conversion in words. I will quote and examine some statements from *Some reasons for thinking, [sic] that the Greek language was borrowed from the Chinese*, by Daniel Webb.

The first innovation of the Greek linguist on the Chinese monosyllable was extremely simple; it was to divide the monad, and give two sounds to that which had but one in the original. This, *perhaps,* was the first attempt at a duad.

The second was more *effectual,* by inserting the consonant between the two vowels: this, probably, gave rise in the Greek to words beginning with a vowel … We may, with some few exceptions, follow throughout the alphabet the Greek verbal roots, *duads* by prescription, but *monads* in structure: for, to constitute a duad, there must be two articulations, _ and _ are of a different mechanism. Now these monads are no other than Chinese primitives, which end as often in two vowels as in one, sometimes in three, and even four, as in the Greek.

One circumstance more – almost all the Chinese verbs end in O, so do the Greek…

Are these the casual agreements of two strange idioms, or unisons _ out of one common process?"

According to this, the Chinese used vowels to alter words. As I don't know any Chinese, I will take the word beauty and dissect it as I did with apple pie. Simple is the best way to go, but remember that simple loses some accuracy. If we take an example of good, better, best and apply it to our chosen word, we can at least make some sense of the process. In this case, *be* will stand for good, adding *a* brings it to better, and adding *u* brings it to best. This should be known as conceptual altering with vowels—discussed in full detail in the appropriate chapter. Looks good, no better, no best = *be* + *a* + *u* = *beauty* by concept.

Again, this is just a tool and not meant to be literal. From this, we can see how two separate languages could grow to be so different. If one language used altering with vowels mainly and another used vowel-consonant or consonant-vowel altering mainly, two different languages would grow, each with its own set of problems. Here the Greeks were said to fix some of this problem by adding consonants between vowels, leading to words starting with vowels.

It is known that the Greeks had a lot to do with the refinement of language when Alexander the Great spread the Greek language throughout the known world. The Romans modified some of it into their Latin, and in English, we have, besides our Germanic language background, many words from the Latin and Greek.

The Chinese having exhausted their vowel terminations on the unmodified signs of ideas, stopped short of inflection, they do not even apply it to the substantive verb, which consequently, with them, has not the virtue of an auxiliary. They have therefore, no other means of expressing the circumstances of the action, than by accompanying the principal verb with other verbs declaring the circumstances, or by particles designed to answer the purpose. (Daniel Webb)

As in verbs mentioned in this quote, if you run out of vowels to alter them, you would need new verbs to alter or describe the first verb in question. I will not attempt to make any examples here, moving on to the next topic instead.

The Interactional Instinct, from which I included a quote in an earlier chapter, argues that language did not evolve separately but came about by our interaction with others as an artifact. I believe that interaction also played an important role in the rise of language. I think that, like everything else, we sometimes overlook the whole picture, though. We would not have language if we did not have noise either. So the ears are the reason for language? Language may not have evolved as some would like to think, but without all these features, we would be dumb. We need hearing, the ability to make noises, the meaning or concept of things in general, a thought process, interaction, and many other things working together for the whole. If you place enough working materials together—functional window, functional door, functional roof—sooner or later they will construct a functional house. So what if they did not evolve together for the purpose of language? Once they have all evolved independently for other survival reasons, they will become selected for as preadaptations going into the makeup of language. You can't just say that language was selected for without saying what it was selected with!

Instead, we must say that because all these things were a survival advantage, their totality led to language. I must, then, at least attempt to show how all the many facets of tools required to achieve language arose in our species. I have not yet read any book on language that has not gone more or less deeply into the workings of the brain and other cognitive studies. I find myself also needing to go there, but I will try to attack the matter with different observations.

There is still much ground to cover, as I must show how all this could have reasonably come about. To do so, we must go into other topics that bear heavily on the origins of language. The brain structure, cognition, types of thought, what we have to work with, and yes, our interactions, are only a few, and I must cover them somewhat before continuing with how articulate speech has arisen from tilogos and sound-clichés.

Chapter Four

The Design Template

This seems more and more likely, there is a specific "language organ" in our brain, analogous to a "language chip" in a computer; this organ is to some degree hardwired, in that some of its neural connections are set correctly without external stimuli.

—John Maynard Smith
Origins of Life

As much as I loathe computer analogies, I must use one. It's difficult to find a book on brains or language that does not use a computer analogy. Mostly, though, they are dealing with intelligence based on Turing (Alan Turing) machines. Alan Turing hypothesized a machine that could reason. I won't use any of the same material here, as I am not looking for reasoning, but a template to convert calls and cries into tilogos and sound-clichés. If I must use a computer description, then it may as well be one that fits the facts best, and I think these will be the only things one will ever have to know about computers to make a comparison with a brain.

I also detest the word module for communicating the idea of separate brain areas or functions. However, most of the books on science, the brain, and language use these terms, and any readers, like me, are familiar with the terms. They are easy-to-use terms and require less of an explanation than the better ways to describe these processes. If you are not a science buff and are reading this book just because of your curiosity of language, then computers and modules might be easier to grasp, than the better but more complicated—in detail—terms would be. That said, I will put my feelings about the poor use of these terms aside and use them. This is why I chose the title "The Design Template" instead of "The Design Analogy" for this chapter.

Computers are designed, which requires forethought. We do not add one byte of memory every time we want to add one byte of programming, so it seems crazy for a brain to be selected for this way. We add huge quantities in one shot, up-front planning for future use. What are we up to now? We are into the terabytes for hard drives and ten gigs of RAM working memory or control systems. When you run out of space, you are stalled. Evolution does not plan, but brains grow through random gene mutation, and the ones with more capability will prosper and propagate.

When constructing a computer, one starts with hardware. Electronic boards and microchips are specifically designed and electrically coded for symbols to be represented in the form of on/off states of charge. The symbols are represented by eight, on or off states, like this one: 00101001—off, off, on, off, on, off, off, on—which the computers are wired for during construction. You need enough of these to allow base programming, done at the factory, and to be able to add other programs based on consumer demand, plus memory. MSDOS control system—the software that is used to load new programs and control the base system commands—works with the keyboard or a disc command only, and with these, any software can now be installed. Microsoft Windows can be installed to control all DOS commands. The names are registered trademarks.

Now we can see a structure emerge in a hierarchy that makes the computer easy to use. One could work the computer by using the preset commands—DOS—which is a lot of work. For example, you would have to press Control-F to reach the find screen to search for a word within a document. Instead, you can work the windows, which work the required commands for you. For instance, clicking on the Internet icon opens the Internet screen. In the end product, all one really needs is a finger to work the mouse. You simply place the curser in the proper place and push the button. I submit for your scrutiny that the finger on the mouse is the finger of the user's attention. This is as much as one can use the PC (personal computer) analogy, and we now go on to the automotive industry.

I am just an automotive technician, known as a mechanic in the real world, and it has earned me a living for a good many years. It is taken in my job as fact that I should know something about electricity. Although as the red line under the word indicates, I can't spell it. That corrected, I am also fairly competent in the computer systems of a good many vehicles. A whole book could actually be written on the computer systems of the automobile. I don't want to do that! I have instead chosen to be the least technical as possible in explaining them, even though I could be considered an expert and should have a more complex explanation. It is my understanding that expert does not mean perfect. It does not mean that you know everything; you are just experienced well enough to be competent in dealing within the areas of your training.

I have used enough of the basics about the home PC; the automotive industry has even a closer template to the brain. I understand it better, and through years of research, I have done much of my thinking and my comparisons to these systems rather than PCs, which is so common in the literature. Vehicle computers are also built on the same format as home computers: hardware, then control commands, then programs—all based on the famous if-then system: if this, then do that.

We have all seen the new commercials about using your cell phone to remote start your car. There is a bigger picture here, and a fruitful one. I am somewhat familiar with the General Motors systems, and they are all patented and copyrighted names and systems, but most of this you can get privy to on the Internet.

General Motors, and other makes, have broken their automotive computers into modules. As we don't really need a lot of detail, I will only deal with a few. The body control module, BCM, is one of them. In vehicles with the new BCM technology, you are not really starting the car but merely commanding the BCM (computer) to start the vehicle for you. The ignition key being turned simply tells the BCM that you wish to start your vehicle's engine. The BCM then checks to see if all other modules are reporting in—that is, did they power up, twelve volts or greater? It then grounds the starter motor circuit, causing the engine to crank over and start. In their new vehicles, you can get factory-installed remote auto starters, which tell the BCM that you want to start the engine, without signal from the ignition switch. It works as part of the key fob—the remote for locking and unlocking the doors. It's only one more step to go to a phone. In GM's case, they also have OnStar.

They also have systems that communicate with each other with their GMLAN, which has two systems in itself: high-speed LAN and low-speed LAN. High-speed LAN has one series wire, either loop or star configuration, which all modules report on. They use priority messaging determined by frequency as to which is the more important message, with safety first, comfort last. In the loop configuration, if the single series-circuit wire goes open circuit, you must check the wire to all the modules. Think of a circle with a bunch of modules hooked into it; if open, all communication stops. In the star configuration, if one wire goes open circuit, you only need to check that one module not communicating. Think of an asterisk button on your keyboard and how the lines run from the center in all directions, joined in the middle. There is no redundancy of communication for GMLAN. In some vehicles, there are over twenty modules instead of one big computer doing it all.

Not to be confused here: the BCM does not control every computer with ultimate power. There is still a module controlling the engine systems (ECM) and the transmission systems (TCM) independently. At any one time, the main power of control could be a different module. The knowledge is just shared between the modules. For instance, if the BCM detects an improper key being used, it will communicate this to the ECM. The ECM will then shut off the fuel pump and the vehicle will not start: theft mode. The ECM reports back to the BCM that theft mode is enabled ... It is this communication part that I will work with throughout most of the remainder of the book.

Modular computerization seems to be the way the brain works also, to avoid having every sense organ reporting to the brain and within the brain all at the same time, in some sort of mass confusion. Lastly, I will mention a sensor or two that reports to the various modules, leaving the decisions to the independent modules and reporting only the conclusions to the main computer, not all the unneeded paraphernalia. A coolant temperature sensor in the engine tells the computer module in charge how hot the engine is and to run the electric cooling fan and regulate air/fuel ratio.

Continuing with the temperature sensor, the ECM needs to know the engine temperature for air/fuel mixture as noted above, but so does the BCM. The BCM needs it to control your air-conditioning. Less AC when your engine is cold ... Why would needless money and resources be spent on having a separate coolant sensor for each module? A second sensor would be a throttle position sensor, which senses how wide—or closed—your throttle is open (gas pedal depressed), which relates directly to engine load. When you are going up a steep hill and need more power, the BCM must know this in order to shut down AC for the extra power needed. If while driving, the air bag module senses a problem, it is a safety issue, so it is given high priority and interrupts communication to put the light on and make a beep sound to signal the driver. Some vehicles even turn the volume off on the radio so you can hear the beep and have your attention brought to bear on the problem. This cross communication freely among modules gives the effect of floating conscious—not literally—as any module could be in control at a given time or place. The automobile does not feel the floating effect. When each module needs the information, it is available and reported. The mouse on your computer as well as the keys on your keyboard could all be considered sensors, or inputs, of some sort. They are what are known as if-then correlations: if air bag, then light; if keyboard letter *a* key pushed, then show letter *a* on Word document.

One more detail about home computers and automotive computers and I will deal with the electrical side of things. After you install Windows on your PC, you can now have many programs or documents running at the same time. As I am writing this, I have two or three Word documents open at the same time. One is this book and another is a document I use to write down ideas as I get them because I don't want to forget them.

The computer does not cross-communicate between these documents at all. For instance, this paragraph or two will not automatically merge into *Tilogos* as soon as I write the appropriate area or chapter of the book where the paragraph should go. I will have to cut it and paste it where I need it. This leads to an outside force being the prime mover. If we want computers to write their own stories, we need more. We need them to understand that I am writing a book and these other documents are part of the book. Then we need them to place like content with appropriate like content. I doubt that this could ever be designed by a master program writer. This is where I leave off on the home PC and begin a better comparison.

Cars learn your driving habits. The home PC does not learn how slowly and poorly I type and make adjustments—although it does perform a spelling and grammar check. The automotive computer does learn. For instance, the transmission on the computer controlled (TCM) vehicles will learn your driving habits and shift best for your performance requirements. The biggest complaint I had for a while was during summer vacations. Trips would be taken, and upon return, customers would phone for appointments to get their cars checked. One of the most common complaints I heard was that the transmission seemed to "shift funny" after a trip. A few days later, when the customer came in for the appointment, he claimed that it was better, and upon checking, we found no problem. Questioning the customer always produced the answer: he would be on a long trip, and when returning, the shift points changed. It took longer to shift into higher gears, a property of highway driving. Quicker shifts are a property of city driving, with slower speeds and more frequent stops. This we call experience as opposed to knowledge. It more closely resembles experience in the brain, and experience is a leading learning factor in animals. The automobile does not know it is learning: it only has experience, not conscious knowledge. We can use it, though, to see what is missing.

This is not technical so by default not very accurate, but it is truth based. Parameters set within the computer preset the shift points. There is also a programmed variance that the computer is allowed to try for any given set of conditions. It might try to shift a little sooner or later and sample the load of the engine, and if the load of the engine is good, alter it again until it gets a bad result. Perhaps more detail is needed here to relate it to survival. If it is allowed to shift too soon, it will overload the engine, shake, and stall, leaving you on the side of the road. If it does not shift soon enough, it will use up more gas, which is energy, causing you to run out sooner, leaving you stranded on the side of the road. Conservation of energy is the basis of natural selection: survival of the fittest. The automobile will thus, through experience, learn where—driver specific—the performance/energy conservation of shifting best suits the driver. If you drive your car for a week, loan it to a friend, and drive it again, you can even feel the difference in shifting after a couple of days. This brings us back to the independent modules.

I just wrote that the engine load was checked for by the transmission computer (TCM) from the ECM (engine control module) for load: if the shift is too early, the engine will lag or shake. If it shifts too late, the engine will over rev. An engineer just has to write the program with the stipulation that load should always be within fifty RPM of desired RPM. Communications between the two allows shared information for learning but also allows for the ECM to "do" engine and the TCM to "do" transmission. There must be communication between modules, at least to acquire and pass on the experience learned.

Looking at the different brain areas, we have the same type of performance. The amygdala has what is known as the fight-or-flight response, and it could, because of safety first, take control of the whole brain/body to flee from danger while sharing this information with other areas of the brain. After another area analyzed the fear response and situation, it might take control again if the amygdala was mistaken: not snake, rubber hose. This also allows learning through experience. It allows the amygdala to "do" amygdala and another area to "do" another area, but also learning and sharing of senses.

Turning to ignition cylinder keys for different language examples, we find that computers have the ability to learn which driver is going to drive the vehicle. This not only solves the transmission shift problem but also seat memory, from the "seat memory module" learned from each driver. Key specific, the seat automatically "sets" to the same position where it was before that specific key was removed from the ignition by that specific driver. We are far enough along in establishing language now, and it will save me from doing it later, to use different tongues as an analogy. Keys have the different drivers with seat adjustments. With words, sounds are the keys: *ve* sets the word meaning one way in one language, and *ev* sets the word with same meaning the other way, specific to the key leading to different tongues, e.g., French versus English. I will touch on different languages briefly in another chapter. Differences in keys are designed, but language is not. The brain can do this without being specifically designed to do so.

Computers can't do it because they don't reproduce after their kind, and it would require ingenious thinking to make it happen, which equates design. Computers would need to reproduce and be naturally selected without interference from a designer, creator, or a god. Computers are designed!

Do we have enough of a template to build a brain yet?

Let's turn to circuitry of the various kinds first and see what we can unearth. There are three basic circuits, and the numbers on the diagrams with numbers are usually there to do Ohm's law equations, but I use it for another purpose below. No math! This is a simple series circuit.

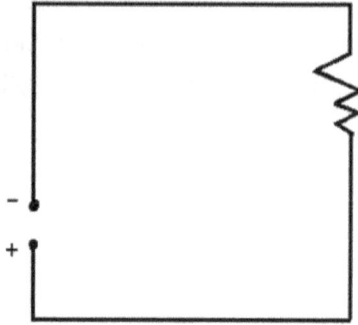

As we can see from the diagram, we have one wire going from source to resistance back to source. This is how basic lower animal wiring of nervation works. Let's say you have a sensitive nerve ending or sensor in your leg. If the sensor is excited externally, the current flows from the sensor through the sensing nerve circuit and into the muscle, causing the muscle to contract, thus causing movement in the muscle and, by extension, the creature in question. If the nerve suffers an open circuit working the muscle, in the end the muscle will not contract. We do not have two or more routes to take in case of an open circuit, as in the following parallel circuit; we only have redundancy in series. We are wired in redundancy also, but this has more to do with evolving higher nervation than electricity.

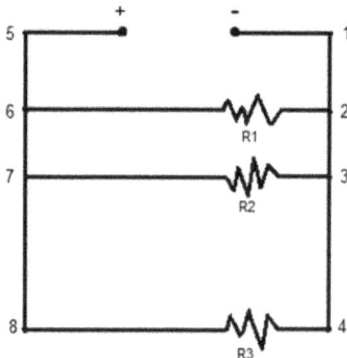

The parallel circuit shown here has more than one path to follow and is supposed to be the way the brain is wired. For one purpose, it could be considered a redundant series wiring system. Let's follow the next step in the evolution of nervation and see what happened. At some point, a brain stem and spinal cord was introduced into the mix and the nerve reported to the brain stem and its automatic nervation of the leg muscle at the same time. So we now have automatic nervation and knowledge of the nervation reported. This made voluntary movement possible, as the new brain stem could "at will" cause the muscle to contract by means of nerve charge from a second source. Actually, it would have started out as nervous system and not brain stem or spinal cord, but I am not going to be evolving a nervous system. Since the standard nervation is in a series circuit, from the sensor to the muscle, adding one more different circuit does not necessarily make it parallel, as they are from two different sources. It would make it series-parallel, much like in the following diagram.

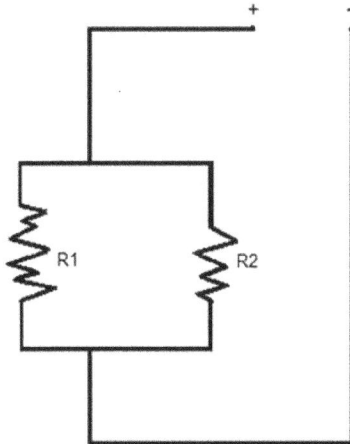

If we follow this diagram and go from the voltage source, the series part, to the first resistor, R1, back to the source, we can call this sensor nervation. Following R2, we can call it willful nervation, being wired into the spinal cord or brain stem—the final step of all vertebrate. This is so important because we need to have automatic reflexes and willful movement. There is no reason to believe that the rest of the brain is not wired the same way—and every reason to believe it is.

I am strictly looking for language and use these analogies to get there, so we must do two things: be simple in our thoughts and, at the same time, be as accurate as we can with these simple terms. If you go to your local hardware store and walk through the wiring section, making these observations as you do, it will help clarify things somewhat. In fact, you should buy a one-foot piece and have it in front of you while reading this. In the commonly used house wire, we have what's called 14/2: it has one copper wire covered in a black casing, one copper wire covered in a white casing, and one copper wire with no covering. The black is live, the white is called common, and the bare wire is the ground.

Generally, the black is powered up, the current sent through a resistance (light) and returned on the white wire, the common. In case of a short circuit, the power is sent directly to ground on the bare copper wire. For reasons that will be dealt with shortly, we don't need the ground in our bodies, as it is only a safety feature. The reason for the color-coded coatings on these wires is for the sole purpose of keeping track of which is "live," or "hot," and which is not.

The reason for the coatings has nothing to do with keeping track but everything to do with stopping electricity from leaking or shorting into the other wires. If you were to imagine that both of the wires were the same color, you could follow the first of the three simple diagrams above and have current flow from the source to R1, say a lightbulb, and return to the source as a complete series circuit if using one light only. I have seen some house lights wired in series, but they are normally wired in parallel. More comments on parallel in a moment.

We also need to consider first conductors, semiconductors, and insulators. Conductors are any material that has the property of free electrons. If there are no free electrons, the current needs higher voltages to push it through the material. If air did not have any resistance, we would never have lightning storms. Lightning builds up electrical voltage until enough pressure (voltage) is there to overcome the resistance (air) and then seeks ground. Copper has a good low resistance to current flow, so it is used to direct the current to where you want it. It can leak electrical current or short-circuit.

A high resistance is needed to stop these leaks and keep the current flowing where you want it to. Plastic is such a material, and it is important to have it wrapped around the conductor to stop leaks as well as provide some strength to the conductors. This is seen in stranded wiring, where lots of bending needs to be addressed. Many smaller wires will not break as easily as one solid one will. At any rate, without both conductors and insulators, electricity would not be possible, or at least it would be very dangerous and *uncontrollable*.

I use the word parallel in two different contexts or concepts in two different areas of the book. Here I use it as wiring. In house wiring, the second wiring diagram is somewhat misleading. If you bought a piece of wire and had it in front of you, you would see that it has two different colors, as mentioned. Look at the second wiring diagram and change the color on the wire, following the resistors R1, R2, and R3 on the same side of the resistor to white. Actually, the numbers one through four would be black, and the numbers five through eight would be white. This would give a truer picture of parallel, and it is generally used in household wiring.

The second use of parallel, which I will use later, is dealing in space/time. If you are still looking at this piece of wire, you will see that it is wrapped in yet another outer case, which keeps these smaller pieces of wire held together in parallel—that is, the same distance apart throughout its length. The space/time will be considered contained in two parallel areas of the brain, but the details are postponed to a more appropriate chapter.

We are dealing with something manmade, and it needs, in order for it to work, an electrical supply, also man-made. It requires a generating station. It also uses parallel wiring, which would be the equivalent of two nerves running through every neuron and muscle in the body. The body is a one-wire system.

In the automotive world, right off the bat, series-parallel is used. Your battery is directly wired in series to the fuse box, which is sometimes wired in series or parallel to the various other electrical parts of the automobile. The positive cable goes to the fuse box only, not back to the source. The source is grounded directly to the body, or chassis. Unlike house wiring, because the chassis is grounded, we can run only one wire to the resistance—light—and then just ground it. This looks a little more like what we are after, but alas, it won't work for the human body. Cars are manufactured with a power supply: the battery. This looks more like our third diagram, though, that of a series-parallel circuit.

Series-parallel is a common electrical term, but it is backward to my thinking on one account. In dealing with the body and brain, a more accurate word would be parallel-series. First, as mentioned, the sensor senses and then enervates the muscle, and then it sends a signal to the brain, and this is series-parallel. Second, the brain can enervate the muscle or the sensor can enervate the muscle, and this is parallel-series.

None of these terms are in the least bit accurate, even as used in electrical theory. Parallel still uses only one wire and not two or more wires from the power source throughout circuit. By opening one wire in the circuit, you open the circuit to one resistor, and that resistor—light—goes out. That, even though it is called parallel, is still series. The difference is mainly that the rest of the lights stay lit. It is only good for an explanation of the types of circuits and not de facto. I use it in this same spirit.

Can evolution possibly evolve an electrical wiring system, insulated, self-powered, and self-grounded? The answer is yes! For the most part, as we shall see, the nervous system has low resistance, coated wiring, and is self-generating. Remember that this is just a template to use to get our language origins, so I will try to keep it as simple as I can. I will deal with how it does it in another chapter of the book, when I examine the soul. For now, I will limit my commentary to the thinking process in communicating with speech.

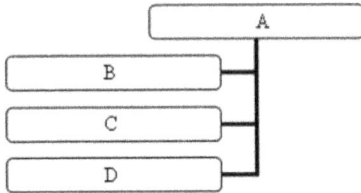

I would consider this a one-wire series-parallel circuit. The line perpendicular to and going from the box A is series and would continue to run as long as needed for adding more information. The other boxes, B, C, and D, have their lines paralleled into the series A line, remembering that we don't need to account for the return or ground, as the body self-supplies it or, properly, does not need one. A is the sentence we wish to utter. B is one thought in word form added to the sentence, which can either be accepted or rejected. C is one thought in word form added to the sentence, which can either be accepted or rejected. D is one thought in word form added to the sentence, which can either be accepted or rejected. Consequently, if we are formulating thought, we can accept placement of D and B, while negating placement of C, into our serial sentence or thought stream. This also gives us our branching effect in synaptic connections.

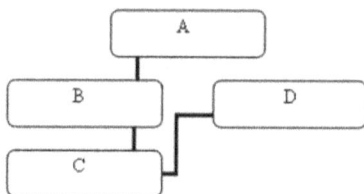

This would be considered a series circuit, and again, A would be the final sentence. The line going to A, being our final thought in word form, is made up of D, C, and B, so if one word were the wrong one, say C, we would not have any control over negation. Whatever thought just happened to pop up from nowhere would be added into the mix, causing poor communication, to say the least. To negate one part for incorrectness would be to negate all. This would also be considered serial thought—that is, a continual stream of information. If B were rejected, everything after it would be rejected too, and you would need to start the thought or sentence over again until you got it right. It also does not account for branching of nervous tissue, or synapses.

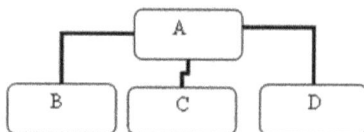

I would consider this a parallel circuit. This is the current thinking in which the brain works—that is, in parallel. Parallel, by its very meaning, is number sensitive: you can't have one! Two, three, fifty, a thousand or more can all be parallel. Problem with the model? It can never fire two separate concepts into one "I got it" or it will not be parallel anymore. It would automatically make it series-parallel. As we can see, all thought would report to the A, being the final thought in word form we wanted to present. There is nothing wrong with this, except that we would have to allow for whatever word came up to be spoken uncontrolled, or longer time frames of thought would be demanded for accurate thought to emerge.

If you add to this one certain neuron to be in charge and choose between all the thoughts in word form placed before it, the neuron in charge would have to sample in series one word at a time. I show here only three thoughts in word form, but the number would actually be infinitely huge. This parallel setup would require all our thoughts to be present at once and pick one from many for the first word, then look them over again and pick one more word for the second ... and keep them all ordered as we speak. This would be time consuming. It also works poorly if you use two in-charge neurons, as which one will have the final say? Bottom line: you need one as an end result for control. You need one for "mind" and "language."

Clarification is needed here. This does not void redundancy in any way. There will be several neurons "in charge," if you will, within the brain and free to give a floating effect to represent the mind.

We are looking for serial thinking, meaning that one thought or word is added to another in their proper relationship, and we have the power to select for the ones we want to use to express ourselves as the words are spoken.

The first diagram I used and called series-parallel would use the entire brain as a search tool and report the findings to the serial A line thought in word form, for rejection or acceptance. It is easier for the whole brain, which knows all we are thinking, to send everything to one place, with final say on the end result, than for one conscious area to do all the searching, and this is reported in the literature:

> Of course, the whole of the mind could not be reported in a part of the mind. This follows logically from the relationship between part and whole. (Gregory Bateson, *Steps to an Ecology of Mind*, 438)

The whole of the mind here is not A, reporting to its parts: B, C, D. The parts B, C, D report to what we only perceive as the whole, but in reality, it is still only a part. You might have to strain a little to get that, but this will be covered again in a later chapter dealing in words.

Also, this might seem a little contradictory, as I wrote earlier that calls and cries were total complete concepts, and I am now writing about one being selected from many. We do need a means of singling out the separate parts of the whole, which I defer to the math.

These are shown on paper with the aid of diagrams to be hardwired into the brain, but it is only a tool and not really hardwired. The information is actually relayed through different synapses firing, which are in no real sense hardwired, i.e., soldered together. They are just there with the coded information from many different modules or areas of the brain, ready to fire into the structure of a sentence if needed or used. This gives us the feeling of thoughts floating around in our brains in a literal sense, or what is called the illusion of mind.

If I am right, the information starts out in the series form or serial data form, with each new word or thought coming into the mind's view parallel to it—many series for the same purpose equates to parallel. The right ones are chosen—allowed to fire—and added to the serial data stream, making up the correct sentence or complete thought in word form. No need for series thought or parallel thought, for both are combined into series-parallel thought or a series-parallel data stream. In case you have not already drawn the conclusion, the emotional center, say, the fight or flight center, will need to report to whatever it needs to report to and "do" its thing at the same time, e.g., utter a call or cry while fleeing from a danger. Also, it needs to be able to butt in. All its calculations are silent to our attention or mind, and only the decision is presented for our final control. We can either go with the emotional automatic response or veto it. This leaves us in a good position for the next chapters.

There are a couple more things to take into consideration here, and they will be well used in application to language later. Analog has different meanings, one for electricity, which I will start with and compare to digital. Analog, in electrical terms, is like a bell curve, and I will show the two pictures of them. It slowly goes from a negative value across a neutral value and into a positive value. When I say "slowly," we are still dealing with the speed of light that electricity travels. Slowly is meant to describe the sixty cycles per second that your lights oscillate in climbing from, positive volts to negative volts and back again. Both the negative and positive values are the same, say 120 volts, for house current AC—alternating current. This type of current is not usable by any part of the body. Nervation is either on or off, electrically or chemically.

Digital current is a square wave, not truly a wave, and has the properties of being either on or off. An example would be that it has, say, five volts on for half a second and then no voltage at all for half a second. The pattern looks square on an oscilloscope, like in the diagram. For practical purposes, it is relatively fast and looks square, still dealing in light speed.

Digital also has more than one meaning, but first the other analog meanings. Another use for analog is in analogy, using one topic to describe another topic that is different but the same.

A farmer who was on his deathbed wanted his children to acquire some experience of farming. He summoned them to him and said, "My children, I am not long for this world, but, as for you, look for what I have hidden in my vineyard and you will find all." The children, imagining that their father had buried a treasure in some corner of his vineyard, hoed deeply all of the ground in it as soon as their father died. They found no treasure, but the vineyard, so well tended, gave its fruit many times over. (Aesop: "The Farmer and His Children")

It also means the exact same thing. That is, we use one topic to describe the exact same topic. If you did not know what a hammer was, I might pick up a hammer and show it to you, then send you to the store to buy a new one. That use is considered analogous. It is what the brain uses to represent images, somewhat like a picture. When you take a picture, it does not show the car parked out back if, in real life, the car is parked in front. (This is not to be confused with the negative images on film.) To be clear, one use of analog is to use something different to describe something different with the same types of properties, and the other use of analog is to use something the same to describe something the same.

Digital is used in electrical terms as above, but it also means something different. It means that objects or data are cut into smaller pieces and stored randomly, or in the case of pictures on film, they are many single dots combined into a solid-looking structure. Electrically, it is in either an on state or an off state.

I am told by a reliable source that this is how computers store data. They break the data up into smaller chunks, assign an address to the smaller chunks of data, and store them at random locations in the hard drive. If you have a hard drive problem, you might still be able to recover some fragments of data this way. If it were all stored in one same spot and that spot had a problem, everything would be lost in that data storage place. I will use these concepts when I am talking about words and the brain later. When the file needs to be retrieved it looks up these remembered addresses and then recombines them into the original document.

I have to reemphasize here that these concepts are not well explained, as it would take a whole book in itself to do so. If you don't completely understand all these concepts, remember that you don't need to. Rather than building an analogy, I'm creating a template to follow in the next chapters. I will explain why I went into electricity before moving on. AC current is no good to a computer system. It needs to be converted to DC in order to be of value and get on/off states. These on/off states are digital. They have to be designed by man, and programs have to be written. I will quickly show here that nature was able to do so without the necessity of design. Nervation is digital and self-powered from the beginning. Design is not needed because the nerves that fire correctly—natural selection process—combine to make the species in question work. Natural selection has produced electrically *self-generating and self-programmed* species.

Before going to the next chapter, I should recap the part of this chapter that relates to the first three chapters. The innate basis, the 01100101, is analogous to the sound-words complete with total concept, which are hardwired into the brain. The entire content of chapter 1 was to show these sounds to be base programming. It takes eight bits to make a byte, and a byte is considered a usable command—just as it takes several sound waves to make a usable call. The 01001101 is compatible with our call or cry in our thinking. The calls are built into the system at the factory! The MSDOS is analogous to the first level of speech, yet to be explained in better terms than V pause, E pause, R pause, and Y pause taken from the previous chapter. The Windows are analogous to the sound-clichés; you don't need to work the sounds separately anymore, as the whole word—sound-cliché—does it. The Windows icon can now operate the whole word without the pause. The electrical stuff helps to understand how the body, brain, and nervous system become combined, shared, and able to become working software. This is, after all, just a template.

There are more accurate ways of explaining the nervous system, but they are also more complicated. Anyone can turn on a light switch and see the light come on. At the expense of greater accuracy, I have chosen to use electricity, even though it has fallen by the wayside in the literature. The true workings of the nerves and nervous system are described in detail more often. This is just one template to use, and we need an even more important template.

Chapter Five

The Placenta Template

It is as though the human brain were wired in the course of human evolution so that the output of an old system for calls and cries were patched into the input of the new system for articulate speech.

—Stephen Pinker
The Stuff of Thought

I have a need for a biological example, and as rich as the literature is, I could not find one to my liking, so with your patience, I will create my own, going from yolk sac to placenta. There seems to be a point, partway between the two, according to *A Treatise on Comparative Embryology* by Francis Maitland Balfour, that some animals have attained. That is, they have a yolk sac but also form a partial placenta, which the author calls a semiplacenta. I will deal here with the placenta in general and quote Balfour:

The formation of the blastodermic vesicle may perhaps be explained on the view that in the proto-mammalia the yolk-sack [sic] was large, and that its blood-vessels [sic] took place of the placenta of higher forms. On this view a reduction in the bulk of the *ovarian ovum* might easily have taken place at the same time that the presence of a *large yolk-sack* was still necessary for the purpose of affording surface contact with the uterus. (Francis Maitland Balfour, *A Treatise on Comparative Embryology*)

Let's start with the egg. If, for whatever reason, an animal born via eggs could not migrate due to underdevelopment and it perished, it would soon end the species. A bigger yolk sac would be required for the same "in uterus" time. If the trend continued, the yolk would be limited by the size of the uterus, as the size of the egg is capped by the space inside the uterus. At some point, the energy needs would overcome the yolk sac supply.

It is a lot more complicated than that, and I will mention just one complication: the eggshell. As the shell of the egg only hardens later, after leaving the birth canal, the shell remains soft enough for veins to penetrate. The softer shell and larger yolk sac would make better contact with the uterus, making a transition easier. When the veins of the developing animal grow into the yolk sac, some, by chance, could also grow into the uterus (problem), making additional nutrition available to the embryo, directly from the mother. As changes in gestation, earlier impregnation, and seasonal changes—pushed for by increased complexity of the animal—took place, more nutrition would be needed sooner, and the full placenta would soon push out the yolk sac. A more complex placenta and vein system would come into being.

The placenta is not, nor can it be, strongly attached to the uterus wall. If we allow for the umbilical canal, stalk, and veins to grow directly into the uterus, removal of the fetus would be impossible. The mother, the fetus, or both would bleed to death upon separation. The placenta needs to grow attached to but not into the uterus. Complexity comes into play here. There needs to be a means of attaching the placenta to the uterus wall, becoming connected enough for blood flow to the placenta and then into the umbilical cord and into the embryo. There would be selective pressure for a complex placenta. If complexity can work its way into the placenta, it can work its way into articulate speech.

To convert this to the language origin question, let the yolk sac be the starting point in the brain—the innate calls, cries, and sounds I went over in the first chapter. If we were to change veins into nervation or synaptic connections, we could establish a starting point for an articulate speech module. It is usually assumed that as the egg gets bigger, it produces larger offspring, which can produce even larger eggs. The language module of the brain would not be doing any reproduction of its own and would rely on a larger brain growing, but if we take it one step at a time, we will get where we want to be. This yolk sac was likely dominated by calls, cries, and maybe other slight sounds with meaning.

If I start with this as a base and use the placenta as a second resource in going from calls, cries, and sounds, one can see that just tapping directly into the brain will not do. It would be just like running the veins directly into the uterus. In the case of language, it would just add more of the same: calls and cries. We need to change these calls and cries. We need our brains to form placenta-type complex transitions. I already gave an example of how to go from sounds into sound-clichés, as I have called them. This, however, is the end result of the process, and we must now find a way of doing the transition. No placenta, no complex change.

There is nothing like complexity to hold pressure. Changing one's own niche would surely keep the pressure of complexity at its maximum. It is commonly said that we were nothing special. We had no long, sharp claws, vicious biting jaws, or super speed. We needed to rely on our wit, whatever that was at the time, and communication with the other members of our tribes or species. Articulate communication became our first unique to human niche change. I will get to the second niche change in due time. First we grew from phoneme concepts to whole word concepts to fluent articulate speech, all driven by niche change. The more we changed, the greater the need to change, just to keep up.

I was sitting on a bench in a park one day and noticed that a robin flew down a few feet in front of me for a worm. I was surprised that the robin did not just eat the worm but started cutting it into pieces. My first thought was, *Do they really eat worms in smaller pieces?* I paid closer attention, and it seemed to divide it into equal one-third pieces. As the robin was picking up the three pieces, it hit me like a ton of bricks that it was food for her chicks. I followed her, and as the trees were low, I could see that she had three chicks. Could she possibly count? Not in our sense! Neither could we count in our sense before something happened to us: we learned to do math. We started out the same as that robin.

According to Keith Devlin, who wrote a whole book on the instincts of different animals having mathematical abilities, dogs can actually do calculus. The book is titled *The Math Instinct*, and no, he does not suggest that they sit down and write out math problems with pencil and paper. They do it mentally and unconsciously to find the shortest way to get to their destinations. It would be a survival advantage to get to your prey in the shortest, fastest, most energy-efficient way possible. The knowledge is all in our genomes through trial and error.

Knowing these mathematical properties innately would eventually let us analyze them and figure out in word form how to do the calculations. It would require the collective work of many, over thousands of years, to give the mathematical symbols we now have:

> I fear, in fact, that at this point the reader may be slipping into the conviction that these ancient and medieval algebraists were not very bright. We started in 1800 BCE with the Babylonians solving quadratic equation written as word problems, and now here we are 2,600 years later with al-Khwarizmi ... solving quadratic equations written as word problems. (John Derbyshire, *Unknown Quantity*)

More on these properties later, when I undertake the properties of analyzing. For now, we should derive the fact that this collective knowledge is stored somewhere in our brains, just waiting to be exploited by cognition.

It has been reasonably shown that we all have an innate number instinct and possibly *two* different areas of the brain in use for each one: one area for small quantities under three—recognized without counting—and another area that actually counts larger quantities. William James, in *The Principles of Psychology*, discussed being able to mentally track six or seven objects before losing count. The fact that we have two brain areas for counting was actually derived from brain scans. Researchers would scan brains with fMRIs—functional magnetic resonance imaging—asking the test subject to either count larger quantities or look at smaller ones and see what areas of the brain lit up.

Remember that knowledge is sometimes all or nothing, as in counting. For instance, once you learn the concept of placing two different names on sticks—the name one if the stick is alone and the name two if you have two single sticks side by side—addition is born, and now you only need to name the different totals. The same can be said of words.

There also seems to be an additional center in the brain for processing phonemes, separately from the one that processes words or language proper. It could also be reasonable to derive the fact that we have two language centers working the same as our two math centers. We could have one language center that related meanings to phonemes and another area that actually took these phoneme concepts and worked them into our more modern speech system.

"Automatic handwriting" is considered by the religious to be an instrument of the devil. Science sees it as unconscious brain control yet to be fully explained. "Speaking in tongues" is viewed by religion to be speaking God's language, because it is recorded in the Bible:

> And began to speak with other tongues … how hear we every man in our own tongue, wherein we were born? (Acts 2:4–6)

In fact, some believers think that you can't get into heaven unless you can speak in tongues! I wonder what happened to believing He was raised from the dead. Interestingly, though, the sides have been flipped in the two cases. Religion believes it is true, and science is at odds with speaking in tongues. In part because automatic handwriting is understandable, you can read what was written and take it as a type of proof. Speaking in tongues is not articulate in any language, and it sounds like a bunch of random noises.

In a brain scan of a person speaking in tongues, a different area of the brain than is normally used lights up. Could it be the first language area—notwithstanding the two acknowledged speech areas Wernicke's and Broca's—that lights up? If so, it may truly be the language of the gods, accessed by unconscious brain control! It would explain the reason you need to be in a different state of consciousness to understand speaking in tongues, understood to be the interpretation of tongues, which according to the apostle Paul is also a gift of the Holy Spirit.

For the sake of convenience, I will call this the speaking-in-tongues module and relay it as being quite possibly our yolk sac, which pushed into a full-blown articulate speech system as it grew into the brain in altered form. Remember that the sounds as calls were already innate with concept and only needed a push to alter them into speech. Complexity needed to be overcome, and we must journey toward that end. In order to answer the question on our language placenta properly, we need to understand what we have to work with, and this will be the topic of the next chapter.

Calls and cries, which are languages' veins, need to be adapted into another type of organ that can grow a new way. We could not allow the veins of the yolk sac to grow directly into the uterus, because the yolk sac and uterus would be one: a chicken permanently growing inside a chicken. We don't want calls and cries permanently growing inside calls and cries. One is biological and formed a complex placenta attached to but not growing into the uterus. Language is not biological in the same strict sense, but we need to have calls and cries attached to, not growing into a new brain area as calls, but in the new form as words. By "attached," I mean conceptually attached but altered into articulate speech, holding the same species of meanings. In the case of language, it must change from analog into digital—better explained later. It will become clear how it is done when I do the math. This was just a means to explain the problem and point out that a change was needed. Some possible sources and solutions within the brain can now be explored.

These same problems occur with not only the placenta and language but also cognition in general, and they must also be overcome in order to learn how to manipulate or influence calls and cries, process the world, and make sense of all the gray areas in learning.

Chapter Six

De Anima

As a Christian, I find the flow of their logic particularly depressing. Not only does it teach us to fear the acquisition of knowledge, which might at any time disprove *belief, but it suggests that God dwells only in the shadows of our understanding. I suggest that if God is real, we should be able to find him somewhere else—in the bright light of human knowledge, spiritual and scientific.*

—Kenneth R. Miller
Finding Darwin's God

I must place this disclaimer here because I don't want those who read this, including my mother, my friends, my children, and the church I serve to think of me as some sort of heathen. I believe in a god. I also believe in a spirit or soul. The soul is what animates us, or *anima* in Greek. These beliefs are by choice. As I work hard here to destroy the idea of having any extra persona at work within the brain or body and try to get down to the bare minimum of what animates us, I draw the same conclusion as many others in the field of science. There is no extra person or persona in our brains, creating the mind or soul. I believe that if there is any proof of a soul's existence, it will prove to be a different state of matter, not an extra prime mover of matter. (A prime mover was a product of ancient Greek thought, used to explain why things moved or continued to move.) This theory of a different state I will not enter into, at least not with the intention of resolve. I will only draw out of it what I need to work with in proving the brain as the prime mover—and only if I need it, with no prior intentions.

The human body has actually been weighed before death and after death to see if there was any difference in weight to account for this supposed soul. In 1907, a Dr. Duncan MacDougall experimented and found that the soul weighed twenty-one grams, which was controversial and has never been proven. There were experiments done by a German team in the 1990s, and they came up with a figure of 1/3,000 of an ounce, a lot less than twenty-one grams, and more accurate, but it is explained as energy loss, not weight loss. There is no real physiological evidence or real proof that a soul has weight, as shown above in the two contradictions of weight.

Let's look at it with an open mind. If your soul truly had any weight to it, it would have been proven a long time ago. I would be gladly writing about the many proofs of a soul and claiming this to be the reason for language, knowledge, and belief. If I won't use the weight of a soul for proof, it is because I need the proof, and there is none—ergo, there is no weight.

Next up, we enter the brain itself and try to see if there is any reason to believe that this extra persona lives there and has any or all of the influence over the matter we are made of. The most celebrated case study was from a railway worker.

Phineas Gage is the best-known case study in accidental neuroscience. Gage was a railroad laborer, and in 1848 the inadvertent sparking of some gunpowder sent a bolt of iron shooting through his brain. He survived, but his personality changed completely. He became surly and difficult and struggled with decision making and planning. Gage's state before and after his injury revealed a great deal about the role of the frontal lobes in the workings of the brain. (Christine Kenneally, *The First Word*)

Everyone who knew him stated that he had changed. His personality changed; he was different. Does this mean that the soul was also damaged and lost control over the brain and body of the man? I thought souls existed forever in their normal shape so a person could live eternally or become eternally damned. The conclusion of an immutable soul has been around forever and written about as far back as Plato. Observations support the fact that when brain damage occurs, both the brain and soul change with the damage, and it is the more current thinking. Many writers and commentators believe in a mutable soul because it has strong, reasonable evidence, and sadly, it is no longer considered a soul.

Do we conclude that if by some unfortunate accident one's brain were to become altered that this soul will be considered evil and damned? Or all its previous evils lost, becoming good by accident and saved into eternal life, all by accident? In sum, is the soul really separate or same, alterable or not? These answers are calling upon religious philosophy and are not to be answered here. If the soul is separate, then why does it not retain control over the body and brain when these altered brain states appear? I will attempt to answer this question, but not just yet.

If a person were to have a stroke, and because of this stroke become a better person, I am sure a case could be made that God had mercy on her and changed her. Everyone knows that God turns evil situations into the best outcome. Two problems, though. One: this would violate free will, as this person in question would have no choice. Two: it shows favoritism, and I want to be shown the same favoritism if I become evil—or eviler, as the case may be.

This aside, it still does not show an immutable soul, nor prove the soul to change with the brain or brain with the soul. What if the change was from a good God-fearing Christian into an evil person? We won't go there. I only want to point out to the reader that if the brain changes, it changes, and no soul or extra persona prevails over it to maintain its previous state. To prove a soul would be to prove a prime mover—something that causes lifeless matter to move—or in this case become animated, and this prime mover would be our answer. End of story.

What is the soul? Dare we take an example from the Bible and dissect it thoroughly and compare it throughout time, up until the modern hypothesis? Let's!

While we're at it, let's use the carbon copy as a basis for comparison, as an extra copy of your body, which is invisible, is the traditional concept of soul in many religious minds. You know the one: white copy goes to the customer; yellow copy gets trashed; pink copy goes into a file. All three copies are identical and formally called a document. Keep this in mind as we discuss Genesis and the creation of man.

> Let us make man in our image, after our likeness ... So God created man in his own image, in the image of God he created them; male and female he created them.... And the Lord God formed man of the dust of the ground, and breathed into his nostrils the breath of life; and *man became a living soul.* (Gen. 1:26–27 and 2:7; emphasis mine)

There seems to be three different statements made within that scripture. One, the word image is used, which deals with what something or someone looks like: the appearance. Two, the word likeness is used, better described as character or what God actually is: a Spirit. Three, the phrase "the dust of the ground" is used, or the material of which he is made, that being the flesh. All three combined into a living soul. Wait! All combined to make one living soul? No separate entity? The case for a different "state" as opposed to an additional "persona" just got stronger. I don't want to deal with religion here, nor is it my intent to convert anyone. I am fact-finding and looking to see exactly what we have to work with here.

We seem to have three different things—the body, spirit, and soul—but all combined into one being rather than separate. Stated in the more modern language of today, we would get something a little closer to this: let us make man out of the materials of the ground, in our resemblance and in our character, so that he becomes a living soul. Amen!

If we move to Aristotle, we find similar thinking, in that we have different parts or a soul.

Further, on the assumption that there are not several souls, but merely several different parts in the same soul, it is a question whether we should begin by investigating soul as a whole or its several parts. And here it is difficult to determine which of these parts are really distinct from one another and whether the several parts, or their functions, should be investigated first. Thus, e.g. should the process of thinking come first or the mind that thinks, the process of sensation or the sensitive faculty? (*De Anima*, book 1, 402b)

Furthermore:

> A further difficulty arises as to whether all attributes
> of the soul are shared by that which contains the soul
> or whether any of them are peculiar to the soul itself; a
> question which is indispensable, and yet by no means
> easy, to decide. (Book 1, 403a of Aristotle's *De Anima*,
> translated by R. D. Hicks)

More important to us so far is the statement made in book 2,
412a, and I quote again:

> Now there is one class of existent things which we call
> substance, including under the term, firstly, matter, which
> in itself is not this or that; secondly, shape or form, in
> virtue of which the term this or that is at once applied;
> thirdly, the whole made up of matter and form.

Here again, there seems to be three different divisions taken
into consideration: matter, shape, and whole. It does not stop
at all with Aristotle, as once supposed. Sigmund Freud tried to
dispel with a soul altogether and came up with the id and the ego,
which he could not make work. Alas, he found it expedient to add
a higher ego, or other self, to explain some of the problems with
higher thinking. Of course, today the thinking is that the brain
creates the illusion of the mind or soul, but the quantity of
factors going into that make-up is not down to just "one" factor
yet. In fact, with terms like emotional intelligence, hidden areas,
math modules, separate thinking hemispheres, and the likes, the
quantity of factors going into our mental makeup gets longer, not
shorter.

We take one more quote from Aristotle to sum it up:

Hence those are right who regard the soul as not independent of the body and yet at the same time as not itself a species of body. (Book 2, 414a)

There must be some sort of reasoning behind this long-held belief in a soul or both a spirit and soul. I do not draw the same conclusion that Julian Jaynes does in *The Origins of Consciousness in the Breakdown of the Bicameral Mind*. He speaks of "many voices" and the need to divide the two halves of the brain to control this anomaly, thus he concluded that growing a smaller corpus callosum through selective pressure would restrict the communication between the two halves of the brain and stop the many voices, leading to our current brain state, or conscious state. True, we all have voices going on in our brains—whether many of them or a few of them. There is a better way to get rid of them, which I will explore shortly. Our brains could and would recognize these voices as other parts of our selves, or literally our souls. As per the computer template of chapter 4, we could even consider a separate brain module as reporting to an "I" on one line of brain communication, and another separate brain module reporting to the same "I" on a separate line of brain communication. By our perception of these separate reports, we consider one to be a soul, another one a spirit or many demons.

The word demon is root based in the Greek word for knowledge. Latin uses science for the word knowledge. This book is about language, and I can't help but add here that while dealing in voices, we would call these voices demons. It is almost as if in man's early ignorance, these voices of knowledge going on in our heads were named after what they did: produce knowledge. Sometimes it is better to make a comment and leave it alone. I will move on to the next topic after doing just that.

If someone was hypnotized by an expert and he ordered her to ignore another person in the room with them, it is true that she must experience that person's presence and location before she can ignore him. For the life of her, she swears that no person is in the room, as she does not see him, but she deliberately walks around the invisible person if he is placed in her path. This is not magic! Her eyes see him and report what they see to her brain, but attention vetoes the report, or rather ignores the report as commanded by the hypnotist. She must pay attention to where this person is so that her attention can ignore his being there to begin with.

This suggests different layers of attention, as some form of attention must be paid to the various brain areas in order to formulate pop-up ideas. In fact, I have had many ideas reported to my brain that, once brought under my higher attention, I have, without reflection, sent whence they came. I don't even remember what most of them were, just that they had flaws worth rejecting. This in itself is worth commenting on at some length, but not just yet.

In the beginning, hypnosis was known as animal magnetism, and it was studied as such. Some experts believed that some objects emitted a force that magnetized you, and observations were made where whole crowds of people were magnetized after sitting for a spell by some tree or other object. Self-hypnosis would be the equivalent term today. How is this even possible?

The use or disuse of attention actually answers the question of trance states or focused states of mind. If you are not paying any attention at all, you tend to drift off to a state of mind idleness. In this state, and it has been reported to have happened, if someone were to ask you a question, you might answer. When a few minutes later the person comes and gives you your drink and finally breaks your idle state of mind, saying, "With ice, as you asked," you might reply, "Huh? I didn't ask for a drink." "Yes, you just said yes to a drink when I asked you; then I asked if you wanted ice and you said yes." Sound familiar? Unfocused attention?

I remember an incident when I was eleven years old. I don't attach any magic notions to it, as I'm not superstitious. I was in the hospital after just having my appendix removed, and it was the first day after surgery. I was a little groggy but was intent on watching cartoons on the television. One nurse came into my room and started talking to me. She left, and a few minutes later, she returned and started talking to me in French. I told her that I was sorry, but I don't speak French. She said to me, "But I was just in here, and you were talking to me in French." I absolutely do not remember her speaking to me in French the first time, and I had my doubts, but she insisted. I will not even attempt to explain this odd situation. I never learned to speak French, but my father frequently spoke French on the phone. I am sure everyone has some such story to tell, more or less odd. I will leave it to the principles of psychology.

Scientific experiments tell us, and it is widely accepted throughout the literature and different disciplines, that the more a synaptic connection fires together, the stronger that connection gets. What decides if it should be fired and wired? Firing is out of our control most of the time, as things happen all around us, and by default, some or most things become involuntarily wired. Out of necessity, however, other things must be wired by our doing.

Could attention have wired our brains so that we ignore the high volume of activity going on in the several areas of the brain and limit them to reporting conclusions on one main line to the higher brain levels, the same as many automobile modules do? This, if you haven't already observed, is just idle speculation on my part, but facts do support it. I believe it to be a better explanation than forced shrinkage of the corpus callosum in later human evolutionary history, as Julian Jaynes has expressed.

How could a brain force natural selection to shrink its corpus callosum? Attention could force unwanted brain communication to be ignored and hardwire it that way.

First, this would form modules only little by little, as required by natural selection, in independent areas of the brain. Second, attention has been around for as long as at least predation. Third, there seems to be some suspicion pointing this way in the form of dreams. Finally, these ideas are formulated and presented to our higher brain function, and we never hear, see, or even know that they are at work. They are completely ignored, and only the results are reported to us. This fits nicely with our template of the automotive computer control modules only reporting the results or emergencies from several independent modules to the one, with no real "one" in charge of all functions.

Actually, there are other differences that require higher levels of wiring through the networks of axons, dendrites, and neurons. In a simple form, I wrote about how these automatic responses took on the ability to become willful responses when a brain stem or spinal cord was conceived in vertebrates. At some point, attention would have to focus long enough to monitor the activity of game, predators, falling stone, or what have you. It would be expedient if you could focus on game and at the same time willfully move in for the kill. If you had to take attention off the game and apply it to your willful movement, then reapply it back to the game, you could lose site and sight of the game. To have another area of the brain say to your focused attention, "Move now," after doing the calculations, would be of great benefit. So attention became able to monitor and control at least more than one process at a time, albeit at a lesser intensity in the conscious mind. It also has independent control in subconscious areas.

A good example would be in the case of defects, nerve damage, or syndromes. Universally, this is where all the information comes from on brain studies: medical problems out of the range of "normal."

> Patients suffering from Alien Hand syndrome still experience the hand as their own hand; the conscious sense of ownership is still there, but there is no corresponding experience of *will* in the patient's mind. As philosophers say, the "volitional act" is missing, and the goal-state driving the alien hand's behavior is not represented in the person's conscious mind. (Thomas Metzinger, *The Ego Tunnel*)

He goes on to describe how a chess player had his left hand make a move he did not want. He corrected it with his right hand, only to have the left hand make the same move again. The left hand's motives were not reported to the conscious, thus there was an open circuit between the left hand controller and the main controller on the information-sharing circuit, in whatever "actual" manner it takes place. Everything else still functions. The brain controls all movements of the body—except automatic reflexes. In these cases, all the movements are not reported and cannot be understood or vetoed by the main conscious, whatever that is.

Before moving on, I would like to point out that it is not possible to have one soul in play here—one soul moving the left hand and the same soul moving the right hand. This would make both of the hands' motives known to the one soul that is controlling them. No one admits that we have two souls. The most likely scenario is that the brain is dysfunctional. If we admit that the soul is the prime mover here, then the soul would know what both hands were doing.

The same process that happens with physical properties can happen with mental properties as well.

M. Mesnet admits, moreover, and repeatedly affirms, that it is an unconscious activity, purely reflex and automatic. In that case he would not have a trace of conscious thought, judgment, or imagination. This explanation, emanating from an authority who had himself observed the facts, is presented with such conviction that several psychologists have had no difficulty in accepting it. It has thus been for some time currently believed that in the case of some patients an unconscious and blind mental activity may, at stated times, supersede consciousness, assuming control of the organism, and producing a series of complicated actions. (Alfred Binet, *Alterations of Personality*)

I found the same unconscious experience stated again in a slightly different form, within the context of an experiment.

When we put a lighted match into the anaesthetic hand, the fingers would back from the flame in proportion as the latter advanced, and would finally relax, allowing the match to fall to the ground, pain caused by burning, accordingly, is actually felt in an apparently anaesthetic limb; there even existed, it seemed, a certain prevision of pain and corresponding defensive movements; yet all this did not reach the principal consciousness of the subject; the sensations and movements of the anaesthetic limb, *by grouping themselves together, formed a secondary consciousness,* which in its development did not amalgamate with the main consciousness. (Alfred Binet, *On Double Consciousness*; emphasis mine.)

If we still want to admit to a soul as an animator of the brain and body, or prime mover, then we, in light of these facts, need to say that the choices of good and evil, as well as those of bodily control, are hardwired into the brain as a soul. If the good brain is damaged, then the soul loses control over good and will only do evil. If the soul had these controls, then the soul and not the brain would need to be damaged. What's that you say? The soul can only control what brain there is. If the soul really did have ultimate control and the brain was to be left only with evil, the soul could ignore the evil and become indifferent to it, still avoiding that evil. Now, do we need to have another brain area for indifference? Surely one can see that these do not make any spiritual or physical sense at all. I conclude that there is no extra persona as prime mover—just the brain. If we want a soul, we are left with a different state of being. For example, solid state versus energy state or whatever you are comfortable with.

We can see from the last quote above that other conscious areas are possible to form. If they can still be formed at this point in human history, then they must have been able to be formed in our past. There is good reason to believe that as these other conscious areas eventually came to report to a more central conscious area, they were heard as voices.

An old Sumerian proverb has been translated as "act promptly, make your god happy." If we forget for a moment that these rich English words are but a probing approximation of some more unknowable Sumerian thing, we may say that this curious exaction arches over into our subjective mentality as saying, "Don't think: let there be no time space between hearing your bicameral voice and doing what it tells you." (Julian Jaynes, *The Origin of Consciousness in the Breakdown of the Bicameral Mind*)

It is a given that all areas of the brain must be in contact with all other areas via some route. This misses the point: that both reporting and ignoring are needed for survival. There is sound reason to believe that the same "ignore by attention" of these voices would have to have happened so that the central conscious area of the brain would not become overwhelmed. Let one voice report at one time, in priority sequence, amygdala top priority.

We have two amygdale, by the way: one "salted" and one "unsalted," in case you're on a salt-free diet. The pun is fitting, as the Greek word means almond shaped. The brain more or less is divided into two duplicate halves. One side is always more dominant for one purpose than the other. In 95 percent of the people, language is a left hemisphere phenomenon. Other control areas work the same for reasons so obvious that I will only mention one. You can't have the right leg worked by the right hemisphere of the brain and the left leg by the left hemisphere of the brain, as in moments of flight, the two hemispheres might want the body to go in two different directions. The hemisphere location for the left leg would have to relinquish control to the hemisphere controlling the right leg. A second way of resolving the problem would be for both hemispheric areas—left and right leg control—to relinquish that control to a separate independent area of the brain in order to favor survival.

If any other area of your brain wants to communicate to your conscious area, it would need to translate the information into the language that your conscious area communicated in. This suggests that the highest form of consciousness was accompanied with language, but no magic is needed. They are all nerve firings, the same as with the programmed 01100101 or on/off states of our computer template. They would automatically be recognized by language, as language arose, as long as other factors, discussed later, were favorable. This could just be a case of other instinctual areas of the brain talking to the conscious or central controlling area of the brain in the form of its calls and cries, which it had all along. These calls and cries already had concepts innately attached, as per chapter 1, such as the innate concept of fear. Is there only one thing in the world to fear? I don't however, suggest that language caused consciousness, or consciousness caused language, but other principals caused both: attention, for one. If this is sound enough of an explanation, then the following would hold true also.

When we look at dreams, most are not recalled, but the ones we do remember are reported to the forebrain from the brain stem and occur in REM (rapid eye movement) sleep only, which can produce lucid dreams, the ones you partake in and remember. Metzinger does a good job describing dreams in his book *The Ego Tunnel*, mentioned above, and gives references to other sources. I will further discuss dreams later.

If they are brain activities, which are normally ignored, quite possibly the particular module of the brain is going over different scenarios that would have been of the strongest survival advantage. It would be beneficial for the brain, and subsequently the species carrying that brain to have different scenarios to choose from in slight variations of the same dilemmas in life, such as avoidance of predators and catching of prey. This does not solve all dream states, but it is plausible. Under this thought, we might always be in a state of dreaming and unconsciously or consciously ignoring these dreams.

Busy equals death if the busy is millions of things happening all at once. I cannot communicate this enough to the reader. Ideally, we need to delegate the busy-ness to other areas of the brain and have these other areas report the conclusions from the sorting process. This was the whole basis for the computer template chapter.

For the perception of mind or soul, attention is the strongest of all the candidates. It can ignore; it can cause a sustained but short working state known as short-term memory; it can place needed knowledge into long-term memory; it can also recall these memories as easily as it has placed them there. If attention wired the synapse, it would have access to recall what it wired. The ones with the longest and strongest attention span would survive and, on average, pass on the genes more often, making it selectable.

> Our brains are always in "ready mode," always tuned in to the never-ending incoming stream of perceptions. Then an event takes place that causes the brain to deliberately pay attention to a stimulus—to put a spotlight on it.
>
> Attention and consciousness are inexorably intertwined, and some scientists now believe that they are actually the same thing. (John J. Ratey, MD, *A User's Guide to the Brain*, 111)

Speaking of William James and his principles of attention being applied to modern-day science, Schwartz writes:

> As he notes, it is entirely plausible that attention may be "fatally predetermined" by purely material laws. In this view, the amount of attention we pay a stimulus, be it one from the world outside or an internally generated thought or image, is determined solely by the properties of that stimulus and their interaction with our brain's circuits. (Jeffrey M. Schwartz, *The Mind and the Brain*)

Elsewhere in the same book, Schwartz says when dealing with tree will and attention:

This notion of mental force fit as the "free won't" version of volition. In a nutshell, "free won't" refers to the mind's veto power over brain-generated urges—exactly what happens when OCD patients follow the four steps.

On the next page, he continues to write:

Yet Libet does not interpret his work as proving free will a convenient fiction. For one thing, the 150 or so milliseconds between the conscious appearance of will and the muscle movement "allow[s] enough time in which the conscious function might affect the final outcome of the volitional process," he notes. *Concluding* Libet's findings suggest that free will operates not to initiate a voluntary act but to allow or suppress it.

"Free won't" is different from ignoring data or at least controlling it. Freewill and free won't are both human attributes that are due to being already wired this way. Paying attention or ignoring by attention is what got us here, the hardwiring. With this control over the final outcome, we not only "feel" as if we have freewill but it actually gives us freewill, as soon as our unconscious learns to control it, making it conscious choice. Here is the important part: once the process of controlled wiring has been established—hardwired—everything becomes available for choice. You just need to tickle the nerve to consciously control your desired outcome, which causes the perception of a floating action within the brain.

I have read many books on the brain: books about female brains, god brains, spiritual brains, wisdom brains, guides to brains, changing brains, and even naked brains. (Who doesn't want to look at naked? Alas, there were no naked pictures in the whole book. I think the author kept all the good pictures of naked brains to himself.) With all these brain books, I grew quite tired of reading about the brain!

To show how strong attention is, I was looking in my favorite bookstore last month and saw another book on the brain—*The Other Brain*, to be exact—and I thought to myself, *I will never survive reading another book on the brain.* By then, my attention was strongly focused on "Other" in the title, and as I tried to walk away, I was compelled, against my desire never to read another book on the brain, to at least read the cover and see what "Other" was in reference to. I am glad I bought it. My language origins still work just fine, but this helps to get the answer to how it is done.

That book was worth reading for sure, and the author explained the technical parts well. I am working on being nontechnical as much as possible because I have to account for my own technicalities with the origins of language transforming into articulate speech. I therefore recommend that you read *The Other Brain* by R. Douglas Fields, PhD. I will, however, apply his idea into the "attention theory," as it shows what attention may be as a mechanism.

I have already read up on chemical generation of electric current in the body from other sources, but he makes a good explanation in his book, as does *The Mind and the Brain* by Jeffrey M. Schwartz, which I read a few years ago. I mentioned that computers and house wiring were man-made and had man-made power sources. In simple terms, I would imagine that nature did it this way. Cells in the body use chemical generation. In nontechnical terms, they lose an electron or gain one to become unbalanced or ionized. In this state of charge or discharge, they have the potential to fire across a synaptic gap, much like the spark plug in an engine. However, some are not electrically charged but chemically charged, or chemically saturated. Nervation uses potassium and calcium ions. There is no need for a power source, battery, or power plant—self-generation by chemical reaction is the way to go.

Next on the list is the insulation on the wires, and I will continue to talk about attention as I explain the insulation. Actually, the longer your attention is paid to something, the stronger the synapse becomes and the more the circuit becomes coated with myelin, which all heavy circuits in the brain are coated in. These coatings are made up of the other brain cell matter, called glial (or glia) cells, or glue, from the Latin glia for glue. We do not need to know about all cells in the body for our pursuit of language, but we need to know about these glia cells.

We have different types of these cells, and they do different jobs. Schwann cells are located only in the peripheral nervous system, not in the central nervous system. Astrocytes, microglia, and oligodendrocytes are found only in the central nervous system and not in the peripheral nervous system, but they are all glia cells. For ease of explanation, I will use the term glia generically to include all the types of glia cells, because after all, we are only looking to establish attention as the base for soul.

The Schwann cells form the myelin that wraps the nerves in the peripheral nervous system and acts as an insulation, which we observed was needed when I wrote about electrical wires needing it to stop shorts and leakage. These were the black-and-white (or red) coatings.

The other types of glia cells (for simplicity's sake, I will call them all glia) are restricted to the central nervous system, but I shall be a little clearer about some of their traits, as they are what we are looking for. They also form a coating around dendrites of the brain. Glias have the ability to cut old synaptic connections. They are used like the immune system and defend the brain against infections.

All cells in the body have the ability to communicate, via ionization. Ionization is simply the nonequilibrium of atoms—that is, they are not in the neutral state but have an unbalanced charge as mentioned above. They are either negative charged or positive charged, which relates to one too many electrons or one electron too few. They do these imbalanced charges with sodium (salt) stored outside the cell or inside the cell, giving them potential for a current flow.

Glia cells do become activated with longer electric pulses to neurons, and longer pulses in neurons translate into attention needing to be applied longer.

> Then after a long fifteen seconds of disappointment, Beth and I were elated as the Schwann cells suddenly began to light up like a Christmas tree. These glial cells had somehow detected the impulse firing in nerve axons and responded by increasing the calcium concentration inside their own cell bodies. Glia, which for so long had been regarded as little more than bubble wrap for the brain, were a party to information sent between neurons. (R. Douglas Fields, PhD, *The Other Brain*)

To me, if you paid attention to something in the natural world for fifteen seconds, it would equal something needing to be stored in a longer-term memory, and from the above quote, that is when all the activity started. Keeping the neurons firing longer means they have a better chance of glia insulating them. Could this activity actually be what we experience as the focusing of attention in the brain?

One more important fact to carry along with us is that these glia cells do communicate with one another.

> For tens of minutes, the researchers watched the light signals pass from one astrocyte to the next, swirling

throughout the dish in a fluorescent light storm. These "silent" brain cells were communicating with one another. More importantly, this communication had been sparked by the same neurotransmitter chemical that neurons use to signal to each other across synapses. The theory that astrocytes might eavesdrop on conversations between neurons had just expanded: not only could astrocytes detect neurotransmitters, they could pass the messages on among themselves using calcium ions instead of electrical signals. (Ibid.)

This has the implication that glia "knows" what neurons are "thinking," what I would call paying attention to the firings. Using these glia cells for brain-wide communication could be the same effect as knowing or "hearing" from these other areas of the brain in natural thought. Then, by extension, the glia could store information anywhere in the brain, know where it is stored, and retrieve it anytime—by default of eavesdropping. Not unlike our computer example from the chapter on design template.

It wraps the brain wiring in insulation: myelin. It cuts the old connections, which I could relate to making a correction in thinking and forgetting the old untrue knowledge. On longer firings, it becomes activated chemically. It repairs leaks in the existing wiring. It has all of the attributes of the effectual soul we are looking for.

Attention focuses over longer periods, long enough for these cells to fire up and wire these newly formed neurons and synaptic connections. Longer used ones would become coated with myelin and become more permanent or hardwired permanently. Gila could, with the smaller things going on in the brain, ignore them, as the nerves would not be electrically or chemically fired for long enough periods of time, and they could communicate across the whole brain unrestricted. In short, they would do everything that I claim attention can do. These "other" brain cells make up about 80 percent of the brain. There are, after all, one hundred billion neurons and many synaptic connections between them to be held in place and wired or coated.

By either ignoring or focusing these firings, they could restrict communication in other areas of the brain when it is too busy and force communication on one line only between these other areas. At this point, I have not finished reading his book, but I hope he has drawn the same conclusions as I have: both brains combine into an effectual soul. It will be one less thing that I have to defend in my search for language. I need attention well established as our prime mover.

I may as well say something more on memory, as I have mentioned it with little comment. According to Fields, it actually takes two "keys" to work memory in the hippocampus. One of these cells is of neuronal origin and one is of glia origin (our generic term for all the different glia cells). These glia cells release a chemical that is right-handed, the only right-handed chemical in the body. All the other bodily cells are left-handed in chemical structure or protein folding. A right-handed one is needed to code for memory. It's odd that the thing that coats nerves under use also codes memory for that use.

This leaves me only to express my concerns about the limiting of our wiring in all the electrical systems I have mentioned. Redundancy is not in the computer system; in the body, it is. We have a patch of skin with several nerve endings close together. We must be able to tell closely where we are being touched, within at least a fraction of an inch. Several nerve ending synaptic connections are needed. They can't all go to the brain, but they do go to the central nervous system. The spinal cords in all vertebrate have one line sent to the brain as a body section. The spinal cord sends the message to the brain as to where it was touched: little toe opposed to whole leg. If one or two of these lines are open, before they go to the spinal cord, others close by may feel them and work in their stead. Redundancy! The brain feels the whole body, and to the same extent, the brain feels the whole brain. The brain is redundant also, but if you sever a main line feeding the information to the brain, it will result in an open circuit and paralysis. In a car, an open circuit means no-go: there is no redundancy. This is why when some areas of the brain are destroyed—say, in the right hemisphere—the patient does not feel the left side, and she might report that her left arm does not belong to her.

Where I shall grasp language conversion out of this will be in the comparison of several nerves in one area of the skin for feeling that area. There are also several nerves in a nerve bundle to feel the different frequencies in sound waves. We will have several nerves in the area of these innate sound concepts to wire freely within the brain and allow for separation of sounds and concepts. This will be a later topic, but I mentioned it here to show that a whole body makes a brain as the interaction of the body with the environment programs survival.

I wrote the following previously:

In fact, I have had many ideas reported to my brain that, once brought under my attention, I have, without reflection, sent whence they came. I don't even remember what most of them were, just that they had flaws worth rejecting. This in itself is worth commenting on at some length but not just yet.

Now I would like to address this. If we are looking for specific problems to solve in our minds, our entire brains will be at work trying to solve them. If we have worked out parameters for the

solving of them, we would expect to have some parts of our brains
ready to be fired with the proper fit of the already known points of
information. There might be, say, ten parameters to consider and
this would leave a solution having to fit most of these parameters.
If six or seven points fit okay and none of the nonfit points were
an absolute no-go, then we might accept and reflect on the idea
presented from another brain area. If one, two, or more points
presented in the offered solution, which is coming from another
brain area, did not fit well with the knowledge we already had of
the problem within the central brain area, then they would not fit
the problem's solution and immediately be rejected. This requires
the whole brain working both independently and together to solve
problems.

An analogy of this would be cookie cutters. If you had a
star-shaped cookie cutter and you tried to place another slightly
smaller star-shaped cookie cutter into it, it would not matter if the
second cookie cutter had one or two pieces missing; it would still
fit. On the other hand, a square cookie cutter would not fit any way
you placed it, all things being equal.

Consider these two symbols: $\pm$ $\neq$. If they represented
ideas, you might ponder the second idea as a fit to the problem
because the two horizontal lines are close enough in idea to
warrant pondering. Let's look at these two symbols: $\pm$ ∞. If
they represented ideas, the second wouldn't fit the first at all,
in any form, and it would immediately be rejected. The ideas,
of course, would not look like cookie cutters or these symbols
but would be in the brain as neurons in sequence, ready to be
fired with the resolve when you hit upon it. That is, the primary
conscious would look for a close match in points of knowledge,
which it already discovered before integrating an idea from
another secondary conscious with what it already knows. The
symbols would look much like our computer analogy of on/

off switching 01100100 and the like. I have written in passing that other attentions would be required, and this would be a case in point: one attention reporting to another attention. It is now accepted that we have these different levels or divisions of attention working throughout and independently in the brain.

William James used the term "fringe" to refer to the border between what the "spotlight" of attention focused on and what was completely hidden from conscious view. This implies that there is a vague area that is close enough to tap into but not noisy to our primary consciousness, much like the actual difference between night and day when viewing Earth (unknown). There is an area that is dusk or dawn: the fringe between light and dark. When in the fringe, we can see enough to make out that something is there—but not exactly what. Because the area is not completely blocked out, it suggests that selection was in force. If the brain completely ignored things, you would not survive. If the brain did not ignore enough, you would not survive. A fringe border would solve the problem. In real terms of life, we see, or rather feel, a fringe in our minds, or illusion of minds, that gives us the impression of something being there, but having to think to locate it. That is, the brain continually has something waiting to pop up in our minds as soon as we are done with the present thought. Good thing or we would never be able to talk. Where would the next word choice come from?

This all brings up complication after complication. For one, what is the central processing area that all the other brain areas report to? Second, there cannot be one neuron firing at the top of the pyramid, as many neurons would be needed. This also conflicts with all the models of thought, including my introduction of series-parallel. Really, one neuron? The automotive computer template has any module being able to communicate with any other module, so at any given time, any module could be said to be in charge. This predicts that the brain might be doing something similar.

I understand that this does not solve the mind problem, but we need to have a light understanding of communication within the brain in order to solve the language problem, which I believe I have done, at least in part.

It is well published that we have what is called an emotional brain, where all our feelings and emotional responses originate, but for the story of language, which is what we are seeking, I need another brain. I hope I have shown that we have several brains to choose from. However, the base will be one specific brain, which I will call, for my purpose, "natural total concept word brain" (calls and cries complete with concepts). Other areas can be included in this mix as long as there is a match for a call or cry concept to arrive at language. This brings me to three independent brain areas, or voices, when we count the brain area that they are controlled by or reported to. You can call them id, ego, and higher ego. The whole person is the same as the body state, brain state, and soul state—one brain does it all.

Even with the sparse examples and evidence shown here, it shows that these voices and communications are within the brain itself; we cannot call upon a separate persona to do the job of conscious, intelligence, language, or soul feeling. We must conclude that our soul is another state, as this is all we have left. After all, another state of the same body, brain, or entity can still be a spirit form of our bodies, brains, and characters.

Before going to the next chapter, I would like to point out what we need to take with us in our search for language. There is only attention—and the fact that we have different parts of the brain dealing with different processes and communicating them within the brain, especially our emotional survival instincts or emotional thought and conceptual thought, which I derived from natural total concept word brain—calls and cries, the topic of the first chapter. The purpose of the rest of this chapter was to establish these main things as ways of doing it. Attention, our potential feeling of soul, will be enough to go from calls, cries, and other noises into fluent, articulate speech.

Chapter Seven

A Human Brain

All the sanctions *of a law of truth lie in the very texture of experience. Absolute or no absolute, the concrete truth* for us *will always be that way of thinking in which our various experiences most profitably combine.*

—William James
The Meaning of Truth

It may seem funny to begin a chapter on the human brain by talking about myths or quotations from the Bible. I take a good look at myths for one very good reason: the people of the myths, and those who passed the myths on, had both cognition and language enough to create them and pass them on.

"Be fruitful, and multiply, and *replenish* the earth, and subdue it." (Gen. 1:28)

It might look like a strange place to start, but we have a good word example here, and I don't want to overlook it. The writer of Genesis used the word *replenish* as opposed to multiply and *plenish* the earth. *Plenish* is actually a real word found in the dictionary. It means to fill up. Replenish means to fill up instead of, or replace, indicating an overtaking of the other larger-brained humanoids.

Even starting back one branch on the tree of life, heading toward a better vocal system, Neanderthal, having evolved a slightly better form of communication, would flourish if its other attributes were more favorable to survival. If the Neanderthal advanced little more in vocal selection, a stalling point, then language would be restricted in the species. Another branch in the tree of life, doing worse in other attributes and barely surviving, but doing better in vocal selection for its collective group size, would at some point, had language taken off, surpassed their bulkier, less vocal relatives. We shall see later that these statements are not completely accurate, as knowledge plays a heavy role in language acquisition.

It is understood that it did not have to be Neanderthal, and I don't think that it was, but Neanderthal did have a large territory and could speak somewhat. Alas, genetically, we are unrelated to the Neanderthal, but we share the FOXP2 gene for some language attributes.

One point at a time seems easier to work with, and I think dealing with beauty first will lend a nice flow to our story. Beauty is judged in one direction, if natural selection is at all correct, and the direction is toward the future, not the past. It is therefore less likely that Homo erectus would find Neanderthal attractive, being an older form of life:

The sons of God saw the daughters of men that they were fair; and they took them wives of all which they chose. (Gen. 6:2)

This seems to be about the time Adam stopped being the son of God and became man, through the fall in the Garden of Eden.

There were giants in the earth in those days and also after that, when the sons of God came in unto the daughters of men, and they bare children unto them, the same became mighty men which were of old, men of renown. (Gen. 6:2, 4)

This could be in reference to Adam and Eve still. If Eve's daughters were beautiful because of an increase in head size, leading to more beauty in those females, the problem would be solved. If Adam or Eve had increased head size and became smarter and more renowned, the smarter and more renowned men would want the more beautiful women. So Adam, Eve, and their descendants might be referred to in the above passage of scripture, with an increase of head size, complete with a change in beauty and renown. There is no need to go outside the species at all.

As I understand the way genes and mutations work, one change could happen to or, more to the point, in the higher structure of the hierarchy in the genes themselves, leading to an increase in some attribute. All of the human genome has been recorded, but not all genes are understood, so I will use the Mendel method of talking about them. If gene M promoted brain size m, here described as Mm, and suddenly mutated to grow a larger size brain, or grow the brain for a longer length of time, which happened to be double the size it was before the mutation, it would now come to be written as Nn in the genome. It could have happened more than once.

As a result, the brain would grow larger, but there is not necessarily any reason for the facial features to change or change much in size to keep up with the larger skull—that is, grow the same exact shape, but larger. The features could stay the same size. It could lead to the appearance of smaller eyebrows, comparatively speaking, to how much bigger the eyebrows looked on the smaller head. The appearance of smaller eyebrows would achieve a better look. Also, the increase in head size could cause the nose to take on a different shape or protrude more, also achieving a better look. The biblical quote I used above— "saw the daughters of men that they were fair"—might have its origins here. As I have no way of knowing this, I will just call it an example, but there is no real reason that intelligence had to be the driving factor for selection. Intelligence was more likely the byproduct of the increase.

I believe the reason a larger, more expansive brain was not weeded out by selection is that it would have become an attractive attribute and selected for sexually, leaving it around long enough to be put to a better use, namely intelligence and speech. I think that sometimes, while trying to follow one selection process, we forget that many things would have to be selected for at the same time: attractiveness, knowledge, language, the best at being biped, hands with opposable thumbs, and much more.

It could also have occurred in one leap from a higher/better food source, or both, as pointed out by Derek Bickerton. Either way, we do have some record of it happening. I quote from *Athanasis*:

The womb was too tight to let the baby out.

And again:

In addition let there be one-third of the people, among the people the woman who gives birth yet does not give birth.

This means that they could not deliver, and many mothers and their children died. (*Myths from Mesopotamia*, translated by Stephanie Dalley)

We also receive some indication of the same event in the Bible:

And unto the woman He said, I will greatly multiply thy sorrow and thy conception; in sorrow thou shalt bring forth children. (Gen. 3:16)

A larger head would not only hurt more during delivery, but it would contain the larger brain needed to perfect language proper. The actual account being true or not, it seems that a few generations later than this point in our history, languages emerged at Babylon.

A sharp reader might point out that the myth being passed along would indicate that they already had a good language system base. Just because the head got bigger in one generation does not mean that language would have happened in that one generation. It is not necessarily true in either case. For one, before they could possible know that it was one-third of all women and children, they would have to have had enough of a sampling from the population.

The maximum birth size of a head is capped off by the maximum size of the pelvic bone canal in the female. Today we have C-sections, but back then, they did not. If the female could not pass the baby through her pelvis, both would die, as has been reported commonly. At best, they would have crushed the pelvic bone, and the woman would have been crippled and childless.

As with all selection in general, the ones who could survive did survive. The females with the larger pelvic bone openings, or pelvic canals, would have had the larger-headed babies. The trait, if you can call it that, would have been passed along; their children could also have larger-headed babies. There would be a generation gap here. The mothers of the first generation would not have had to have larger heads, just larger pelvic canals. The second generation now grows to maturity and starts to have their own babies, and they survive. These are the third generations now being born. Remember that the only survivors were the babies born to the women with larger pelvic canals.

In the meantime, the second generation could start the process that I am suggesting, in evolving language. They would have no idea what happened in the previous generations, but they would know what was happening in their generations. The females with the smaller pelvic canals would still be in the process of being weeded out. As we are the direct descendants of our grandparents' genes and not our parents' genes, the germ line mentioned in chapter 1, women with smaller pelvic canals would still be born for at least a few generations.

The people being born to the females with larger pelvises would in the meantime learn improved language, and it would be refined for two generations at least. A few generations of ancestors are plenty to notice that there is a high rate of deaths at childbirth, due to an increase in head size. This knowledge, if it were true at all, would be passed down from the third and fourth generations at least. There is plenty of reason to believe that four generations would coexist if we use a mean average of fifteen years' reproduction rate. By this time, there is reason to believe that enough population sampling would exist but would not be accurately counted.

It might have been remembered by another means, as they would not have had a counting system yet. It might have been remembered by means of a coupling versus one death: a coupling being a husband and wife or, more accurately, a pair bond. They did not have any writing either. We are not given these myths by word of mouth, but they are written on clay slabs, presumably generations later, when writing was invented. Even if language took a few generations to get respectable in size, it would have been well enough established both in myth and language to be recorded many generations later in the better form of remembrance: writing. The only requirement is that they developed language before all the deaths (one-third) had taken place. From analyzing these myths, I conclude it to be at least possible that a larger brain size and language proper could have happened within a few generations. There is also reason to believe that beauty was a factor in the selection process.

We will now discuss brain size. Earlier I mentioned that *The Math Gene* by Keith Devlin gave me another idea to use. Well, here it is:

> Imagine now (and this is the fictional part) that a second brain grows, parasitic on the first. This second brain has a similar structure to the first, except that its world is the first brain. Where the first brain receives its initial stimuli (its inputs) from the physical world, the second brain receives its stimuli from the first brain; and where the eventual responses (the outputs) of the first brain are physical actions in the world, the responses of the second brain are further stimuli to the first brain. We might then be inclined to refer to the activity of the second brain as "symbolic thought." Whereas the function of the first brain is to manipulate physical objects in the physical world, the function of the second brain is to manipulate symbolic objects that arise in the first brain.

Notice that Devlin stipulates that this is the fictional part. It is true that this cannot be exactly the way it works, but the second brain could be used for higher analysis, higher attention, and a higher form of manipulation. All these higher forms would still be based on the old brain functional capabilities.

Devlin said it is as though we have two brains. If we were to have one brain increase, completely free of the functional demands that fills the smaller brain, to its functional capacity, it would act like the freed jawbone becoming an ear: it would be as if we have two brains. That said, this "fictional" story could have happened. It is important to realize that even a doubling of a brain does not take it from small to extremely huge. It could be the same in relationship as imagining the peel of an orange to be an increase in the orange's size. Volume is what counts, and an increase of double the size of our cortex is not going to make the head three or four times the size, just add layers enough to become well used. The doubling here could have been from the original size and not the combined size. Double a quarter of an orange and you get half an orange. Double the original quarter of an orange again and you get half an orange. Add the doublings of the two oranges and you get three-quarters the size of an orange, not four quarters of an orange, as the first quarter was already there. It doesn't count. In this way, it is possible to get a buildup of layers. The following quote should clear this up.

> The cortex is a continuous sheet of cells from 2 to 3 mm thick on average, and for the most part made up of six sublayers which have in them a variety of types of neurons … Pyramidal cells that have their cell bodies in the more upper layers of the cortex (layers two and three) connect to other parts of the cortex itself while those lower down (in layers five and six) send their axons to places outside the cortex altogether. (A. G. Cairns-Smith, *Evolving the Mind: On the Nature of Matter and the Origin of Consciousness*)

Notice that the lower layers wire outside the cortex and the upper layers wire into the cortex for communication within.

If there were to be an increase in brain size at different periods in our history, as already hypothesized by others, we could have made the leap needed to go from calls and cries into sound-words and from sound-words into sound-clichés and from sound-clichés into articulate speech. The second leap would be the ability—paralleled with vocal development—to use single sounds to form small word concepts, discussed below.

This would be a fair communication system, but of poorer vocabulary. Thus the sound concepts would depend on vocal ability selection and not brain size, i.e., extra brain space, for the vocal neurons to wire into would already exist. I see no real or imagined reason that would prevent "module" migration within the brain. It would also make use of a larger, more energy-consuming brain, which would have to develop to relate, adapt, and control the new vocals while keeping track of the meanings of each of these different sounds.

Better communication would lead to better selection for a good vocal system—the only thing in need of selection. This sounds as if I am saying that as soon as man had the last brain increase, the selection for sounds was started. I mean it in a different way. Calls and cries would have been selected for all along, and man would have already had more vocal abilities than any other animal. They would have had to select for the vocal ability needed for control of what we refer to as digital sound. More on this later.

Manipulating the knowledge learned by the first brain into doing the same job without the environment being present at the time would naturally ensue. If one learned slightly better than most other animals to manipulate his environment, while in the environment only, with the normal sized part of the brain growth, then the enlargement of the neocortex would act as his second brain, allowing the speech symbols to become our main off-line thought process in analytical digital form.

It must not be forgotten, however, that chimps plan raids on their neighbors without actually seeing them, indicating "off-line thought," so an accumulation of brain increases are more likely to have happened, until the final one produced our high level of speech consciousness. As per our computer template, huge storage capacity is needed up front, and we don't grow one new cell every time we need one more storage unit of space. In fact, infants are born with more neurons than ever needed, and the unused ones die. More on this later.

It is also recognized by science that language is not the sole means of thought. As I discussed in a previous chapter on grammar, we think in concept, object, emotion, and other means, as well as with language.

Manipulating the knowledge learned by the first brain into doing the same job without the environment being present is called off-line thought, and this brings us back to our analogies. Homogeny is usually used to depict *same as*, but I have chosen to stay with the same word throughout the text: analogy, which I used for *same as* also. Homogeny is also used under a different sense, which I don't want to leak into my meanings.

This is where my prior description of analog and digital comes into play. This analog is "same as," and I used the hammer as an example earlier. Hearing is being able to locate a sound within a degree at several yards away, and the sound can be placed within the scenery very close to where it originated. By scenery, I mean exactly that—when you look at something around you, what you see in panoramic view with nothing out of order and nothing missing. Hearing can place a noise within the natural surroundings at a close proximity and direction of the source's location.

A tree may be ordered also. You might have in the scenery a rock, some grass, a pond, another rock, more grass and the tree, and then another pond or rock. Real objects are seen by the brain as they are, where they are. Things are heard as they are, where they are, within a degree or so. They can be placed within the scenery. So the brain can see them as they actually are. Smell is not like this at all. We can't tell the exact location in space where a smell is coming from in order to place it into the scenery. They say that smell, by the way, came first. We need smell; it is important to our survival.

We must then have a means of recognizing the smell and storing it in the brain, where it can be analyzed and communicated from where or what the smell is from. You can't place the smell of an odor in the air at a certain rock the same way hearing a noise can be placed into the scenery. If the smell is a predator, you must now look and listen to find it. The brain must then break up different smells and store them randomly in the brain to see which predators or foods they are. Smell is needed to identify the type of odor and determine whether it is present, but it can't be used for location with any real accuracy.

It stores each individual smell digitally, in on or off states, randomly in the brain according to Gary Lynch and Richard Granger in *Big Brain,* due to the properties of smell not being analog—that is, with sight we see things in a completely oriented way. We can tell with sight where everything is in our physical surroundings, so our brain can store it as we see it, in the proper order: analog. With smell, we can't tell exactly where it is coming from, as it could be carried for miles in the wind, so we store it digitally.

The initial sensory cortical expansion was based on the point-to-point organization, sending faithful representations of images and sounds forward into the neocortex that was, as we have indicated, set up with the random-access network designs representative of the olfactory cortex. Thus, the point-to-point world of the visual system becomes abandoned after just the first few connections of processing in the rest of the visual cortex. We have already seen that the same thing occurs in the olfactory system, where neat spatial organizations in the nose and the olfactory bulb are replaced with scattered random-access representations in the olfactory cortex. As neocortex grew, it mimicked just this arrangement. (*Big Brain,* Gary Lynch and Richard Granger)

The olfactory—smell—part of the brain is what has grown into the neocortex (actually the whole cortex) in all higher animals. Paraphrased, this gives the brain the ability to store information randomly and have it available for any other part of the brain to use—it can form modules and communicate between them by growing new connections—in point-to-point form or digital form. Hearing, sight, and smell can be stored as information together anywhere in the brain. We can still see in analog and hear in analog, but they are stored in analog digitally, so we can think about them digitally. Now we have the unused property to be able to speak digitally; the sound can be handled within the other areas of the brain.

[I]n perception the brain breaks down sensory information into the smallest of elementary units, tiny parts that are seemingly unrelated. The brain then distributes these bits of information and some how reassemblies them, according to a persons memories, past experiences, and possibly even wishes. (John J. Ratey, MD, *A User's Guide to the Brain,* 91)

This fits nicely into our computer template of random storage. In case it is not immediately obvious to the reader, if your brain can divide sights and sounds and store them randomly in digital, it can do the same with concepts. This directly relates to storing total sound concepts, our calls and cries as well. We need to have continuity in analyzing things. This continuity is the changing of analog sound into digital while still holding the complete concept as a whole, plus the divided parts separate for our individual use. This analog form, like an assembled jigsaw puzzle, holds the information true but separated into chunks or individual pieces in the new form of digital, still ordered; it is the cutting of the picture into its puzzle pieces. A completed jigsaw puzzle looks like complete scenery, but it is made up of digital pieces. Now any piece of the information can be separated, used, and mixed.

Mirror neurons and super mirror neurons exist in different areas of the brain and do two completely different things. Mirror neurons code our brains to mimic others, like from my example above. Saying *tik* while pointing would produce the same effect in other people of pointing and naming the gesture, thus completing the phoneme concept. Super mirror neurons would at some point stop your actual actions of pointing and let you, without actually moving, say the word or concept. This is the probable answer to the problem of off-line thinking and for sure the answer to understanding another's speech, without seeing the person, a great survival advantage.

According to the embodied semantic hypothesis, when we say, hear, or read these expressions, we actually activate the motor areas of our brain concerned with the actions performed with those body parts. When you read or say "the kiss of death" your brain activates the motor cells you activate when you actually kiss someone. (However, let's hope you won't think about death the next time you kiss someone.) There is convincing empirical evidence in line with the predictions of embodied semantics, although it generally does not involve kissing. (Marco Iacoboni, *Mirroring People*)

I included this quote to show that we have some disconnect from actions, and it is a real science. I also wrote earlier in the book that all other areas or instinctual areas were reporting to a central area for language and hinted that it was not really needed in the language of that central area. It would stand to reason that if our language were to be innate based, we would need our senses, responses to stimuli, and sounds, if any, all present to form any meaning-based language facility. Therefore, something must have happened to change our thoughts into linguistic thoughts. In the form of mirroring, actions can receive sounds, and actions do exist without language. Also, actions can be disconnected from the sounds.

As mirror neurons seem to code actions, there is increasing evidence that they also code the meaning of the actions with the sound related to the action, and that increased experience reinforces the association of the acoustic signal to the action. (*The Interactional Instinct,* Namhee Lee et al.)

This, as I have suggested, would automatically be done anyway with the sound-to-complete-concept base, and it would further need to go into every action without sound, not just, as language dictates, innate representations with sounds. That is, anything can now become mirrored with the meanings attached. Anything can have sounds attached to the meanings and, by extension, concepts.

It then would allow for alterations of concepts as they arise, and additional ones that are not inherent in the genome but pushed for by selection of naming.

A minor point to be made here is that it appears to be the same thing I was writing about earlier: ignoring something by attention. We cut the action off from the word while still retaining the meaning. This is important because calls and cries would be total concept represented in the brain and part of the action taking place. A growling wolf would be ready to fight if needed. Not only the sound would be aggressive, but the action would be as well. In order to talk freely about the past situation, you would not want to relive it every time but just explain it. "I growled at him in defense, and he went away." This cannot happen until words are uncoupled from the actions.

Imagine that you were out hunting and in the open. You were able to keep track of the hunting party and the game hunted. You could point—signal to them where the game was going, where you were planning to go ... This would be fair as long as you were in the open. If you could communicate well with sounds, one person from the tribe could stay in one place—in a tree, for instance—and keep track of the game and every other hunter. Even if the game avoided where he was because he was shouting commands, it would not matter. He could talk you into trapping the game between all the members of your group, and victory would ensue. He might not be able to communicate well with his hands while gripping the tree, but unattached sounds from actions would win the day. This is also known as niche change, one of the strongest selection factors in evolution—sexual selection being the first within control.

Mirror and super mirror neurons are only the uses made with the neurons, and they do not affect what I have written in the previous chapters. They are properties of the respective brain areas and are seen in other primates as well. This has nothing to do with language or communication in our high-level form. They must have been originally used for another purpose, as monkeys have mirror neurons but don't speak. I suspect they are very important, though, in language development after the fact.

We can use body language to communicate many concepts silently, which transfer from individual to individual through the mirroring effect but are also conceptually innate, as per the same effect as chapter 1, without the sounds. Any concept can have a noise placed upon it and be understood with some effort, as long as the body language occurred with the noise. This makes learning new noises possible with their concepts. Other properties are needed, and we continue to seek them out.

We seem to have, possibly unique to humans, the ability of both top-down learning and bottom-up learning.

If you consider that most of the things we know exist outside of our conscious awareness; we always know more than we can say ... we can successfully ride a bike or drive a car even though we aren't able to describe exactly how we do it.

In essence, our brain is organized so that once an activity becomes routine it doesn't require conscious effort but occurs automatically." (Richard Restak, MD, *The Naked Brain*, 24)

Notice that there is very much a conscious effort—cortex—in learning to ride a bike. This effort is negated to the lower, if you will, brain functions and becomes automatic. Nature did not produce bikes, and mastering them meant little to our distant ancestors. With attention and repetition, these and many other skills and knowledge are learned. This is top-down learning.

Bottom-up learning is different in that it is the environment that teaches a species to avoid a predator or advance in the direction of food. It is completely "unknown" to the species and is instinct wired, only becoming cognition when the top-down and bottom-up processes merge.

Unbelievably, there is a theory that during the course of evolution, our heads actually rotated 180 degrees to face what is now our front. The reason for the explanation is that the left brain runs the right body and the right brain runs the left body. It looks as if learning was reversed in direction at some point in our history. We look at the letter x here and use it for a template. If we allow the bottom of the x to represent bottom-up learning and the top of the x to represent top-down learning, we have an inversion. Both merge and unfold into the other learning type or method. For one, this in part seems to be a setup for our placental change in growing words from calls and cries. Where the two merge produces some form of change, if only a directional one.

I must suppose from this that the brain looking in on itself would start the process of allowing what was looking in to start to make changes and another type of learning possible. This other type of learning is cognitive learning, and it too allows what is learned to become hardwired.

From a previous quote, we saw that the first of the six layers were wired into the cortex, and the lower three layers were wired outside the cortex, into the old brain. We now have two different types, or species, of human learning to work with. I will quickly, but without the details, show a transition for calls and cries. Calls, learned bottom up, as per chapter 1, can now be separated, recombined, and more importantly, learned as being analogously the same or analogously different when transformed into words. This separation and recombination is top-down learning or speech development. The details will be explored in greater detail in another chapter, but for now we continue with the thought process.

> The old brain had been assembled there as a vehicle of instinct, and remained vital from one heartbeat to the next as new parts were added. The new brain had to be jury-rigged in steps within and around the old brain. Otherwise the organism could not have survived generation by generation. (Edward O. Wilson, *Conscilience*)

"A vehicle of instinct" is a good way to put it, but through the course of time, several instincts would clash and decisions would need to be made. The run instinct seems clear enough, but running to the left or running to the right is only a random, blind guesses if we don't have the ability to chose the best one for the current crisis. If we go back to the vervet monkeys and their concept-specific call for leopard, "jury-rigged" might begin to make sense.

Now she sits in the tree, watching as, sure enough, the leopard roams around. She also bears her full attention to this dangerous predator. Do you think there is room for other "goings-on" in the brain? She could look for a better place to wait out her enemy. Say for the sake of extra work here that she found herself in a poor "safe" area. The tree was low, not very strong, and she needed to get to a higher, stronger tree. No instinct in the world will send you automatically through the right path. One must be observed and chosen. This requires deliberate thinking, whether it is conscious on not. Does it not seem to you, as it does me, that this requires firing some nerves (generic term) to make the willful selection of an alternative? Does this not sound like planning and choice, being born within the brain? It also sounds like the eve of a higher form of reverse wiring.

If you look at a tree, it might give you some idea of what I am talking about. The reason I spent so much time on series-parallel wiring it that this is actually what it reminds me of. So I will base my examination on this observation. The roots of the tree can be considered in concept, to be parallel in feeding the trunk of the tree as a whole. Different roots lead into the tree trunk and feed it. Converting the thinking process into the use of neurons as trees, setting signals from each root in the tree trunk would set off a different signal or combination of signals into the trunk as a whole. Sounds with meaning would be one good area to think about, as we are looking for language anyway. Now the signals travel through the trunk and into the branches at the other end in series, and they—the branches—are then separated into parallel paths again, redividing the signal. Some of these "brain trees" are several inches long as they extend from one brain area to another. If you like, you are welcome to insert the proper names here: axons, neurons, dendrites ... but I estimate it would require adding ten to fourteen extra paragraphs for the most accurate explanation.

If each individual root represented a different aspect of a total concept, then growing them into the trunk would be to combine the individual elements of the concept into one total complete concept. Branching the trunk again at the top of their delivery point would be equivalent to separating the concepts into their smaller parts again.

Actually, trees have these qualities naturally, which is the reason I chose them. Each root feeds its own separate branch through the tree trunk fibers. A maple tree is different from an apple tree. One sound is different from another due to the formation of columns.

The cells in these columns are very sensitive to specific differences in sound frequencies, and changes in frequencies cause different columns to fire. In order to come up with the tremendous range we hear in sounds, columns fire together in deliberate mixes. The cortex then compares the patterns of firing to stored patterns, or features, with which it is already familiar. (John J. Ratey, MD, *A User's Guide to the Brain,* 95)

I need to tie these together and gain some simple understanding of how it could be done. It is not likely that we used one single neuron—again, my generic misleading term—to wire for a whole complete concept. Actually, I should be a little clearer here. Neurons grow several dendrites and synapses, so the neuron could be a complete concept, with the separate parts represented as dendrites … Water, let's say, as a concept, covers a lot: wet, thirst, cold, bad tasting when bad, good tasting when good … We could make a fairly long list. Some parts of these concepts would be in other areas of the brain by means of our senses. Cold, for example, would be felt; taste would be different; and so on. Several dendrites, synapses, and neurons, de facto, from different senses could be used just to contain water concept. Dealing in space/time would be better for me but much harder to explain, and my poor brain is already getting blisters and becoming callused. I must work with what I can dredge up in order to communicate these ideas.

Letting the several dendrites of a neuron stand in the brain for the larger concept of water leaves a way to separate these secondary concepts out of them. The whole is a given and will be taken along with us as a given, as per chapter 1. This will free us to work with the several parts. I must choose a quantity to work with, and I will make it the arbitrary number of twenty-five. Twenty-five dendrites come to represent the whole concept in the neuron. Attention, as I have suggested, will be our wiring control mechanism, and I will again use glia/myelin as a generic term.

154

This is the reason water does not work quite as well: it did not necessarily have to have an innate word (call or cry), but we will treat it as if it did. Every time this word was used, of the entire secondary concept would have become excited in the brain. If attention was fixed on, say, wet, then cold would have been ignored, but it would still be present and excited. To alter the sound from *wa* to *we* while focus was placed on the wet portion of the brain excitation would tend to wire these dendrites as a separate secondary concept, complete with a new slightly altered sound. Every time wet was now used as a word, it would cause excitation of this dendrite concept in the midst of the neuron total water concept. All the other dendrites would give the different meanings attached to the sound—call or cry—words. That is, water would still contain all concepts, but wet would contain wet.

This could be repeated with coldness, saltiness, or what have you. We could use a 25:1 neuron firing or a 25:2, 25:3, or so on to get the different concepts mixed or separated and recombined to perform any duty we needed, all using altered sounds. These are not ratios. The first number represents twenty-five dendrites in the total concept of the neuron, and the second number represents one part of the total concept by means of one dendrite—nothing whatsoever to do with math ratios. For example, the 25:4 dendrite could come to be known as brackish (bad-tasting) water. These neurons would become myelinated with our knowing glia cells and forever become associated with the different parts of the whole.

When you heard the word wet in the future, it would automatically bring to mind water, as would the word brackish. To be clear, the parts are to the whole what the whole is to the parts, only from two different directions—top down and bottom up. For example, activate dendrite four of the twenty-five dendrite neuron set, assigned to the concept of water, as a secondary concept of brackish. Dendrite four then becomes activated within the twenty-five dendrite neuron set to be recognized as the water is brackish, within the brain every time you taste bad water. This is all possible because you would have had the whole concept in one neuron cluster of the brain. Therefore, combining a concept from a neuron cluster in the emotional brain module with the same concept neuron cluster of the calls and cries brain module would become wired into another language cluster brain module in an articulate speech form. This other module would be a digital, analytical extra area, where they could become cross associated. Cross association would allow the meaning to become manifested whenever the word was heard, or whenever the meaning was implied, the word would appear.

Back to the trees, we can see that the roots feeding the branches through the trunk looks the same as this model for concept separation. It seems hard to believe, and is only speculation on my part, but we see more examples in nature. We have what is called the jet stream, a current of air moving within the air as a separate entity. We have what is called the Gulf Stream, which is a current of water moving within water as a separate entity. We have roots to the branches being fed through the trunk fibers of the tree as a separate entity, as different roots feed the different branches of the tree. No one questions these! Why is it so hard to believe dendrites feed dendrites through nerve fiber? We actually do have, and it is believed only human brains have, special neurological dendrite, nerve fiber systems located in our cortex: prefrontal lobes:

Perhaps the most notable transformation that has taken place in the human brain is the expansion of fiber bundles underlying the frontal lobe—they are larger in humans tha[n] in any other primate species, even after correction for an overall change in brain or body volume. Some long distance connections, such as those that link the inferior prefrontal cortex to the occipital pole, *may exist only in humans* ... their dendritic trees, which receive incoming inputs, are bushier, and synaptic contacts are massively more numerous than those of other primates. (Stanislas Dehaene, *Reading in the Brain*; emphasis mine)

To try to clarify some of this and bring us a better understanding of how I believe it is done, I will elaborate some. If we place these trees from root to branch in several stages—that is, several root to branch connections—a mixing pot emerges. If the roots of the first tree enter into the trunk and become a concept, then what of the second tree? The second tree does not, in anyone's greatest hallucinations, have to wire the same. By example, root one can be wired into branch one and then crossed into root four of the second tree, root seven of the third tree ... When we look at this statement, does it not seem to be our placental problem fixed physiologically? If nerves wired for sounds were to wire directly into calls and cries, then directly into language as one longer nerve fiber, we would have calls and cries growing into calls and cries. Because of these naturally occurring shorter root-to-branch nerves, this is not the case. In fact, neurons grow dendrites into other neurons' synaptic connections, further adding to the mixing bowl. It would probably be better to replace the term mixing bowl with the term separating bowl. In terms of sound, we can now have different calls and cries, which have some overlap of sound and concept, becoming mixed and fixed.

This chapter is on the human brain, and I have spent so much time on wiring of neurons into fiber clusters, as this might above all else be the answer to language. If, from an earlier quote, we have nerve bundles coding for sounds, and I have shown sounds to be reasonably innate to concept, we just need to reseparate everything. This will wait for another chapter. Meanwhile, we continue to look at the human brain.

On several occasions, while reading the works of other authors, I have noticed comments on there being a smaller area dealing in sounds, I believe, located at the bottom tip of Broca's area, shown in brain scans. If Broca's area were to start small, with calls, cries, and other sound concepts, a fair innate communication system would be present. Now, singling out smaller concepts from larger concepts and recombining the separated smaller concepts into different total concepts would appear. As this is now a new process of conscious speech, it would invade this new area of the brain or our second brain, and in the process perform the placental conversion needed. I might remind you that it would need to be changed from analog to digital.

Two areas have been more specifically located (see again figure 4.10). One of these is "Broca's area." It lies close to the lower part of the motor cortex, the part which mediates movement of the face, tongue, jaw and throat. The other is "Wernicke's area" situated further back in the temporal and parietal lobes closer to the lower part of the somatosensory cortex. Damage to either of these areas produces distinctive speech difficulties. Patients with Broca's area damage have trouble with grammar: they may know what they want to say but have trouble getting the words out and in putting them in proper grammatical sequence. Patients with damage to the Wernicke's area have trouble with meaning, with formulating what they want to say: their speech may be grammatically correct but nonsensical. (A. G. Cairns-Smith, *Evolving the Mind*)

This, of course, shows that there are many different complications to getting language. It almost shows that the order of the world and words are combined with the meanings of these words placed upon them, from two different areas and wired into new neurons as a proper word connecting both properties: name and meaning. Remember, I briefly mentioned wiring into another area in the last chapter.

A suggestion would be for scientists to scan the brains of other primates while making meaningful noise: a snake call, for instance. Then they could compare these to brain scans of persons speaking in tongues and the separate area of the human brain dealing in phonemes. There must be a correlation between all these, showing that meaning transfers directly to the sounds made. Humans just have more of them. If it has been done, sorry; I don't have the information.

We have two acknowledged speech areas in the left hemisphere of the brain, with the Wernicke's area controlling speech and writing. Why speech and writing? I suggest that the same process of relationship between symbols to sounds has taken place that happened when going from cries to articulate speech. Now we are going from speech back to silent symbols: writing. Speech was established by going from seeing the world to speaking what we saw. In writing, we go from speaking the world back into seeing it in the form of letters: symbols. More on this writing topic later in the book.

We seem to be the only species to have any real language areas at all, or at least any of notable size. The placenta template seems to be, at least in part, the answer for this anomaly. The anomaly, in my opinion, has always been how to change innate sounds into articulation, and I believe the answer is to grow a bigger brain. This brings us full circle back to larger brains.

Make no mistake about it: if we have extra brain space, something will wire into it. It is important that the same preexisting functions don't overtake the brain. Equally important is the fact that if change is needed, the change is different in species, as discussed in the chapter on the placenta. I am trying to build a human brain here, and it is important to show where things come from, but more important to show where they are going. It is likely the reason that redundancy is stronger in the human brain—wire invasion due to the extra space. We don't automatically grow extra limbs because we have more space in the brain, so redundancy would ensue.

> Any aggregate of events or objects (e.g., a sequence of phonemes, a painting, or a frog, or a culture) shall be said to contain "redundancy" or "pattern" if the aggregate can be divided in any way by a "slash mark," such that an observer perceiving only what is on one side of the slash mark can *guess,* with better than random success, what is on the other side of the slash mark. We may say that what is on one side of the slash contains *information* or has *meaning* about what is on the other side. (Gregory Bateson, *Steps to an Ecology of Mind*)

I not only feel that calls and cries can be divided by a slash mark, but I also feel that the meanings are innate within the brain, and the observer—in this case, one's own mind—does not really need to guess. This ensues naturally, as per my above tree analogy that these synaptic gaps are the slash marks. They are also redundant, which leaves plenty of room. Redundancy can be invaded and replaced with different species of actions, knowledge, and speech without crippling the actual species of animal. It has come to my knowledge recently, that invasion of redundancy has a name. I must credit Stanislas Dehaene for the proper term of neuronal recycling, which basically, only better, describes what I am saying. His previously cited book is a must-read, and I will need to defend slightly my idea in another chapter on reading and language.

That said, there is reason to believe that calls and cries would tend to invade the brain increase in redundancy, and this brings up a concern that should be discussed here. The first is that it is known that genes actually code the brain cells for on or off states of "learned," but I have enough to deal with without going too deeply into this other area. Some of the genes themselves take an active part in learning by being activated under the proper stimuli. We have many things going on in our brains that nobody fully understands yet, but this is understood. There are not enough genes in the human genome to code for every single brain neuron, group of neurons, or specific structure of neurons. Genes instead make general areas, and the individual neurons wire in learned progression.

The FOXP2 gene has been discovered in the Neanderthal genome, but that does not mean that anything remotely resembling our speech proper was possible. As I read it, the gene only directs the wiring of the brain for the use of the tongue and vocal system, and involved in language are other genes yet to be found. Also, it does not control all of grammar; however, when defective, it does make some words lacking in speech—that is, you can't articulate the sounds. It could conceivably be only one step in a hierarchy of speech acquisition. If a part of this larger brain increase were to become used for wiring the vocal system, causing other different sounds to be made, and these new sounds became conceptual alterations, as per my theory, then these neurons would become well used.

If, when defective, the FOXP2 gene were not to wire properly, you would not have "voice" of, say, the letter *g*. By extension, you would not have the wired paraphernalia needed to innately understand the sound-words, or tilogos, as I have called them. Neither would you be able to mirror it from others making the sound, thus becoming oblivious to what *g* meant.

Humans have some 140 sounds that would not be wired for if they were not needed for survival. Why would these sounds wire the tongue, voice box, and brain control if not of some value? It's not as if one nerve in the tongue, the voice box, and the brain do all the sound controls so that when you get one, you get them all. We would also not need 140 separate concepts to be innate to survive, as I will discuss later. So at least some of these sounds could have become altered for another reason. I suspect that if actual calls or cries were discovered, they would have redundancy of sounds within them and not be all completely different. Further, the division of these calls and cries are likely the product of our vowels and consonant productions. The FOXP2 gene, then, likely started out as wiring for calls and cries and was also inherent in the Neanderthal genome at our common split in ancestry. In our line, it was further developed in the brain within the mixing abilities and became trained as digital sound.

There are certain things that I cannot prove here but merely speculate about. However, I can give the reason, I believe, for the lack of proof. We have the largest brain-to-body ratio of any other animal on the planet. This has a price to pay. As mentioned above, our head size is capped off by the pelvic cannel. Most of our growing in brain volume is done after birth. This poses a huge problem, several in fact, but I will mention only a few. Dependency for your survival, I will not look at. These complications also turn out to be an additional placental change discussed below.

It was five o'clock on the Friday afternoon of March 4, 2011, and I was rushing to the hospital after taking my youngest daughter Alicia home to get ready for work. My oldest daughter Tiffany was in the hospital giving birth to my granddaughter. While I was on my way back, I got the call: she'd just given birth. It was six minutes after five, and I was just pulling into the hospital parking lot. I rushed up to the delivery room to see this new package of delight. Much to my upset, she was delayed in being brought out for our viewing pleasure. I was told that she was fine and the mother was doing well, and I was relieved, as we all were.

As I watched my granddaughter, just two hours old, I noticed that she was calm and sleeping, yet she was making faces. I recognized one expression as one of surprise, and another was just a wince. Her mother (my daughter) watched her little faces with amusement and said with adoration, "Look at all those funny little faces she's making." I couldn't blame her! My biased opinion is that she was one of the cutest babies I have ever seen.

At fewer than twenty-four hours old, she was still making the expressions, and I showed her new grammy. She agreed that they were cute. I also noted some minor noises she made; none were phonemes proper. One sound was a slight bark type of noise, not at all like a dog, and the other was a cooing noise. By this time, they were the only sounds that I could hear her produce. I will likely have finished writing this book before I can discern all her sounds for myself, but no phonemes so far, which I would expect if I am right. Those will come later. I am just so glad that she is healthy and content to lie in my arms from time to time so I can adore her.

Both these expressions were being wired into her brain, as they had saved the life of her distant ancestors. One of disgust might have saved the life of a child whose mother saw it eating something toxic and stopped her from eating it. The wince I saw might have saved one of her ancestors if something touched her and her mother took notice and saved her from contact with some parasite or other threat.

Wait now. I just said "being wired into her brain." How can this be possible without external stimuli? Instinct, of course! Most of our behavior is instinctual and must be *wiring reinforced* before it can be second nature, as they say.

Also from watching her while asleep, I had the impression of a thought that she needed to be "wired" physiologically to stay awake for longer periods. Note to self: think on this for a while.

At just more than one month old, Hailey has already learned a fake cry. We get much pleasure from watching this fake cry for attention. She is already learning how to communicate well with what she has.

If we compare the learning of children, infants practice saying the sounds they hear from their parents (language specific) in their first months before speech, which are, I believe, repeated *dadadadadadada* and *mamamamama*, long vowel cries like *aaaaaaa*, and so forth, and they don't attempt to speak in articulated words before these are mastered. Actually, I find these theories to be a little off, but I will include them anyway. Children speak with proper grammar, as mentioned in chapter 2, but poorly stated phrases, such as *goed store*, *him falled*, and so on ... to the final stage of properly learned speech: three steps. Why not three brain-wiring events? Maybe we only need two and a different explanation for the final stage of speech. Let's head to this end:

> It seems indeed that a small baby does all that touching baby stuff—kicking, sucking, gurgling, mewling and puking—without seriously engaging her neocortex. (A. G. Cairns-Smith, *Evolving the Mind*)

This seems to suggest that the new brain (neocortex) needs to be taught from the old brain and the child's surroundings as well as receive input from the parents. An unprogrammed neocortex learning from a programmed older brain, environment, and parents would solve many problems. I will take into account a few of these human brain attributes.

One of the ways that the larger brain problem was solved is that it grew many, many more neurons than needed. We need the extra neurons to wire the brain, in part so we can all be different. I will get back to that in a minute. Our brains need to have the capacity to learn both old things and new things. Interesting, for example, that sight has to be learned somewhat. Babies see things differently. They do not yet have depth-of-field vision when first born; everything looks the same distance from them. Even when they are a little bit older, they may walk into things and have puzzled looks on their faces. They are still learning how to navigate the environment through sight. Not withstanding, shapes are innate somewhat, per chapter 1 of this work.

Babies also have the instinct to feed—that is, suck for food—but they still have to learn to suckle properly in order to get the milk. Neurons need to be hardwired for proper control of the mouth; the mouth must learn to suckle properly. So, with this said, in some real sense, we need to both have it innate or instinct, and learn it as well. The neurons that get used the most for these simple tasks are the ones that become hardwired and permanent. The ones that do not get used die or become weeded back from disuse.

The reader is probably asking what this has to do with language. I have heard several babies in their early life stages making noises. The first noises they generally make are a cooing type of noise, and often the mothers return the noises. Steven Pinker was the first, I believe, to use the term "motherese" when mother and child first communicate vocally, and it is quite unlearned and natural. Babies then learn how to make all their separate phonemes that will be required to speak their language. These are specific to the language they hear their parents speaking. It is only then that they say their first words. This is the conventional wisdom of language, and I challenge it.

The crying of infants has been studied, and they are innate instincts. I have mentioned these earlier as proofs of concepts, with sounds being innate. These I have no problem with. Phonemes I do.

The placenta required a change in substance. It grew attached too, but not into the uterus. I started out this chapter with larger brains and reasonably showed that, via myth, language occurred as a result. This is the change in substance. All other animals are born ready to survive, or are isolated a few months before being exposed to nature. Deer and their kind are born standing and ready to run within a few moments of birth. Wolf cubs are sheltered in dens until they can reasonably survive. Humans are the only mammals who are born defenseless for so long.

Infants' brains are large for their body size, but the brains are still not fully grown to their maximum. The brains do grow fast but are interrupted. I will discuss this interruption shortly. I mentioned earlier about the experiment on rearing infants without hearing any language at all and stated that it was a botched experiment. No other noises were recorded. How, then, do we know that some form of calls and cries did not develop naturally as the brains developed?

I can't help but think that they could actually learn these calls and cries first, in the same way they learn to suckle: hardwiring of the innate instinct. They must have, as per my theory, some basis for the concept-to-sound mode—then separating out the different sounds into phonemes and finally organizing these sounds into words. The last two parts of that statement are true. I have never read anything about the first part of the statement, about learning the calls and cries first. I can only ask the question and hope to get an answer: Does anyone know?

Sight needs to have its basics wired and trained, even though babies are born with sight. Vision needs to be learned by the neurons to work the depth of field and the focusing of the eye so the world is not blurry. Why would it be any different for the neurons in our language facility? This would put them into the proper order of acquisition: calls, phonemes, and then speech—all our speech organs would need to have their control learned by the neurons in the brain. This learning calls and cries will not work in the form I have written about above, as there is a new difficulty introduced with brain size and learning.

The difficulty is that babies, to my ear, untrained as it is, do not really make what we would consider calls or cries. Unless we count the actual crying types previously mentioned and some grunts, cooing, barks, gut sounds, screams, and such. I attribute this to the immature brain at birth and a new factor introduced into the mix. This new factor is what I mentioned above as interruption. Adult humans do not use calls and cries anymore, so these calls and cries cannot be reinforced in infants. Truly innate ones as per chapter 1, with the factoring in of learning to hardwire them, are no longer possible with nonuse. They don't become perfected, like the instinct to suckle.

Instead, it is more probable that the articulation of these calls and cries as digital phonemes have taken over as representing the calls and cries in a shortened version—still, of course, with the complete concept attached. This, if you have not already figured out yet, requires learning. Learning requires teaching, and there must have been a first to avoid the "chicken or the egg" problem. I will not deal with this here, but deal with it I will.

Here we truly do have an exact placenta transformation. The brains must grow so huge, that an early interruption sabotages the natural process. Calls and cries are eliminated and replaced with the phonemes, which are language specific from the parents.

Finally, we must consider the deaf and the problems of brain damage. The deaf issue is hard to deal with, as deafness was not selected for as a survival advantage, at least not in primates.

Sometimes we need to be blunt for the sake of accuracy. Therefore, with my apologies, I will state the facts. Selection is cruel and has no knowledge of its cruelty. In the beginning, there would be no such thing as the deaf surviving, or surviving well. Deafness is a defect in genetics or other developmental properties. I suspect that deafness in higher animals would not have existed in the wild until compassion or maternal love drove devotion to aid offspring. That said, there is no reason that a language instinct would not exist in a human brain just because an eardrum did not form. In this case, the brain would be looking for a way to represent these concepts. As soon as one person found a means to which the deaf could communicate these concepts, the brain would be just as elastic, and articulation would follow. This we know as sign language.

Reported in the literature, but I will not cite anything here, is this very ability to learn sign language. In some schools, as sign language is beginning to be taught, the students actually learn their own signing and make up their own form of communicating. All a student needs to get started is an example: talking meaningfully with her hands. She then interacts with other students, learning to use gestures instead of sounds on innate concepts. These students make them up with agreement to a common sign. What is so different about this as compared to sound language? Once it became a human trait, language would always be a human trait.

While on the human brain, we should question genetic wiring.

First Word by Christine Kenneally has an example of two different people having two different hemispheres of the brain removed, and both learned to speak well enough. So something must be wiring the brain for speech, and generally it happens to be in the Wernickes and Brocas on the left side, but it doesn't have to be. If the brain is becoming wired for speech with the area removed, then it makes sense that something else is wiring language. This is the harder obstacle to get over. I quote the same point taken from another source. The UG stands for universal grammar.

> If we look at these results from the theoretical perspective of UG, the left hemisphere and the right hemisphere in children appear to be identically equipped to acquire language ... UG is supposed to be a genetically based neural module that is uniquely dedicated to grammar. Why would the module be available bilaterally? Another perhaps more plausible explanation is that language can be acquired in various neural tissue, and that tissue does not have to have domain-specific wiring for language. (*The Interactional Instinct*, Namhee Lee et al.)

I dispute the UG part as occurring naturally as per chapter 2, and that leaves only language. I think that a baby being born with only a partial brain is no real problem here, as she will still be born with a tongue and voice box that need to be wired into something. This is different from being born without a tongue and voice box, as these actually make the sounds. The brain is plastic enough to take the neurons from another area and use them for tongue control.

I suggest that all that goes into making language in the first place, calls and cries, world-ordered structure, and whatever else is required, grows together into its module in the actual state of language as realized by the brain in learning these firings. If the usual part of the brain is missing, then another part will be used, but less so due to competition for the other purposes of that same brain space, needed also for survival. The fact that the brain is wired almost exclusively into the same module specific place is no real inscrutability, but there is something guiding the process. This other guide is the back on which it came into being in the first place. The same as sight grew into its own area, sounds grew into theirs, and meanings with them. The domain or module would only come into being when enough information was being processed in the first place to call for separation and communicating in an isolated area, which would not interfere with other thinking processes. The processes drive the modules, not the other way around.

If we are to evolve language at all, we must admit into our process, at the very minimum, that all the senses are involved. We feel heat; we see light; we hear sound; we taste sweet; we smell scents. These are all concepts also. If we started to place sounds upon our entire world in any central area of the brain, then the other areas of sense would have to wire into this same brain area if those other areas are to have their concepts receive names. Removing one hemisphere, under the right circumstances, would not stop the brain from wiring into another area, albeit a smaller area due to competition for space. This would be just a duplicate of the original process. As I wrote above on the FOXP2 gene, it directs the wiring into the brain. If less brain, it will still direct it somewhere.

We see that language built the language brain, not the other way around. How could a brain ever invent language and force a voice box and tongue to grow into a species with supreme control? If the latter were true, then it would be a real puzzle how a left hemisphere removal would allow language into the right hemisphere. Reasonably, it is not a puzzle at all. We should look at how I think the brain has adapted to the task of higher speech.

None of this is actually contradictory. The concepts and sounds wire the brain, and the brain then puts to use the sounds and concepts. In the case of the deaf, the concepts are still there, and the hands are learned for communicating. This is a byproduct of being the same species: human!

If any of my extra speculation on these facts is true, we have extra brain space, digital brain space, a disconnect between sounds and actions, a small area in the brain just for sounds, a mixing pot for placental template change—and we are ready to take the next step. In the next chapter, I will try to show how these large concepts could become separated into smaller, more accurate ones.

Chapter Eight

Leaving Natural Thought Behind

The method is the same in all cases, in philosophy, in any art or study. We must look for the attributes and the subjects of both our terms, and we must supply ourselves with as many of these as possible, and consider them by means of the three terms, refuting statements in one way, confirming them in another, in pursuit of truth starting from [premises] in which the arrangement of the terms is in accordance with the truth, while if we look for dialectical syllogisms we must start from probable premises. (Aristotle, *Prior Analytics*)

I needed some form of expressing how the thought process has changed over time from a natural complete concept form into a more rational form and thought that I would create a mathematical analogy that was not really a math using numbers. It is only a means in which to express the complex changes in the thought process. I have not been able to find one, or at least understand one enough to use, so I will cheat and make one up.

I was looking for myths and other older information and stumbled upon a book by Graham Hancock titled *Fingerprints of the Gods*, which turned out to be a great read, as I found a perfect analogy:

> Under the grooved edge of the gilded casket on which his effigy now crouched was found an inscription: "initiated into the secrets." Alternative translations of the same hieroglyphic text render it variously as "he who is upon the secrets" and as "guardian of the secrets."

Total sound concepts would tend to be the same as hieroglyphics: too vague to be of perfect use and poor grammar present. We must include under this category calls and cries as too vague, which I discussed partially in chapter 2. We need a method of dividing them, refining them, and adding them together into words and sentences. I suggest that there was introduced a new selective pressure: the refinement of vague, for a better understanding of what we mean exactly. Bear with me as I take a detour to establish other areas of knowledge within the brain. It might seem redundant, but it will be used differently here.

We are often advised to follow our hearts, particularly in the case of love. What does your heart tell you? In order to know if this advice is warranted, you would have to have had two types of marriage: one where your heart said, "Get married and don't look back," the other where your head said, "This is the right thing to do," but your heart was not in it. I think that if your heart were in it all the way, your mind would make the necessary compromises to make it work for you, or kill you in the attempt. Only if both were willing to make the mental compromises from the start would it succeed. You would less mind giving something up or putting up with something irritating.

Feelings are often more powerful than logic. This is because we have used feelings, our feeling brains, for longer than logic. Logic is something new to us, as is reason, if there is even a difference between the two. The amygdala is the older part of the brain that deals with emotions such as the fight-or-flight response. In order for a species to survive, it must feel its universe. It must also ignore most of it. This is what we refer to as white noise, the constant vibrating of the earth beneath our feet, the motion of the planet while it rotates on it axis. These are all constant, along with many other things. The absence of the smell of oxygen or hydrogen, but not water—oxygen and hydrogen combined—is another case in point.

If we had to concentrate on the movement of the earth and try to offset for the imbalance while walking, and all these other things that we ignore, we would be too busy to pay attention to anything else. This is one way to start from nothing and ignore it completely but still know it by having a feeling somewhere in an ignored area. As brains get bigger, they are used for other purposes, and the information is not generally reapplied to the new options of the brain. What would be the advantage of having several copies of the same ignored species of knowledge?

Not one of us would survive even one day on planet Earth if we did not know everything needed for our survival. Just one moment of inattention could end in fatality. We know the earth moves, but our brains and bodies ignore it by compensation, to the end that it took four generations to bring this knowledge into acceptance: Copernicus, Bruno, Galileo, and Newton. Having this knowledge reconciled to our consciousness has done nothing to make our brains and bodies feel that movement.

In fact my own theory of savant numerical abilities draws on this very analogy between the mathematical complexity of language and savant calculations. In order to describe this theory, I need first to explain a little about how brains function. In most people the major cognitive tasks—such as understanding language, figuring numbers, analyzing sensory perceptions, and so on—are highly specialized, preformed separately in different regions of the brain. This specialization of different mental activities is effected by a process known as "inhibition," which prevents one area of the brain from interfering with the activity of another. (Daniel Tammet, *Embracing the Wide Sky*)

We have several brain areas performing several different functions. If we want to mix within these special areas, we need to have another area available to do the mixing so as not to interfere with what is already established. The previous chapter concluded that an extra brain via a larger brain increase combined with the following is a way around this problem. I will return to "inhibition" later for another reason, but for now extra unused brain space partially solves this problem. I will use this extra brain space to grow the properties of analyzing language problems.

We have an emotional center of our brains, which contains all the knowledge needed to survive, our fight-or-flight responses or emotional intelligence. We have the effect known as the feeling of knowing and many hidden layers, which give us the sought-for answers as if gifts from the gods. Then we have the more analytical part of our brains, which has come to be called reason. We also have the area of the brain that contains all our total sound concepts, mentioned in the first chapter of this book, on the innateness of language, all innate.

I have established that attention is wiring for brain silence and restricting communication to smaller single wires or neurons. I left off that chapter with "emotional thought" and "natural thought," and I will clarify them here. Emotional thought is the knowledge just commented on, or the feeling of knowing. Natural thought, I suggested, would be our total sound-word conceptualization area and will become our second persona, the first persona being emotional thought. I head for the third persona, which we know as rational thought. I will call it analytical thought.

This will probably give me a headache, but I think that "analytical math" might become my answer. A concept is wide, generally speaking, and must become narrowed to be of any real value, such as my commentary at the beginning of this chapter on the vagueness of hieroglyphics. The concept of sight contains much: light, seeing, dark, insight, and the like. Water contains as much: wet, thirst, cold or damp, ice, liquid, and the like. To go from analog to digital in this context would give us many more digital parts than its whole.

Let a whole concept be admitted by one letter (it is analytics, after all) and for my purpose, different ways of writing them will be the separate parts of the concepts, thus A, a, *A, a, A, a,* and the like. Remember that the following discourse is in reference to different brain areas.

If you remember from Aristotle's "Analytics," if A has a property, and B has the same property, and C has a property of A, it will also have a property of B. So, then, A, a, *A, a, A,* and *a,* will become the wide concept of our first persona. A will become the narrower concept of our first persona. We will let a B in as the same second persona narrower concept of the wider second persona of B, b, *B, B,* and *b,* just for the contrast. Got that? The letters and not the sounds in this case are not dealing in language but in personas. Each way of writing the letter represents the different, separate concepts in the larger concept. The letter A being, in this example, water, the different ways of writing it being the smaller concepts included in water: wet, drink … We sneak

177

a C into the equation as the third persona needed to make the transition, and hopefully it will become self-explanatory.

If we have the one total concept as Aa*Aa* and Bb*Bb*, causing C from Aa*Aa* to arise and c from Bb*Bb* to arise, we get Aa=Bb=Cc into Cc, the third party, or third persona. If the total concept of both parties is water, then we might get a secondary concept of water is wet, into AaBb. Now we could raise it again from AaBb into C, the third persona, as AB equaling C. The third persona, C, treats the AB as a higher level concept, or secondary concept of wet, complete with the sound change from wat, to wet, in the third persona, C. Wow, and I thought reading Aristotle's *Analytics* was going to kill me!

I will recap the last part for my own benefit, if not yours, using language and trying hard not to lose my mind. Water wet becomes the new topic of the new word represented in the third persona C. It gets it from the agreement of the first persona, A, stating water wet the Aa part and the second persona stating water wet the Bb part of the combined personas. Then the third persona, C, casts out the water part, so to speak, and gets wet only from the first persona, A, the A part of the first grouping, and the second persona, B, the B part of the second grouping, leaving only wet, complete with a sound change. To be clear as mud, the first persona, A, knows it as a call, cry, or other sound, via the innateness of language from chapter 1, in a total concept form. The second persona, B, knows it only as a feeling of knowledge.

Remember, we are here strictly talking about going from wide concepts, which both personas A and B know, into narrower concepts, which persona C comes to know. So then, with the parties included, attention bearing on the first and second parties singles out wet from the water concept, making it a third party higher or separate concept from the totality of the water meanings. This smaller concept change would be accompanied with a slight sound change or a little more exaggerated one as long as it was different enough to be a separate sound. The separate sound would need to be related but distinct in concept from total primary concept to partial secondary concept. Ouch, that hurts!

The first persona of emotional intelligence here is not at all contested by anyone, to the best of my knowledge. The second persona of Natural thought as I use it here might become so, but hidden areas and the feeling of knowing are not contested either. My third persona might become contested, so I should be a little clearer before moving on. The idea is that this fictional story of the two brains would actually work with the one unused brain increase I proposed if we allow for the invasion theory mentioned in the previous chapter. To be clear, this does not in any way restrict itself to emotion, and language-minor module—any module—as any part of the brain can now use the same process. We could call the extra modules persona D, persona E, persona F … and only require persona A, the language-minor module to be included every time. Thus our persona C would become our language-major module or area.

If persona A fired (physiological) I got it, that is a sound alteration representing the same or varied concept and the persona B fired the same "I got it," that is, to allow a variation in a concept and accepting a sound to be placed as a marker, there would only need to be one more "I got it." If persona C were to be the persona that actually made the connection between the two concept changes and fixed the sound marker change onto it, thus firing "I got it," the light would come on and reasoning would be born with lots of extra brain space to wire into. Conscious is from the Latin word for science, meaning knowledge; adding con changes the meaning to awareness of the knowledge. If the other two parts of the brain reported differently, then a conflict would arise, forcing a conclusion to be drawn and more knowledge sought to resolve the matter. These are known as gray areas where faith and reason conflict, not discussed here. It's not that far-fetched, because as we all know, there are many voices going on in our brains all the time, and one of them just needs to be called "I." We may have several layers of this reasoning built on the back of lesser layers, after the same pattern described. In the final analysis, I suggest they were all wired by attention, and attention will become the "I" in question. This does not restrict the "I" to one place in the brain, however.

Going from thinking in huge concepts into thinking in smaller parts of the same concepts is reasoning or analytical thought. Basically, we are dissecting whole complete concepts into several of their smaller particles and, in the process, naming them, or sound-symbolizing them.

> Not only are facts sovereign but there are more of them. Facts breed facts, and as knowledge of facts burgeons the domains into which they are organized are severed into yet smaller pieces, as individuals and their knowledge become increasingly specialized. (Roy A. Rappaport, *Ritual and Religion*)

What are we doing if not analyzing the wet from water? To go from silence to sound requires it to receive sound-symbols: in this case, phonemes. Altering the sounds to alter the concepts from "total" to "parts of" might not be that hard, as I will attempt to show.

If we were to take here the "analytics" Aa*Aa* and Bb*Bb*, we could form the "reasoning brain," and it would eventually lead to an "I" or, in the case of split personality, several "Is" or an analytical brain. Only when the various parts of the brain can openly communicate using symbolic language or sounds can a central processing area be formed in the brain of what would come to be called "I," or the "mind" in control of the other areas. It would force control in one area over the whole system of language. In other words, both analytics and articulate speech are based on separation of wholes. This separation forms the working area of the conscious "I."

In part, the structure of calls and cries governs the structure of speech but also logical thought:

> Acquisition of the rules of sound structure, in turn, depends on fixed principles governing possible sound systems for human languages, the elements of which they are constituted, the manner of their combination and the modifications that they may undergo in various context. (Noam Chomsky, *Language and Problems of Knowledge*)

One part of this brain I suggested already had a sound-word language—sounds, calls, and cries—that only needs to be conceptually altered. The starting point of the alteration process being an innate sound, representing an innate concept of time and containing, say, the V sound for *time*, or the R sound for the concept of *place* instead of time. The concepts from the two different areas in the brain begin firing together into the area of the brain where it would become a higher persona, C nerve firing. The series nerve firing would combine the two parallel nerve firings into series-parallel—from our electrical diagrams. The series nerve firing would come from two parallel nerve firings, personas A and B, meaning its concept name is time or place, going from meaningless to symbolic: a symbol can be a sound. Actually, even a puff from the gut, as it were, in addition to grunts and sighs could come to mean something and in time have its sound change into a better one, until finally it reached what we would formally call a phoneme. The original sound-word in some cases could have become completely lost (totality), as we no longer *tik* but say *tik* instead.

There is also place here for error, which I have not mentioned, and it would be best to go to the source of analytics and quote Aristotle from *Prior Analytics*:

> But if the premise is not wholly false, a true conclusion is possible. For if A belongs to all C and to some B, and if B belongs to all C, e.g. animal to every swan and to some white thing, and white to every swan, then if we take as [premises] that A belongs to all B, and B to all C, A will belong to all C truly: for every swan is an animal. Similarly if the statement AB is negative. For it is possible that A should belong to some B and to no C, and that B should belong to all C, e.g. animal to some thing, but to no snow, and white to all snow. If then one should assume that A belongs to no B, and B to all C, then will belong to no C.

I am probably more confused than you are, so I have decided only to show these possible mistakes when doing the analytical math. I only wanted to point out that mistakes could be made. I am hoping that after someone reads this book, she will be able to explain the whole book to me.

So I attempt to combine analytics with the yolk sac. Without using all the technical paraphernalia, I will be quick and to the point, without the accuracy. If Broca's area were to start small, with calls, cries, puffs, or grunts, a fair innate communication system would appear, but like the hieroglyphics I started this chapter with, vague and needing context. As per my analytics, singling out smaller concepts from larger ones in these calls or cries, and the recombination thereof, would appear, bringing with it the conscious process of articulation, or digital speech. These new digital sounds would invade this newer area of the brain in a different type or species of language. The newer brain area generated from our last brain increase in size, as mentioned in the last chapter, would house this new enlargement of language into what is called Broca's area. Broca's area would then take its enlargement from the smaller area at the tip of Broca's, which recognizes phonemes, which in turn was developed from calls and cries.

This would be no different from veins growing into the uterus and forming a placenta. With the placenta, I did not deal with the complexity, but I must with language. I use attention, as it is free to do anything, to take care of some of the complexity, that is to say, actually do the separating of the concepts in analytical form. Because the brain areas that do this are digital, any two personas can fire into one persona going from a parallel (two persona) thought to a series (single persona) thought, or series-parallel thinking when combined into its finished state.

It has been shown by the aid of various pieces of equipment like fMRI that speech and thought, and action or reaction, both start in the body/brain before we have time to actually think them. If all we have is one brain, logically, to call the automatic response instinctual thought or natural thought as I have done, then granting attention, thus control, the power to override these thoughts, creates a more accurate picture of what we perceive to happen. This was the chapter on the soul.

I spoke of love at the first of the chapter, and now I want to relate it to knowledge in general. We all know everything needed to survive, but the knowledge is hidden. It has not all become analyzed and integrated into our common thought. To convert it to our common thought, things must happen; they must be observed, taken apart, checked, and revealed. We might see one thing that does not quite make sense to us because it was ignored for our survival. Think of the earth moving. It takes much thinking and observing to place theory as fact; this is where gray areas come into play. You feel in love, but your mind has to adapt to the other person, not your heart.

Your mind actually has to adapt to your own heart also. They say that when you first meet someone, you know by the sight and smell of her that she is the one. We hear it said that love has little to do with your brain, but in fact, it has everything to do with your brain. You want to be with her, and we can attribute this to love. You also want to know everything about her, and that cannot be attributed to love. Your reasoning and your emotions are at work here. You are unconsciously checking to see if you are compatible. Both areas of your brain must reconcile with each other, and compromises must be made if a relationship will ever ensue or last. These areas of your brain must have a common battlefield where they can weigh out information. In order to weigh out information, the brain must be able to bisect or dissect all the knowledge it has, in whatever form it has it.

This is just a way of bringing up the topic of attention again. When anything new is learned—and make no mistake about it: you must learn to love her mentally—you apply more attention. You also analyze every aspect of this person and then decide whether your intellect will allow a compromise with your emotions. The four of you must be compatible: your emotional brain and your natural brain in addition to her emotional brain and her natural brain. The properties of each of these brain functions would become entangled in your analytical brain. Love made the best example here because more people feel and think about love than they do about language or how our minds work. This love commentary will make practical applications possible in the last chapter. I will prepare you for it now and ask the following: What is the minimum number of people you need to have in order to develop a language? How well must they know each other to develop a language?

The same thing applies to what we feel about everything else in the world. No less would it apply to language. We heard our parents telling us to slow down and "think" about what we were saying. By this, they really meant to pay attention to what words were being formulated and produced. Are your words consistent with your feelings and knowledge? We will reflect on this in the last chapter.

We know that we each have a mind floating freely within our heads because we feel it. This does not make it knowledge. Man has been working toward this end for a long time now. It has been written about since at least Plato. Lesser things also have been studied and found out, bringing forth a better understanding of nature. In fact, it has become our nature that we must now derive the truth. We must have several smaller dawnings of some untrue knowledge before we count it as wrong and get the truth to actually fit better with the newer idea than with the old idea. Once these observations are singled out in nature, we already know them to be true someplace in our brains, before it becomes rationalized knowledge. I will cover this in more detail with examples in another chapter.

Ignoring would indeed have had to be around at least as long as attention itself. How could any animal ever survive without the ability to ignore? I started right off in the book with how sounds and hearing could have evolved innately. I now ask the reader: How could you ever feel your own vibrations if you could not ignore the constant movement of the earth?

I might place under the microscope for your scrutiny that any discernment of different vibrations would only need to be pointed out if they became either a danger or opportunity to mate. This would let them remain in some isolated area of the brain. The only time it would be necessary to report it to a higher level of attention would be when the imminent danger was unavoidable. This would only need to be communicated with one act of nervation. One act of nervation only needs one line or a series link to the higher attention, much like the separate modules in the automotive computer systems. This process is completely selectable, by small steps as required by selection, right from the beginning, and needs no more complication of explanation than this, at least to get language, our goal.

This, I suspect, is how the other parts of the brain have become silent, and we are only fed information from them as needed. How else can our brains, unconscious to our minds, think without our knowing it? It would seem to me quite insensible to think that we could only pay attention to one thing at a time and survive. If there was too much going on at one time, we would always be lost in confusion. Attention would have to be able to handle the here and now. Some other part of the brain would need to handle, or rather record, what was happening. Yet another part would need to compare it with previous experiences, all while vigorously fleeing for your life.

Dreams just might have come about by tapping into this emotional area of the brain and allowing the viewing of what is being analyzed, as I have mentioned. It would need to be recorded somehow if experience were to ever take hold and produce what is called conditioned learning. If we did not want attention to be dealing with all this and much more going on at the same time, then attention would need to wire some things for us to ignore. Selection would encourage survival of the brains, which could solve and report solutions the fastest without the need to pay attention to every detail.

To put it in perspective: if a rabbit being chased by a lynx or mountain lion were to use its attention to navigate the immediate course it ran, it could survive a spell. While running the immediate course, the rabbit also has a separate area of the brain, using the same eyesight and scenery, without strain to the immediate attention. This separate area points out to the rabbit's immediate attention where a hole in the bush was—big enough for the rabbit but not the cat—and the rabbit would survive better yet. The repetition of this chase and escape, ignored, might be repeated within the brain, ignored, with different possible outcomes, ignored again, until the ignoring part of the brain became unconscious enough not to ignore it any longer. This would be the dreams we have while asleep. This would allow for long-term storage in memory and, as noted previously, provide an arena to participate and alter outcomes in dreams, what we call lucid dreams.

These would all be, strictly speaking, our old natural way of thinking, which we still somewhat have. Many areas are built to do certain functions outside our immediate conscious areas. Remember, these are only examples to get to our old natural way of thinking in its many established forms.

If this makes any sense to you at all, then you can see that when it comes to language, it is not different. As language arose to a more articulate form, the old calls and cries would be ignored and lost to one's conscious, but the concepts would remain as part of the new sounds produced. Thus the new system of articulate speech would replace the old calls and cries. An innate base would always be in the brain with the newer, different sounds, which have gone through the newer analytical thinking process. It is then likely that we have this area still within the brain set on ignore, maybe our speaking-in-tongues module I mentioned previously.

It also explains why we have an ability to learn articulate speech as knowledge.

> Similar problems arise in the area of vocabulary acquisition, and the solution to them must lie along the same lines: in the biological endowment that constitutes the human language faculty. At the peak period of vocabulary growth, the child masters words at quite an astonishing rate, perhaps a dozen a day or more. Anyone who has attempted to define a word precisely knows that this is an extremely difficult matter, involving intricate and complex properties. (Noam Chomsky, *Language and the Problems of Knowledge*.)

Most people suggest that language is actually learned. Children never learn to speak on their own. The first of our ancestors who started this process would have had to pass these accumulated word growths down to their offspring and cross cultivate them among their clan. I hint at this in other areas of my book, but here I flatly state it for clarity. Having these concepts innate, with a general sound, would be of the highest aid in getting them passed on as complete words with meaning. We would be able to understand these meanings without having to allocate a difficult statement explaining the meaning, as it would be intuitive. These intuitive meanings are innately part of our natural thinking or natural thought.

If this seems like reasonably sound thinking to you the reader, then add the language. Analyze calls and cries from their total concepts into the lesser concepts within, and you can "get it" reasonably well, which makes the transition better than anything I have read or heard on the topic. At some point, we would actually "get" that we "get it," and this would become our higher thinking.

That said, with every sound alteration, a mutual understanding would arise of what was actually being said about the whole concept, by its individual parts. Actually, mirror neurons have been shown to aid in understanding one another's form actions, sounds, and even facial expressions—lots of tools. These tools would be detrimental in getting the different sounds from a call to mean the same part of the call/concept sound transition to the different individuals interacting in communication, i.e., they would aid in "I get it." I here add this quote as an insert and ask you to read the appendix II for the details.

Perhaps most significant about this arrangement is the fact that the brain structures involved in basic biological regulation are also part of the regulation of behavior and are indispensable to the acquisition and normal function of cognitive processes. The hypothalamus, the brain stem, and the limbic system intervene in body regulation *and* in all neural processes on which mind phenomena are based, for example, perception, learning, recall, emotion and feeling, and—as I shall produce later—reasoning and creativity. Body regulation, survival, and mind are intimately interwoven. (Antonio Damasio, *Descartes' Error*)

I hope that it is understood in this chapter that we naturally have thoughts, actions, and individual brain areas promoting our survival. These I call natural thought. There is overlap, redundancy, and priority within these brain areas. I started off with vagueness, leaving a need for clarity, and showed that it is possible, at least in concept, to have the brain self-analyze with three different personas. It requires an "I get it," though, and I am not happy with the traditional take on "I get it." We will need to examine this also.

The following chapters will deal with more things needed to work with before I go on to do the math. This way, when you read the elucidation, you will see why I have set them up the way I have. We need to have a better understanding of "I get it" and some concepts to work with, which can be taken into the math for analyzing. These will be the respective topics of the next chapters.

Chapter Nine

The Dawning

We routinely disqualify testimony that would plead for extenuation. That is, we are so persuaded of the rightness of our judgment as to invalidate evidence that does not confirm us in it. Nothing that deserves to be called truth could ever be arrived at by such means.

—Marilynne Robinson
The Death of Adam

Have you ever been with another person and were taken in by someone, and when it dawned on you what had really happened, you looked at each other and knew that you both knew that you had been duped.

I can't think of a better story to use than this one. Moreover, I doubt that you, the reader, no matter how well educated, could come up with a better story. If it is not true in some form or other, at least it is so very well constructed that one would do well to better it. If you remember from the preface, I mentioned that I used to argue creation versus evolution. This is one of the arguments that I made to myself.

Personally, I think that both sides of the creation-versus-evolution argument miss the importance and significance of the story. If I am right, you will forever look upon it with new eyes. It deals sometime after some form of communication was established, as they were talking in the narration, but it does not have to be full-blown articulate speech. They also had some form of knowledge, but not necessarily the consciousness of that knowledge. Let's peek at the fall in the Garden of Eden as I dissect the hell out of it. (Is that going to get me an X rating?)

> Of every tree of the garden thou mayest freely eat: but of the tree of knowledge of good and evil, thou shalt not eat of it: for in the day thou eatest thereof thou shalt surely die. (Gen. 2:16–17)

> It is not good that the man should be alone; I will make him an help meet for him. (Gen. 2:18)

My first set of observations: Adam was told that he should not eat from the tree of knowledge. The tree of knowledge was not really a tree of knowledge but knowledge of good and evil. Finally, Eve was not even made yet, as these two scriptures are in the correct order of their happenings. That's three observations to take with us as we go.

> Now the serpent was more subtle than any beast of the field which the Lord God had made. And he said to the *woman*, Yea, hath God said, *Ye* shall not eat of every tree of the garden? And the woman said to the serpent, *We* may eat of the fruit of the trees of the garden: but of the fruit

of the tree which is in the midst of the garden, God hath said, Ye shall not eat of it, *neither shall ye touch it*, lest ye die. (Gen. 3:1–3; emphasis mine)

A couple more points here. The serpent came to the woman and asked her if she could eat: hath God said, Ye shall not eat ...? How did the woman know what God said if she was not around when God said it? Adam told her! They must have had a good conversation over it, because they were so fearful that it would get eaten, that they somehow added: "neither shall we touch it." God never said anything about touching it. Remember this for later.

And the serpent said unto the woman, *ye* shall not surely die: for *God doth know* that in the day ye eat thereof, then *your eyes will be open*, and ye shall *be as gods*, knowing good and evil. (Gen. 3:4–5; emphasis mine)

Tradition has it that this was a complete lie that the devil told her. After all, the devil is a liar. Was it a complete lie? Read on.

And when the woman *saw* that the tree was good for food, and that it was pleasant to the eyes, and a tree to be desired to make one wise, *she took* of the fruit thereof, and *did eat*, and gave also to her husband *with her*: and he *did eat*. (Gen. 3:6; emphasis mine)

Note the following: First, when the woman saw is taken as fact—that they avoided even looking at this fruit. This was the first time she even looked at it, as denoted by it being pleasant to the eyes. Second, she touched it and nothing happened. Third, she ate of it and nothing happened, but the command was not to her, so nothing *should have happened*. Fourth, her husband was with her and witnessed it—that is, nothing happening to her. Now the fear left Adam, as it was obliviously harmless to touch and eat, so he did eat. He was the one who was not supposed to have eaten it, not Eve. When he did eat comes next.

> And *the eyes of them both* were opened, and *they knew* that they were naked. (Gen. 3:7; emphasis mine)

> Behold, the man is become as *one of us, to know good and evil.* (Gen 3:22; emphasis mine)

Depending on your view of death, neither one died, except unto God as far as a relationship. So there was some truth to what the serpent said: they were as gods, knowing good from evil. Remember that the serpent asked if she was free to eat everything in the garden; she answered no. In truth *she was.* She could touch the fruit of the tree, as could Adam. *She* could eat it or *they* could do anything they wanted to with this fruit, such as use it as ornaments. *He* alone was not to eat of it lest *he* die. Note: it was not likely an apple as has been supposed, but that is another story in itself.

This is not a story of knowledge at all. By some accounts, Adam was reported to have already named all the animals. They were obviously talking with each other and sharing this knowledge. They were both naked, and likely they knew they were naked. Let's be clear: the man knew he was naked because he was not wearing any clothes. The woman knew she was naked because she was not wearing any clothes. The most likely scenario to the story is that this was the moment of their both knowing that the other knew—or the theory of mind happening. The possible dawning that they had been fooled at the same time opened their eyes to the fact that they each had the same knowledge; they each knew themselves to be naked and knew the other was naked and covered their shame. This has become known as self-consciousness. When finally enough "I get it" moments have occurred, you must come to know that we have reached the ability to "get it."

I must also point out that they immediately sewed fig leaves together and made aprons. So the idea of sewing was known. We must not allow this knowledge of sewing to enter here as unknown before the fall, because it leads to a bigger question needing to be answered. If the knowledge was instant and a result of the fall, then why did they not know everything at once? Why instant knowledge of sewing and not instant knowledge of electricity? I don't think either side—faith or reason—wants to get into a pissing contest over this question.

Both of these terms—theory of mind and self-consciousness—are derived from another source. The other source is what Eve was tempted with in the first place. She was tempted with *your eyes will be open*, and ye shall *be as gods*, knowing good and evil," or in her thoughts and words, "make one wise." Please correct me if I am wrong, but you can't truly understand this without wisdom. It has to be a hindsight revelation. Looking back at the story, you could just about put any event into it and have the same result.

What is wisdom but knowing the difference between good and evil? In fact, the best definition of wisdom is to know what best to do with the knowledge you have, or application of knowledge. So we have knowledge and we have the ability to best apply it. They knew that each other knew that each other was naked and covered up because they were self-conscious of the other's consciousness.

Wisdom was not instantaneous either, as the story goes on to include the next quote directly below. Very likely, it is a parable to describe to Adam and Eve's descendants how realization and wisdom came into being. Adam and Eve finally realized that they knew they were communicating and understanding each other. Because each knew the other had the same knowledge, creating more knowledge became possible: learning, and learning takes wisdom. With wisdom and learning, your own behavior comes into scrutiny. Behavior now demands excuses:

> And the man said, The woman whom thou gavest to be with me, she gave me of the tree, and I did eat. And the Lord God said unto the woman, what is this that thou hast done? And the woman said, The serpent beguiled me, and I did eat. (Gen. 3:12–13)

As we already saw above, it was neither the woman's nor the serpent's fault. That said, they lacked wisdom as a tool, as I have tried to convey here. Wisdom was the product of their hindsight opening their eyes. Before moving on, I should add a couple of notes.

Noteworthy here is that as wisdom dawned, so did labor, in both senses of the word:

> Unto the woman he said, "I will greatly multiply thy sorrow and thy conception ..." (larger-headed babies would definitely hurt during delivery).

> And unto Adam he said, "Cursed is the ground for thy sake; in sorrow shalt thou eat of it all the days of thy life.... In the sweat of thy face shalt thou eat bread ..."

Agriculture, farming, and animal husbandry, and many more labors and insights are the topic of another chapter. For this chapter, I plan to see if something is missing from our model of knowledge.

While I usually only use my computer for research or checking my e-mail, one day I decided to look over the home page of MSN. I just happened to see a headline about a cow working a water pump and thought it would amuse my idle brain. It made it work harder.

It was a video of a cow drinking from an old-fashioned water pump—the kind where you pump a handle up and down to draw water from a well. This cow would place its head under the pump handle and lift the handle. Then as the handle fell, it would lick up the water coming from the spout. Wow, what's next for cows, nuclear fusion? Cows, for the most part, are just as dumb as the patties they leave lying in the fields. This cow seems to have mutated into one intelligent cow.

This bears the need for closer inspection, though, and we must examine how and what happened here. We can think this through reasonably well without actually seeing how the learning took place. Very likely, the cow happened by when water was dripping out of the spout and took a drink, as little as that might have been. The position of the pump handle was facing the cow, and if the cow naturally lifted its head to walk away, the handle would automatically be lifted. The cow, ready to walk away, smelled and saw the water so drank more. This pattern, occurring naturally, would allow the cow to drink all the water it wanted as long as it continued to raise its head to leave. Getting its fill of water, or at least some water, that day would lead the cow to "know" there was a water source there for future use. The cow wandered by the same well again, and going to the spout, it placed its head under the handle again, allowing for a repeat. The cow then began going there repeatedly for a drink.

There was something learned here, and I don't pretend there wasn't. The cow does not know that this is a water pump and pumping it will produce water. What was learned is that this is a water supply and, we could add, if you don't lift your head to walk away between drinks, it won't produce more water. The learning is strictly physiological, even any part that could be called known by the cow. It's unlikely the cow would bring its calf to the well and lift the handle for the calf to drink. Its head would not be positioned correctly. To go from physiological to conscious has problems plaguing it, and we must now examine some of them.

It is hard to believe that some scientist, somewhere, is making a living studying sea slugs (sorry, but I will not be using the proper Latin name). He sits on the beach with his cooler of beer, ordering in pizza for lunch and getting a tan while waiting for a sea slug to come out of the water to study. Wow, I need to get me a job like that! Actually, I just had a funnier thought than this one. Some reader might think that I am being serious here and complain to some agency that his tax dollars are being wasted. Its time to get serious again.

They study it by placing negative stimuli to work and seeing if they can "teach" them to avoid certain conditions. Without anything one could call a real brain—they are slugs, after all—they do learn to avoid the negative stimuli. With many tries, eventually they unconsciously get it and avoid the negative stimuli, and this is referred to as nervous system learning.

It only makes sense that if we can teach these slugs, nature can teach these slugs. I will use two different terms to keep it straight in your minds (in reality, my mind). We can use direct evolutionary learning (programmability), where selection weeds out the ones who cannot physiologically perform a necessity for survival. We can use learning proper (learnability) to relay learning over and above programmable necessities and call them benefits. Surviving would only prolong your life and not favor it above the many others of your species. A better capacity for learning would favor your survival in the selection lottery. This is slightly different from direct evolutionary learning, which is not really learning, per se. Any slug that came face-to-face with a rock and stopped, doing nothing to escape its predicament, would perish on the spot. Any slug that changed direction and went around the rock would survive. This is blind evolutionary learning. It is innate in the genomes of all animals that survived. Sea slugs have only nervous systems and no real brain: if a nervous system can learn, a brain can learn better.

The question to answer is whether it is possible to evolve I get that I get it from nothing. The answer is in the affirmative. Sometimes you only realize something is happening when you word things differently. It is in this different wording that I will proceed to show its happening. I already made a slight differentiation between learning for survival and learning for advantage in survival.

If a condition that is not deadly but favored, say, eating a better meal by avoiding the thorns, were to become learned by a member of a species, unconsciously of course, then she would feed better and survive better than her siblings of the same species. She would also tend to be healthier and more fertile, thus passing on her learnable genes more often on average. Eventually, her offspring would outnumber the competition's and replace them in their environment. This would not in any way be considered an "I get it" in anyone's understanding of the term. It might be just a different way of eating, which avoids the thorns: as long as it was a learned behavior, it will promote learning. Think of the cow. This learning is strictly physiological in nature and must be present and selected for. That is, nervation must be programmable for learning conditions and not innate, as in chapter 1 of this book. That's two conditions being utilized, innate programmability and innate learnability.

If-then is what we are truly referring to here, and it is not argued by any evolutionist—that I know of—that it does not exist in nature. To keep us on track, a small recap is in order. We have normal programmability and advantage learnability, neither cognizant but physiological in nature so far. When brains are added to the picture, it leaves room for more unconscious events being learned.

Snakebites are avoided not because every animal has been bitten by a snake but because the ones who avoided them did not get bitten. The ones that were bitten became food. This is a case of programmed behavior, but the behavior need not be anything conscious to the animal either.

In order to get it to become conscious at all, you need to have it under attention. That is, you need to see the snake and not only automatically avoid it but know that you need to avoid it. This is where brain learning has the advantage over nervous system wiring. Once the behavior is learned, it can become permanent within the synapse and available for recognition. Recognition is the second, third, and so forth, number of times the event has been cognized after the first event. We could call this an unconscious "I get it" moment. The reason that I say this is because whatever species we are talking about here does not have to know *why* it is so, just *that* it is so.

Those who saw another member of their species bitten by a poisonous snake and suffering, succumbing to death after many cries of pain, would, upon seeing the snake, learn of the reason why it fears it so. The learning could be produced by mirror neurons. Learning the behavior and learning why for the behavior are two different things. One is conscious, and that's why we fear and avoid snakes. This process of understanding why something happens is an "I get it" moment: it is the knowledge of the instinct becoming manifested. Now you have two learned synapses in the brain representing the same thing: avoid, and why avoid. These two will thereafter fire together whenever a snake is seen. It is still if-then in character and not what would be considered a true higher conscious experience. It is, however, one step closer, or intermediate in nature.

Attention would be the reason for the second learned behavior, though not for the first programmed behavior. The species in question saw firsthand why avoidance was prudent. It also heard from the screams of its suffering comrade that danger was present, and this would yet become one more firing of a synapse for the same reason: snake. If our species in question were also to wire the sound for a warning, we'd be one step closer to "I got it," with language attached.

The cry or call in question would become the concept for snake and the action of behavior to take, which fits nicely with my thesis. By the third wiring, there must be some kind of hint to the animal to make it realize it. A vervet monkey who cheats uses her leopard call, without a leopard being present, to scare off others of her species so she can claim her freshly discovered food supply and not share. This behavior has been studied in vervet monkeys. In turn, the others discover that they have been tricked. Our species in question has become borderline at knowing what they are instinctually living. Even though I have not written in great detail how to evolve "I get it," we can see the seeds for its happening from what I have written and the conditions needed to evolve it.

As with the chapter on the placenta, I did not evolve it completely, nor did I evolve the ear completely. I did, however, mention that there is a difference between stimuli learning and willful learning. The reader might remember my writing about two paths of nervation—one from sensor stimuli and one from willful nervation. Place this in your mind and think that there is no real difference between stimuli inducement of "I got it" and willful nervation of "I got it." The wiring is now there because of ...

Once the act of getting anything is hardwired—that is, stimuli produced—the act can also be blindly, unconsciously produced. If the event learned can be blindly induced by the brain willfully, then the brain must blindly know what needs to be done to perform the act. Attention can now make the observation of what is being done and the steps revealed to performing the act in question. Under this method, automatic willful nervation becomes intentional willful nervation of the act, and at some level, intention equates to some level of consciousness.

As brief as that explanation is, it is beyond the scope of this book to follow through on the process or spend several pages here in detail. As I did with the ear and hearing, I will show probability and leave the rest to your imagination. I do have enough information written now to get where I want to be. There are also plenty of theories on the topic anyway.

Higher animals have the ability to "get it" as well as humans. Experiments with chimps, monkeys, and most other primates all show that most primates are well able to "get it," at least after some practice: even language taught to chimps. Whether they are actually aware that they got anything has yet to be factually proven, but I don't see why they couldn't get it at some level. Thinking about all that I have read on these experiments has had me draw another conclusion about them in general. What is so different about other animals and humans? Darwin said we have more instincts, not less. We also have more brains and not less.

There are still problems with this model, though, and they need to be built upon first and then questioned. More ability to get it leads to more "I get it" moments, and layers can be built, or rather instead of getting a dozen things, we can get hundreds. I suggest that if chimps—or other animals, for that matter—"get it" with effort, and we have more brains than any other primates, we would by default "get it" more often. I get that I get it is just one more form of the same species of thought. If "I get it" is possible, then "I get that I get it" is possible with the same process. Instead of getting it, well, you get it, which is the same. You are just getting that you are getting. Get it?

Many dozens of layers (not literal layers) of "I get it" just produces more "I got it." From necessity, there must be something else at work here if we follow the logic of the placenta template. Growing veins into the placenta will only have chickens growing inside chickens. Growing calls and cries into more brain space will only give more calls and cries. This is perfect logic, as far as my numb brain can calculate anyway. Applying this same logic in growing different levels of " I got it" into more "I got it" will still only give you "I got it" in higher form, not different form, never producing true consciousness. We can search for some other property that can make the transition.

Attention can produce the "I got it" and it is highly likely that it did at one level or other. Attention can for sure follow the process while watching, then duplicating the process in the brain repeatedly until you get it—if for no other reason than because it is by then committed to long-term memory, recalled at will, and duplicated exactly, with the intent to duplicate it. Ten thousand "I got its" later and attention can surely follow the same process as above, say, "I got that I get it." Great! So what? What did you get, really?

Attention is definitely needed per this line of thought, but something else is also needed. Let's add something else. Sugar! We add sugar, and this idea becomes sweet, but not a problem solver.

Try something else. Memory! Well, memory is also needed, but I already used it as part of the explanation above.

Try something else. Details! The details of every cognitive act must be at some level important, but from the above description, we included details with duplicating the exact process.

Try another approach and hit other known factors and I list them here: nurture, learning physiologically things from the environment, genetic predispositions, if-then, context, hormones, and whatever else you can imagine. To add to this list, all can be adduced as very much needed. We must try something else and keep trying until we get the answer.

No, we must stop here and admit that anything we place into the exercise will come up with the same response: yes, we need it. Every single attribute you can think of is known to man, believe it or not. Many I have not covered and will not cover. I am not looking to have a five- or six-hundred-page book here.

Different types of brain scans, taken on many brains, show nothing in those scans that is uncommon to all conscious areas of the brain. Brain scans can't explain consciousness because there is nothing there in excess of the brain activity to show. Scans do not show a soul either. No one can think of any additional attribute needed to produce consciousness because we know them all already. In fact, some scientists are beginning to see this as a problem and are searching for a different explanation. I agree.

Actually, this is not within the scope of this book, and I shall not use quotes. The problem is that cognition of cognition does not show full support for consciousness. I must put my lack of money where my mouth is and back up my statements.

If everything I say is true, and it is true, then we must reexamine everything that *we have* for clues. The reason I say "we" is that I mean *you*. I have no real intention of doing so, so I should have written, "*You* must reexamine everything." I plan to only reexamine one thing here, as I believe "I got it" is the most fruitful avenue. We humans quite possibly have learned proper so many things that our brains became specialized in getting it. That is, level one. Whether level two or level three thousand, they are all the same, as mentioned above. I get that I get that I get that I get that I get … It means nothing in reality. I suggest a different "species" of kind or a different "kind" of species of "I get it." Let's try on for size the notion of one of those "I got its" being "I got that I can get it" and see where that puts us.

After this thought, we can begin to see that nothing special must happen. It is simple in nature. It only requires time until this needed different species of "I get it" is hit upon and no other magic is required. It does not require finding any hidden traits or missed attributes of the brain, which stupid man cannot find or has not found yet, but look what it gives us in return. We can now call it questioning, as this is what it produces. Why does this happen this way?

Actually, for your information, as I was sitting here typing this, I was thinking about what the other ingredient might be. I typed in "why" and thought, *No, because this would imply the species to be capable of questioning before consciousness arose.* It might sound fearful to suppose that the first time a prototype human, not conscious, or only semiconscious, asked why, the full light came on and consciousness was born. I don't believe it's possible. However, a form of analyzing will avoid the questioning problem. I left this area of the book and thought about it. I get that I *can* get it was my epiphany, and it led me to believe this is the reason for "why," or questioning in general. It also, which must be obvious to you by now, solves the biggest problem with my language origins. I get that I can alter, first calls and cries and then, shortly after, words. I have invented a huge word for this: wisdom. Well, I didn't invent the word; I just called it a niche change to drive knowledge. Socrates is reported to have said, "Wisdom begins in wonder."

The theory of mind has only one requirement: that we both know and mean the same thing—that we are thinking the same thing—but we are separate entities. I covered "mirroring" in the chapter on brains, and this mirroring ability gives rise to *copying* other members of your species and promoting their "I get it" moments to be your "I get it" moment. Attention, focused on the watching of an event while learning that event, might just begin to divide the whole process into its separate parts or functions. In this view, someone else's learning can become your learning as well.

A different kind of thinking with the same material has transpired here again, by default, this extra characteristic of getting that I can get it must have become specialized in causing the light to come on. This is a different species of thought. A different species of thinking gives a different species of communication (speech) and leads to a different species of animal. Before I get that I get it can become useful, a different type or species of thought is needed. The brain, due to the selected properties encouraging survival of species in the first instance of blind unconscious learning, now has the ability to consciously learn other novelties.

There is far greater complication here than I can ever hope to settle, but there is not enough to have layers upon layers of "I got it," or cognition. The cognition must somehow change. Like the placenta template, it must become more complex and change species of processes in order to work the same but differently. If we are to become the highest form of species and rule over the earth, we must change this species of thought into another form altogether. It is not acceptable to say "cognition of cognition" and leave it at that. I must also show how the change was done and why the change was needed.

When we use the proper term of cognition of cognition, of cognition, of cognition, of cognition … instead of I get that I get that I get, we see that cognition does not in any way need to be conscious. If first level cognition is only learned by the nervous system to produce this or that in accordance with the stimuli, then it is stimuli produced and stimuli recognized only. This was covered in a previous chapter. You need a second means of firing the stimuli-produced effect. I mentioned nerves going from sense nerve to muscle only and the effect producing only a contraction of muscle. Then a system for willful nervation, in the final form of a spinal cord and brain in all higher animals, which started out smaller and evolved into that, of course. This gives us another means of making muscle contraction, which I claimed to make the nervous system wired in series-parallel. Series produced to the muscle, but parallel produced from the automatic nerve charge from sensor and willful nerve charge by the act of brain. These are two different means of charging one system with nervous movement.

We now need two different means of cognition. One stimuli produced and one willful stimuli produced—that is, the creature in question needs to be able to produce the stimuli mentally in order to think about it. The problem is that it is more of the same: cognition growing inside cognition; veins growing into uterus; calls and cries growing into calls and cries ... It won't work. Attention alone won't work either, even though I have used it in bisecting sounds to form different sounds, thus altering meaning: vowel altered and vowelized. You need to have some recognition of what is taking place before it can work. What would it take for a change? I often ask myself this question in vain.

I can only offer speculation on my part for an answer. As noted, there are some different cell types in the brain, but they don't involve different species of thought. The same neuron cell types are used for the brain process of seeing, hearing, feeling in general, and any cognition that takes place. Not to be confused with the actual difference of cells doing the actual seeing ... What the eyes are wired directly to is different, but the brain that interrupts these signals in the cortex is the same. Life would be so easy if a different type of neuron cell looked after cognition. The change could be explained genetically by mutation. As it is, it would be like asking mutation to change sounds in their frequencies.

Conventional thinking has the top of our pyramid capped with "I get that I get it," or knowing that you know, which I have partially selected for. I suggest that it does not work, and explaining why is difficult. One immediate reason is that it does not have to lead to anything. However, with a slight alteration, we can get it to mean something. By adding "can" to the equation, we can say that I get that I can get it, and this makes all the difference. If you have the ability to get something and know you have this ability, control is turned toward your favor.

As soon as you make the transition to I can get something, your knowledge changes from unconscious if-then into a conscious knowledge, as you now have the power to perform logically and analyze, to know good from evil. From what theologians call the word, and scientists call a myth, we discover a reality in our nature: wisdom.

For the first time, we can now say, "I can come to know anything and apply it to everything." This is different enough to change our thinking or, in reality, start our thinking. So wisdom is born, as is conscience, and with this, the story being true or not, we can venture into the next chapter. We depart with these words:

But after their gratification when past and weaker impressions are judged by the ever-enduring social instinct, and by his deep regard for the good opinion of his fellows, retribution will surely come. He will then feel remorse, repentance, regret, or shame; this latter feeling, however, relates almost exclusively to the judgment of others. He will consequently resolve more or less firmly to act differently for the future; and this is conscience; for conscience looks backward, and serves as a guide for the future. (Charles Darwin, *The Descent of Man*)

Chapter Ten

How Many Concepts?

The greatest common-sense achievement, after the discovery of one time and one space, is probably the concept of permanently existing things. When a rattle first drops out of the hand of a baby, he does not look to see where it has gone. Non-perception he accepts as annihilation until he finds a better belief. That our perceptions mean beings, rattles that are there whether we hold them in our hands or not, becomes an interpretation so luminous of what happens to us that, once employed, it never gets forgotten.

—William James
The Meaning of Truth

I could not resist reading *Adam's Tongue* by Derek Bickerton when I saw it on the shelf. He brings up many excellent points. He uses one on niche change quite well and drives home an important point: we effectively made a niche for ourselves in the language department, which drove the need for a better language faculty. He also recommended reading the book *Niche Construction: Odling-Smee*, which I have not read. Bickerton talks extensively about niche construction and about the real problem with language, which I did think of and read about somewhat before. He also brought up another good point that I would never have even thought of: how many concepts would you need to start a language? Try to make a list of ten. I will even try to show a transition.

Before I get lost in the concept world and can't find my way back and they have to send a search party, I will have to point out something that should be obvious. There are at least two different kinds of concepts. I will only deal with two and leave the "at least" part untouched. There are primary concepts and secondary concepts. Primary concepts, I believe, are as I have thus far contended. They are complete, total concepts that have become innate in our genotype and grown into our phenotype. I have frequently used space/time as an example of a total concept. There would be selective pressure to learn our space well, for example. There would also be some selective pressure to learn time. If you got to the same place every day and the same prey was available for your consumption each time, you would eat well. If you could not discern this, you would be on a schedule of hit or miss.

Primary concepts are possible to learn from another route, I believe, and would still be complete in nature or species, but have not become part of our genotype and, by extension, our phenotype, as in chapter 1. They are learned and do become important in navigating our world, but we are not born with, or set to trigger with them under the right stimuli. They more or less dawn on us from learnability.

I will use the example from the opening quote. If you closed your eyes and you still survived not seeing the world, there would be no harm, no foul. Or would there? If a predator approached you and you closed your eyes so as not to see it, you would still likely become supper. It would still be there, whether you see it or not. This looks like selective pressure to make it innate. Any creature that closed its eyes and "thought" it was safe would probably perish, but any creature that intently watched and avoided the predator would prosper. To survive, do you need to know that it is still in the world after it is out of your sight? That would be what I would still call a primary concept. Both of these concepts are different from the concept of an apple.

A secondary concept would be one that was derived from a primary concept. Like time, a primary concept has past, present, and future as secondary concepts. As a primary concept, space has up, down, forward, backward, and side to side as secondary concepts. The world still being there when you can't see it would still be derived from space/time, and we would call it perception and nonperception, but perception is a different concept than time.

How many primary root word concepts would we need to survive on? I have absolutely no idea whatsoever but guessed at a few. As I am looking for innateness, and it has been shown that both monkeys and apes have some form of innate communication for naming things (calls or cries, for example, when seeing a snake), I will leave out names and comment after.

A concept for time
A concept for distance/space/weight
A concept for water
A concept for food
A concept for danger, nonpredator (could have come
from cry for help)
A concept for negation, thus good/evil, true/false
A concept for vision

A concept for hearing
A concept for number: singular, duality, and plurality
(amount of three may be added); first, second, third
A concept for life/death—animate/inanimate
A concept for emotions
A concept for cause/effect

There is a list of twelve, but I have no idea if we would need more concepts or different ones than I have selected in this list, and I fully admit it. Some of these I will deal with and get out of the way fast, as I don't plan to work with them.

Water is physiological, and the brain represents it as thirst: water quenches thirst. Because it is biological, there does not have to be an innate name for it.

Food works almost the same as water. We all need to eat, but it has become apparent that objects and food are separated in the brain. It has been shown by studying the many patients with brain damage that something thought impossible was happening in the brain. One patient with brain damage from a drug overdose would drink anything and eat anything, whether it was food or not. Could we actually have an area in the brain that differentiates food from other objects as an innate process? It could be secondary, that is, for survival: we would need to have the innate inclination to eat. Babies put anything in their mouths and have to learn what is nonfood. Do we need both these concepts of food/nonfood to survive? No!

In the case of food, we would be accustomed to eating what we were fed as humans. In animals, strangely enough, I can't think of any reason for it to be any different. Bugs are hatched on their food, as one example. To explain the problem of eating anything only means that the patient lost his ability to tell the difference between food and objects and treats it all the same. So hunger would be the

concept and food from nonfood the secondary concept, maybe. There is reason to believe that a hunger cry exists in almost all the species of primates, for babies cry when hungry.

Other patients lose the ability to name living things, as was the case with Flora D., who could name any inanimate objects but could not name animate objects at all. In the case of us humans, in earlier times, either we would have eaten animate things or they would have eaten us. The same holds true for inanimate things: we would have eaten them or they would have been separated out as nonfood.

Everyone has the propensity to call the different species of animals that have feathers and fly birds, but not insects, some of which also fly, because they lack feathers, are smaller, and so forth. We have cat families to describe lions, tigers, and so on, and we consider them related by some means. If we did not know that they were derived from the same source, how would we place them in family? The names and families would come as part of naming, but the naming would be a part of the animate/inanimate concept.

Predators could have become innate (naming habit) via another route, as is probably true of distress calls in general.

> Whatsoever Adam *called* every living creature, that was
> the *name* thereof. (Gen. 2:19; emphasis mine)

There is a difference between having a concept innate and having an innate concept with an innate sound representing it. Even a shiver from the cold could come to mean "I am cold" if accompanied with an audible sound to use as a word.

This is not the hard part: going from calls and cries to articulate speech. Getting words like for, to, under, of, the, and the likes is more difficult. Wave your arm three or four times in a direction and you have the basis for the start of distance as long as it is accompanied by a sound, which I mean as literal. Others, I believe, have used it as protoword. Honestly, I would not even know where to begin, but once it did, it would evolve. I will try to show how some of these concepts could evolve from one meaning into a different meaning.

I used as an example already *ve* and *re* in the third chapter to get here and there, ever and never, and the like, but I would like to use a more flowing example here to show crossover. I will use the word *verse*, which has one definition from Latin: *versarus*, of *versari*, to be active, to be occupied in. That fits our *v* theme quite nicely and is workable into concept changes with the following. Activity is usually forward: compare Eve, as the mother of all living. This would account for the starting with the sound *EV* followed directly with the sounds *ER*, as I will use these sound concepts to depict the place within, and we can kind of, sort of, see where it goes in meaning, or what it states. Maybe we can loosely settle on this: from the length of my life, I am actively at such and such a place in time, while continuing in a forward direction.

Adding the sounds *re* to the front of it now changes the state of our direction, and we get reverse, thus the secondary concepts of forward and backward are born. For my purpose, other things are born too: past, present, and future; the concept of universal, all in one; and a nice small word to use as a meaning for a change of direction or *re*do. *Re* can be added to any other word—to get rewind, renew, replace, refocus, and revamp, for starters—and of course we no longer call it a word but a prefix.

George Lakoff's book *Metaphors We Live By* gives many other examples of how we use a small number of concepts to relate other ideas: more notably virtue, a *v* word is up. Depravity, also containing a *v*, is down. I have become a "sicko," and I don't think I can look at another word again without psychoanalyzing it. Help!

Let's see how much grasping at straws I can do. Combine time and space—eve + ere—and we can construct *very* from maybe *vere*, or *vr*, which would pinpoint a position in time and space, becoming verified or past tense verified, to confirm a location in space/time. Later, it would evolve into verifying anything needing to be verified, a change in use and meaning.

From this, we have various, variety, and verity. Maybe we can also cross over into *ov*, or *of*, meaning the result, or piece, and venture, to come out into. Again, according to Bopp quoted from earlier, *dve*, *dva*, and *dvi* all point to two: dvi-matri, which means having two mothers, and quite possibly the word divide itself could stem from cutting in half or two. Finally, we can make a permanent word, which can be added on to any other root word, thus adding to the words, meaning a continuum, inclusive, or partaking of: *ive*; relate = relat*ive*, demonstrate = demonstrat*ive*.

It may be, but it is not of much consequence to us, that *geresnis* and *gariyans* (strong theme) are also connected in the positive base; so that, as according to p. 398, in Greek and Gothic *goodness is measured by depth*, in Lithuanian it is *measured by weight*. The Sanscrit comparative under discussion means, also, not only "heavier," or "very heavy," but also, according to Wilson, "*highly venerable*." (Bopp, 414; emphasis mine)

Note that venerable has both the *v* and *r* in its spelling. Compare this real work with my made-up example on *eve* and *ere*. You have part of a concept added to part of a concept, meaning the whole word is something different. Maybe my list of concepts is too long.

We can easily go from *v* to *f*, which both sounds have the same, or only differ slightly in the position of the mouth. *V* is a vibrating sound with the mouth in the *x* position, but leaving the mouth in the *x* position and puffing air without the vibrating noise produces the *f* sound. The state of a word is changed by going from *v* to *f*, as in leaves to leaf ...

True
Truth   of the true
Trugen   "to deceive" or negate true—German, I
                believe

I want to point out a transformation here: if we take the T in true as having a meaning of its own, then readding it to the same word narrows or widens its meaning. *T* ru *t h* or truth, meaning a sample of the true, would be like saying this true part of the true, being stated as *TH*, singling out a portion. This is awfully close to "the" pointing to a specific object or "thee," pointing to a specific person. Not for all the tea in China will I attempt to reconcile "gen" from Trugen, the negation, but I will poorly attempt to reconcile this as a buildup point with the following:

Th   to single out part of
The   to single out a specific object
Thee   person singled out
Other   o + the + r
Mother   m + other
Brother   br + other
Daughter   ugh has close to or the same sound (in German?)
                as oth
Father   Fa + the + r

Am I losing my mind?

The "th" was used, at least in English, from whence it cometh, who knows, at the end of many words: forth, cometh, truth, entereth, climbeth, openeth, calleth, leaveth, and so on. It is used in numbering: fourth, fifth, and the likes. It became continuum, as with "S," as in eats, and remains selective as in fifth, to single out the fifth from the sixth. It also has continuum in runneth, which is also replaced with the "S."

I will look at more concepts here but only mention this one and refer the reader, as I don't want to deal in these concepts beyond getting language out of them. "Animacy, definiteness, and participant roles" are discussed on page 166 of *Typology and Universals (second edition)*, by William Croft, showing we have a concept of animate, which was one on my concept list, and I wrote some on it already. More important to me is that Croft also shows that "*conceptualization* plays a role in *language order*, and *psychology* should be used in the studying of language," p. 202. (Emphasis mine.)

Biblical Hebrew uses words that have two different senses. One sense is causative, and another sense is permissive. This happens to be a concept on my list, but it shows that there had to have been, at one time, one word meaning both and taken in context. One sense is that one can cause something to happen and in the other sense one can prevent or not prevent something from happening, and both relate well into effect. If you were not there to translate it later, it would lead to some confusion.

They also never used any punctuation or vowels. As a result, there are those who think that God does both good and evil. It is worth our time to use a couple of scriptures here for the examining of poor communication by poor or limited words. I chose one that had both the word *cause* and, in my opinion, improper punctuation, placed as they were translated into English. The translators placed the vowels and the punctuation marks into the text at the same time the translations were made, as I understand it anyway.

But though he *cause* grief, yet will he have compassion according to the multitude of his mercies. For he doth not afflict willingly nor grieve the children of men. To crush under his feet all the prisoners of the earth. To turn aside the right of a man before the face of the most high, to subvert a man in his cause, the lord approveth not. Who is he that saith, and it cometh to pass, when the lord commandeth it not? Out of the mouth of the most high proceedeth not good and evil? (Lam. 3:32–38)

The first *cause* in this scripture seems to be in the permissive sense, as indicated by "doth not afflict willingly nor grieve the children of men." It seems to indicate the allowing it to happen and not causing it to happen. The last sentence quoted has a question mark: "Out of the mouth of the most high proceedeth not good and evil?" The answer is no, absolutely not! Does it not fit better as a statement? "Out of the mouth of the most high proceedeth not good and evil!"

In fact, using the battle of good and evil, the best rendering would be: "Who is he that says and it comes to pass, when the lord commands it not? [The devil.] Out of the mouth of the Most High proceeds not good and evil!" That was not so bad, was it? I refer you, the reader, to reread the first pages of the third chapter for the commentary on time and day. The Hebrew word for day had no quantity with it: not second, minute, hour, day, month, year, nor millions of years—just a period of time.

The important point here is that having the two senses in one word, being secondary concepts, they would have to eventually become divided into two separate words, one for each sense of the word, if it were not to lead to any confusion. In addition, both senses have the ability to relate to effect—one by aggressive cause, the other by passive cause, not stopping something from happening.

I must make some more comments on different things needed to make my imaginary sound-clichés work properly. Beginning on page 69, Lakoff talks about causation, which is one of my concepts on the list I just went over. This is a good quote:

> It might seem as if there were a clear distinction between directly emergent and metaphorically emergent concepts and that every concept must be one or the other. This is not the case. Even a concept as basic as CAUSATION is not purely emergent or purely metaphorical. Rather, it appears to have a directly emergent core that is elaborated metaphorically. (George Lakoff, *Metaphors We Live By*)

More importantly, *gestalt* is spoken of and defined on page 71, which of course he uses for his work on metaphor, but one could easily take out his words and install phoneme concepts, or sound-clichés. The basis being that once all the categories that go into making a phoneme concept were, let's say, vowel altered, such as Ev having a slightly different meaning from Av or Ov, Ve, Va, or Vo, without reflection on what was being said, we would automatically name things appropriately with the base concept V becoming varied with the vowels.

Lakoff used the example of birds. Any bird that looks like a bird would come to be called a bird. Any sound-word that used the sound *v* would be associated with that concept.

> We experience them as a *gestalt*; that is, the complex of properties occurring together is more basic to our experience than their separate occurrence. (George Lakoff, *Metaphors We Live By*)

A long time ago, we knew this and called, for example, ivy, ivy, because IV or VY meant to spread out or climb up. Either this appeared without reflection in the mind of the person naming it, or we did not know the basis of it and the V is just coincidence.

There are a few reasons for using the citations of other authors. One, it saves me a lot of time explaining everything in complicated detail, as you only need to read their books to get additional details. Two, most of these other works were already "defended" or "approved" by their peers before they were books, and it leaves me to defend my own original ideas only.

That said, on page 94 of the same book by Lakoff, we find him using terms like "overlap of entailments" and "fit together" in referring to consistency of combination while talking about metaphors. First overlap of entailments:

> It is this overlap of entailments between the two metaphors that defines the coherence between them and provides the link between the amount of ground the argument covers and the amount of content it has. This is what allows them to "fit together," even though they are not completely consistent, that is, there is no "single image" that completely fits both metaphors. (George Lakoff, *Metaphors We Live By*)

Lakoff is talking about using a metaphor to compare an argument, but in reality, whole concepts are being cut up and different secondary forms of the concept are being used to make the argument. The argument uses one metaphor being adopted with the secondary concept of, the amount of ground you cover, taken from the whole primary concept. Then, with a second metaphor adopting another secondary concept of, how much content the argument had, taken from the same whole primary concept. The two metaphors would have to combine into the same text. Ground cover and content fit together when used in an argument. Ground cover and apple do not. My argument covered a lot of ground, but he found it to be apple.

To use the same principal in words, there must be a certain amount of "overlap of entailment," as in the sound-word overlap, and they must fit together to form a meaningful sound-cliché. These are my examples of how they would be, versus how they would not be: transverse, traverse, adverse, with the base of verse, reverse, and universe all fitting together. These do not: foodverse, loveverse, sexverse, workverse ... They are different topics that don't fit with "verse." After all, if it were available, who would not want sexverse? If sound-cliché is close to the right answer, we would only have words made up of topics that "fit together," even though for the purpose of example I may have used others that don't fit.

Now back to concepts in general. I have mentioned primary concepts and secondary concepts and how they differ slightly in concept form. With some of my examples in this chapter, I have reasonably shown that we can change one concept into a different concept using metaphor. I actually consider myself lucky enough to have found examples of it in the literature of other authors and did not have to make up my own. I have shown that most of these concepts exist in one form or another, but I did not cover all of them. I pointed out that not all the concepts on the list had to have had any sound-word associated with them. Those would have evolved words in another way.

A concept for negation would be directly related to stopping one's behavior if it were undesirable or in some way nonproductive to, say, eating. If you had to stop yourself from jumping too quickly at prey before it was close enough, you would learn negating your actions or starve. This would lead to wanting others to negate their actions in some other way and would eventually be named. It could also have some sort of sound attached with it. Children often whine if they are bugged by other children and want them to stop.

Concepts that we have, such as sight, can be unknown. Eyes are named after the fact, as is sight in general, but light is not necessarily the case, as I have mentioned in the first chapter. A sound, call or cry, which would become innate with the concept of time, would hold the secondary concepts of it's time to get up and eat; it's morning, and so forth. With the concept of light, we can evolve sight, eyes, dark, and other meanings.

These transformations can be seen in the next two chapters. The first one is on the math and then on growing these words.

Chapter Eleven

The Math

This means that vocalization is a good candidate for increasing fecundity and thereby winning the battle to become the better replicator. How, then, could the fidelity of the copies of sounds be increased? One obvious strategy is to make the sounds digital. As we have seen, digital copying is far more accurate than analogue, and genes have certainly adopted the "get digital" strategy. I suggest that language has done the same. By making discrete words instead of continuum of sound, copying becomes more accurate.

The Meme Machine
Susan Blackmore

I have read several accounts now from other authors, mostly scientists or philosophers, stating that there is great difficulty in describing new concepts, as we do not have words that we can use to describe them. This makes it obvious that we can't just make up new words for new concepts as they arise. New words have to be learned, as do the meanings for them. So with this, new words are not really the problem. The meaning that these new words represent is the real problem. How do you place a meaning on a word if you don't really have a meaning to begin with? We first start as our ancestors did and use an analogy to describe the concept the best you can until your understanding of the concept improves and better words are used, weeding out the less accurate words in the process.

It was probably quite difficult to explain the concept of an inner planet orbiting the sun and what it would look like if it were going back and forth in the sky, stopping to take its breath before returning to the other side of the sun in the opposite direction. You need to explain that not only is the planet going around in an orbit, but that it is not orbiting the earth but the sun, inside our own orbit. Wow, no wonder it took several generations to catch on to the true concept.

This too is one of those concepts that takes a lot to explain, and several other topics need to be brought into the mix. I found that I had to keep them extremely simple in example, using slightly wrong terms when explaining things like wiring of the body, computers, electrical circuits, placenta as a biological template, and much more. Yes, I do know that some of these things are less than accurate, but they are not really untruths either.

Just because I have been trying to be as nontechnical as possible does not mean that it did not happen as I have vaguely suggested. Time will be the final judge, and if I am close, someone will come along, an Einstein, and correct my grievous errors. If it becomes a huge embarrassment to man that someone would even think of such a thing, there is also good in that. While correcting me, someone might stumble upon the real truth.

That said, I think I have commented enough on all the properties needed for the evolution of language to take place. I do realize that the information within this book had no clear flow to it, but I needed all of these theories in place before doing the math. To do math, we need rules, so I will attempt to write the proofs in Euclid form in this chapter. I use his terms, but some of them are arbitrary.

As I was looking for myths and other sources of older information as a research tool and comparison of older language with modern language, I read *Fingerprints of the Gods* by Graham Hancock, from which I will now insert this quote:

Another possible legacy of Tiahuanaco, and of the Viracochas, lay embedded in the language spoken by the local Aymara Indians—a language regarded by some specialist as the oldest in the world.

In the 1980s Ivan Guzman de Rojas, a Bolivian computer scientist, accidentally demonstrated that Aymara might be not only very ancient but, significantly, that it might be a "made-up" language—something deliberately and skillfully *designed*. Of particular note was the seemingly artificial character of its syntax, which was rigidly structured and unambiguous to the extent thought inconceivable in normal "organic" speech. This synthetic and highly organized structure meant that Aymara could easily be transformed into computer algorithm to be used to translate one language into another: "The Aymara Algorithm is used as a bridge language. The language of an original document is translated into Aymara and then into any number of other languages." (Emphasis in original.)

It made me think of another algorithm, a natural one. Sounds—that is, calls and cries—are analog by nature. They start out low in volume, rise, and then taper off again. This is like the diagram I showed when writing about computers and wiring. I showed that analog was in a waveform or bell shape, like making the sound of the vowel *o*: oooOOooo. To use analog while trying to say words like sssSSsss, pppPPppp, eeeEEeee, aaaAAaaa, kkkKKkkk, iiiIIiii, nnnNNnnn, and gggGGggg would take forever if it did not become digitalized.

Digital form will allow the smoother word: speaking. Digital words would need to have had their sounds become digitalized. What are we doing but digitalizing them by adding the vowel sounds in naming them? It shortens them from *vvvvv* into *ve*, or properly, *v* small and digital. Now the brain can store them in digital, altered in meaning from the one large primary concept into the smaller secondary concepts of *va, ve, vi, vo,* and *vu*. All these "words," *va, ve, vi, vo,* and *vu*, when combined into another word, would have a meaning dealing with time or space. The brain can now pick which one it wants and combine it into words and sentences.

I mentioned emphasis in the chapter on grammar, and I think now is a good time to finish the discussion. When we teach our children to speak or learn the alphabet, we emphasize our letters. We teach the sounds like this: *veeeeeeeeee*. Why we emphasize the *e* more might have something to do with naming them, or I propose that it has to do with a concept change originally, thus the emphasis on the *e* to point out the change. I have heard many parents do the exact examples I am using. For contrast, I have heard children speaking words incorrectly and being corrected differently with the sounding out of the letters, or phonemes. "Are you going to bacuum the floor?" "No, honey, the word is *vacuum*: vvvvvvvvvvacuum."

With the alphabet, perhaps we should be doing the same: *vvvvvvvvvve*. In vacuum, the letter *a* follows the *v*, and we tend to describe it with the emphasis on *v*. It is logical, but not necessarily true that the *e* alteration was first, as it is also the name of the sound *ve*.

It struck me that there could be some form of algorithm, mathematically interpretable, in all languages. I have no means of proving this whatsoever, but I will write it out mathematically anyway, in word form. Maybe someday someone might find a better answer. If you never ask a question, you will surely never get answers. I chose to write them out in word form and elucidation style, using mostly his terms, but the terms can be considered arbitrary. The terms do fit nicely, though. I want to remind the reader that I was going to leave the "mistake" mentioned in chapter 8 on analytics for clarification when doing the math. I actually wrote this: "I am probably more confused than you are, so I have decided only to show these possible mistakes when doing the analytical math. I only wanted to point out that mistakes could be made." These mistakes are under the heading of irrational.

~ Let rational be correct and selectable.
~ Let irrational be incorrect and nonselectable.
~ Let medial be indifferent, therefore selectable, with no good or bad effects (it could survive as a meme).
~ Let parallel be the total concept.
~ Let the parallel side be part of the total concept.
~ Let the individual part of the total concept be called point of bisection.
~ Let sound concept thought be complete concepts.
~ Let emotional thought be complete concepts.
~ Let analytical thought be the divided portions of complete concepts.
~ Let thought be changed from total conceptual thought into analytical thought.
~ Let total conceptual thought be called instinctual thought
~ Let analytical thought be called reasoning.

~ Let attention be manifested to focus for the same reason that analytical thought was manifested.
~ Let attention override instinctual thought.
~ Let the paralleled concepts be represented as series in new brain area.

First order rational *vowel altered* (my term)

~ Let the sound *v* have the concept of space/time—starting point, distance, height, complete, void—but let it also stand in two areas of the brain (paralleled).
~ Let attention be brought to bisect the total concept at the point of bisection, "beginning," and let the new point of bisection be called *e*, thus altering the sound and giving us the word *ev, in one series area of the brain* (other words like ve, av, va, iv, vi...).
~ Let it be called rational, as concept is to concept, thus correct and selectable.

First order rational *vowelized* (Bopp's term)

~ Let the sound *v* have the concept of space/time, but let it also stand in two areas of the brain (paralleled).
~ Let attention be brought to bisect the total concept at the point of bisection "place" and let the new point of bisection be called *r*, thus *vowelizing* the sound and concept fittingly.
~ Let it be called rational, as concept is to concept, thus correct and selectable. In addition, it becomes a starting point of place in space/time (instead of sending it back through to first order rational vowel altered to receive the *e*, we can add higher levels like nominal and do it in one step), giving us the altered *re, (er, ar, ra...)*

First order rational *consonant altered* (my term)

~ Let the sound *b* have a concept *x* and let it also stand it the two separate areas of the brain.

~ Let the sound *t* have a concept *y* and let it also stand in two separate areas of the brain.

~ Let the concepts be complementary and thus joined into an appropriate meaning slightly altered. All I am looking for is an end result, and this would give us something like "slightly obvious" or subtle in meaning.

~ Let it be called rational, as concept is fitting to concept in a complementary way, therefore correct and selectable.

First order irrational or medial

~ Let the sound *v* have the concept space/time, but let it also stand in two areas of the brain (paralleled).

~ Let attention be brought to bisect the total concept at the point of bisection "food" and let the new point of bisection be called *q,* thus altering the sound, giving us *vq.*

~ Let it be called irrational, as concept is not to concept, thus incorrect and nonselectable, or at the least medial and indifferent. I shall not dwell further into either irrational or medial.

Second order rational sound-clichés

~ Let the two new sounds *ev* and *er* be combined, skipping steps, into the word *ever*, and since concept is to concept, let it be called rational, thus as per chapter 3, after repeatedly saying *ev* pause *er,* being two separate words, they are permitted to become the sound-cliché *ever* represented in the brain as rational and fitting, thus correct and selectable. Thus we can go from phoneme, call, or cry into articulate speech. So this automatically gives us syllables, complete with emphasis. They could be considered binominal and ready to combine.

~ Let x be anything you wish to construct:

$\{(ve) + (ri) + (fy)\} + \{(x1) + (x2) + (x3)\} + \{(x1) + (x2) + (x3) + (x4)\} + \{(x1) + (x2)\}$ = articulate speech: this is more like what we see in our language structure than anything else hitherto suggested.

A more complex version and quite possibly a more accurate one would be $\{(ve) + (ri) + (fy)\} + \{(X x1) - (X)\} + \{(X2) \div (x3)\} + \{(x1) + (x2) + (x3) \times (x4)\}$ = whatever sentence uttered. This is the whole reason for getting into any kind of math at all, which I could have avoided, but it is the best way to show "a sentence within a sentence" as mentioned above. It is also the best way to show our analytical speech, analytical thinking, and how they arose.

This is the first word we can get some clarity on, as I have used both examples: V, representing time, and R, representing place. (ve) + (ri) = (time) + (place). What are we really saying when we want verification but give the time and place as proof.

I must make this comment, lest you become confused as to my terms of multiply or divide. To multiply would be to make a word plural. To divide would be to make a word singular in meaning. Do I have that right? Going from many to few, or one. Going from one into many or some.

I have used the sound or phoneme V as I have worked with this letter throughout the book, but it will work with calls or cries as well.

First order rational *vowel altered* (my term)

~ Let the call or cry have the total concept of intruder/protect: so defend, fight, or whatever ... but let it also stand in two areas of the brain (paralleled).

~ Let attention be brought to bisect the total concept at the point of bisection—"defend"—and let the new point of bisection be called *d,* thus altering the call or cry, giving us the *d* sound-word, or tilogoi.

When we put it back through the rest of the process, it would end up giving us the word *de*; therefore, as concept is to concept, let it be called rational, thus correct and selectable.

Now let us see if we can modify them into forms of concepts altered for other purposes or different concepts. I will use the same elucidation method I have already used—that is, writing them out in word form as high as I can take them.

~ Let it be proven that time and space, by means of relativity, are parallel. Therefore, concept is to concept: they are correct and selectable.

~ Let it be proved that space is parallel to height or width for the same reason ... Therefore, concept is to concept: they are correct and selectable.

~ Let it be proved that height is parallel to status—for the same reason, which is venerable, previously discussed and explained better in the next chapter. Therefore, concept is to concept: they are correct and selectable.

Actually, with a little imagination, any word with the letter *v* in it can be reconciled. That is the topic of my next chapter, but first I will finish this one.

As a total concept is parallel in two areas of the brain, as expounded earlier in the book, so too have the sides become parallel. I use the term sides here to represent the secondary concepts, which were stripped from the primary concept. The secondary concepts hold the total concept plus the point of bisection, the part concept, derived from it. It would be like saying from Aristotle's *Analytics* from above that if A has a property, and B has some of the same property, and C has a property of A it will also have a property of B. This resolve comes from two brain areas being utilized from our hidden areas, as mentioned earlier, and attention being applied. As attention was brought to bear on the parts of the total concept at the point of bisection—the wet from water—we now have a mode to go from total conceptual thought to analytical thought, with attention being or forming the final layer in series to the synapse.

Euclid's Elements, Book XII, Proposition 18 starts out, "Spheres are to one another in the triplicate ratio of their respective diameters." He deals in two spheres within one another, not touching, but what stuck out to me were the words "in triplicate ratio." The easiest way for me to get higher in explanation and keep it simple would be to use three spheres as follows. The center sphere or first sphere would represent the emotional brain. The second sphere would represent the sound concept or natural thought brain. The third sphere would represent the analytical brain.

Now, if the thought in the emotional brain were to be triggered and it passed through the second layer or sphere, with a sound concept of time attached, it would be the setup. If the third layer or sphere were then dissecting the concept, selecting wet from water, and wired with a new sound, like vowel altered, then the third sphere would become analytical in processing, thus going from knowing in a natural form to a sound-altered separated concept form into the analytical language form in the brain. Then it would form these into altered sounds that would have altered concepts.

There would be more, smaller concepts, wired into the analytical brain, and at the same time, they would be analyzed into articulate digital speech as they evolved.

The easiest way for me to get higher in explanation and keep it simple would be as follows.

~ Let x be the first layer of the brain (say, emotional: fight/flight, digitalized).

~ Let y be the second layer of the brain (say, tilogoi, or innate sound-word brain, in digitalized format).

~ Let z be the third or attention layer of the brain, actually analytical attention.

~ Let x and y have the same concept; therefore, they are parallel, with parallel concepts.

~ Let x and y be fired together—if they fire together, they will become wired together—into one series path, or synaptic connection, into layer z of the brain, with attention fixing it, complete with the altered sound.

We now have a means to build other types of words, as in words proper—what we speak today. Back to the tilogoi as a word, we can convert words—tilogoi—without vowel altering them, as we can also consonant alter them. We can create words—tilogoi—with both vowel and consonant alteration. Tilogoi have been vowelized, vowel altered, and consonant altered and it is now possible to form and convert these alterations into sound-clichés or words proper.

It is likely that language started completely with verbs—and verbs only. By language, I mean one of two different types: common language and uncommon language. Common language would be any sound produced for a purpose, as I have covered in innate concepts, plus any inadvertent names of places or animals that would be, say, named for the sounds they produce or place where they produce their sounds. The place would come to be called tanana, for instance, after the animal that is called tanana, which makes the sound tanana. These would be inevitable to have happened. The word common only depicts that they are common to our species. Uncommon only depicts that they were not normally used.

Uncommon language would be naming the time of day or a part of a whole: the leg of a tanana, for instance. It also would include the more important words for explanation: to, for, under, over, before, after, the, and many more words that I have used as examples throughout the book. These would have started as verbs, I am sure, as time and space are ever moving—in action, which is the definition of verb—as we are in the constant state of living, and our whole lives are one action after another. As we see so many times in many myths and throughout the Bible—in fact, in any source—names are placed on things as nouns. To name a soul he or she is to place a noun on a living, active soul. To place the name Eve on the first woman was to name her after the verb, begin, which became her name proper, or noun. In fact, grammar itself is ordered, making it a verb.

The best words would be the best memes, but I understand that the meaning of meme has been stretched.

> The definition of meme I suggest is nevertheless more focused and somewhat different from that of Dawkins. It is the one posed by the theoretical biologist Charles J. Lumsden and myself in 1981, when we outlined the first full theory of gene-culture coevolution. We recommended that the unit of culture—now called meme—be the same as the node of semantic memory and its correlates in brain activity. The proposition, or schema, determines the complexity of the idea, behavior, or artifact that it helps to sustain in the culture at large. (Edward O. Wilson, *Consilience*)

To have memes is quite fine, but they too should become part of man's genome. It would not do to have a meme war over the best words if they did not innately mean something at some level of cognition.

I now attempt to show how the mind sees words appear and the recognition of them as meanings and not just words.

In the chapter on computer analogies, I used this diagram in explaining how serial data was compiled in the brain. This is just another tool, and it is in fact not hardwired into the brain in any of these methods. It has been demonstrated that when we have words revealed to us one letter at a time, we have placed before our cognition different possible end results. As the letters are revealed one at a time, different words appear in our minds, and the correct word is slowly chosen. I will try to duplicate this within the context of the diagram.

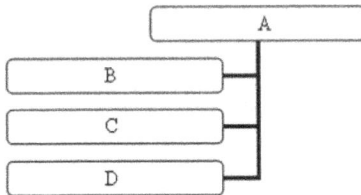

Let A be the final word. I will use the usual example for clarity. Verify will be the word that will appear in box A as a final result. If I at first place the letter V only in box A, then boxes B, C, D, E, F, G … (not shown here) will come up with all the words that start with the letter V. When I add the letter E into the A box, it will cause all the other boxes that contain any other vowel to become ignored by the brain. It might hold B, C, F … as still being the possible word and eliminate the rest. When I place R next into the box at A, it again eliminates all words down the line as stated. When I install the letter I into box A, your mind, while attempting to establish the word, would now be close enough to make a guess at the word, as there are only so many words matching in the boxes B, C, D .... As the letter F was written in box A, the word would have been guessed at already as verify, verified, or verification.

Today we have too many words to work with, and it would take pages to write out a single word starting with the letter S in any detail. There have been actual experiments showing this to be the case. It could be written off by some other means, but what is interesting here is that as soon as the word is made intelligible by the brain, it automatically inserts the meaning. The meaning in this case would be "He wants me to prove the space/time of what I have alleged to have happened," from the sound-cliché *verify*. This happens before the whole word appears. Why, if not due to the fact that these letters represent concepts in the first place?

These next three diagrams show the process a little more clearly to eliminate any confusion. The A represents again the word being spelled out. The other letters are showing what words they could be getting ready to call into action.

VER	A
VERY	B
VERTICAL	C
VERGE	D

As soon as the next letter is written, some of the words are lost and the possible words it could be are fewer.

VERI	A
VERIFICATION	B
VERIFY	C
VERIOUS	D

238

Each letter added reduces the possible word in our minds.

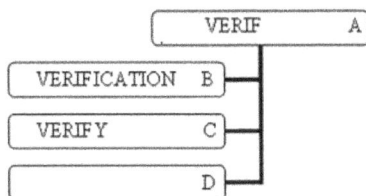

In the end, we have in my example only two words to choose from but will still need the last letter Y to make the final elimination. Both words, however, have the exact same concept in our minds and we immediately start to think of how to verify what is in question.

One more matter needs to be settled here. Bickerton does a great job of destroying a theory on word origin. I will quote the theory because it somewhat resembles mine, and I must defend my own idea. It does differ in other ways, and it is not where I got the idea in the first place. Note that the two calls Bickerton uses in his critique are already in digital form and already had complex meanings attached.

Suppose that the holistic signals were phonetically complex—in other words that they consisted of a number of segments that could be distinguished from one another. Two of Wray's examples are hypothetical holistic calls, "tebima," meaning "give that to her," and "matapi," meaning "share this with her." (Why anyone would develop two holistic calls quite different in structure that would largely overlap in meaning is one of the things about holistic protolanguage that remain unexplained.) These calls happened by pure chance to share a syllable, *ma*.

The sharing is, of course, coincidental; there is nothing about *ma,* or any of the other segments of these calls, that yields any kind of meaning in itself. In Wray's own words, "The whole thing means the whole thing." However, the double coincidence—that the syllable occurred in both calls, and that both calls contained reference to an unspecified female recipient, or potential recipient—would be picked up by some smart hominids. They would then begin to use *ma* as a signal for "female recipient," joining it with other fragments similarly gleaned, to start building a stock of words. And that is how language took on the compositional structure—isolated words having to be put together to form sentences—that we know and use today. Instead of starting with words and building them into sentences, you start with sentences (or rather the semantic equivalent of sentences) and broke [sic] them down into words. (*Adam's Tongue*, 67).

I don't suggest sentences as concepts being broken down into words but rather calls and cries. I am forced to use an example here, but I don't want to. So I will compromise and make my call more of an *m* sound—*mmmmmmmm* being our call. There is danger in placing artificial sounds on these calls because you, the reader, might think that these sounds I am producing might have been the original. Don't! If we were to digitalize this *m* sound into articulate speech, we would possibly get *ma* out of it. In any case, the sound would need to be innate with its meaning—strictly for starting language—and I chose to use the concept of space/time instead of mother.

My theory will not become as easily destroyed because I don't have to contend with any of the digital forms before the word's origin. In fact, the reverse is true. I have produced a digitalized word out of the sounds being used, and these have their meaning already implied with the single sound *m*. M is already short, making it digital and ready to combine with whatever other sound-words—tilogoi—make up the rest of the sound-cliché, becoming another meaning. This is not to say that my idea can't be destroyed.

Note that he uses holistic instead of total complete concept. I also don't need two calls to mean the same or close to the same meaning to draw a conclusion and make words. I certainly don't need to purpose "phonetically complex" calls or cries: any call or cry will do.

I find myself having to explain this in word form, with only a slight diagram to use for show. If you were to have *v* represented as a whole, complete concept, it would be permanent in the brain. There would be other sounds, not permanent in the brain but learned. With *v* in the middle of my diagram and surrounded with the two different forms of sounds represented as small case or capital letters in the forms of long or short sounds—hard or soft, if you prefer—they can now be separated into different concepts portions of the total concept. Thus if two were to understand, say, Adam and Eve, then they could now teach their offspring their language.

Since there are many smaller concepts within a huge concept, as I have shown to be the case many times over, we have many alterations that can take place. Just in space alone, liberally, we have height, width, depth, distance, up, down, through, under, and more. If we accept that we can only use each vowel once in each of its states—long, short, or silent, again being liberal—we can at least set before ourselves a template.

I suspect that the emergency room at my local hospital is getting tired of hearing from me. Every time I think of a new idea that is quite complicated to explain, I end up there, complaining that I might be having a stroke. They say that my brain going numb is not a sign of a stroke.

The problem here is that I want the explanation to be small rather than having to explain a lot of math. I also want to keep in line with real math. I tried to use what they call "Gaussian elimination," which is a real mathematical principal, but failed. I will briefly explain the process as well as the reason I failed. If you place three rows of letters and three columns of letters—all different letters, of course—and resolve that you can only use a letter from one row and column one time, you have a method for solving the weight-volume problem, which Gaussian elimination does.

I will sneak in a quote here, and if you are interested in more of an explanation, I will refer you to read the book:

> Look at the *ahm* term, for instance. Having picked *a* from the first row, first column, it's as if the first row and the first column are now out of bounds. The next number, *h*, can't be taken from them; it has to be taken from elsewhere. And then, having taken *h* from the second row, third column, that row and column are then out of bounds, too, and there is no choice but to take *m* from the third row, second column. (John Derbyshire, *Unknown Quantity*)

If that was a little clear to you, it won't work for assigning vowels while constructing language. The reason is that you need nine, sixteen, or twenty-five boxes for the algebra letters: three rows and columns, four rows and columns, or five rows and columns. With the vowels, we have five, ten, or at most fifteen, if we do a silent *a, e, i, o, u.* There are other problems too, but we don't need to get into those, for these first problems prevent it from working.

Finally, I settled on this diagram, which could serve the purpose.

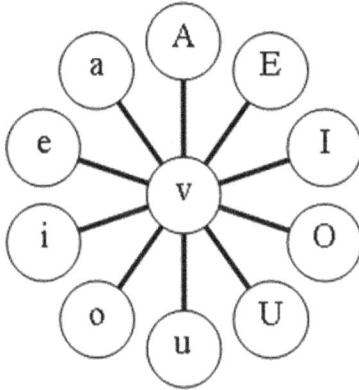

All the capital letters will represent the long vowel sounds, and the lowercase letters will represent the short vowel sounds. As mute vowels are only a requirement of spelling and invented as a rule, or the placeholder for concepts of them in the brain, I shall ignore them.

Now if we let *v* be the whole complete concept and we rule that we can only use one exit for a concept change, we would have the possibility of ten secondary concepts. If these were learned as the vowels originally for changing purposes, they would remain in the brain as the movers of language and only need to have the center consonant changed to evolve different secondary concepts from the original whole concepts.

I suggest that the dawning could have been as easy as a stop short—an abrupt stop before the completion of a call has transpired. We often stop short in midsentence when something occurs to us or our thoughts are disrupted. It could have happened that a call was stopped short in midsentence and formed a digital sound. This digital sound was then interrupted to have a slightly different meaning than the whole call. Other sounds within the call are now free to be stopped short and form different varieties of the same concept associated with the call. Digital calls, or what I have called tilogos—that is, sound-words—are born.

The stop short, defined above, could have been contingent on some different aspect noticed about the reason for the call ... You would think that being a wrench turner, I could use tools better than this. You would be wrong, and I have the scarred knuckles to prove it. Our example of the Chinese using vowels to change verb states led me to this thought process, but I am not sure how to proceed to gain the best understanding.

If we look to the wild, we might begin to see some places where they might have transcended from. If you remember from an earlier chapter, I mentioned that chimps have all the vowel sounds within their calls or cries. I also mentioned that we were not chimps and therefore had more sounds to work with. If, by chance, and it is a fairly good chance, most of our calls were significantly vowel based, the manner of my explanation would improve. Take a made-up call and examine it. I'll make one up with one consonant and some vowels, but remember that the call is made up for the purpose and not in any way real. *Vaaaaeeeeaaaooo.* You don't like this one? Make up your own!

Now that you have made up your own, examine it. We see one and only one consonant—and for good reason. Consonants are hard to "hold" in voice and prolong in loudness; they can't be varied well either. Vowels can be "held" in voice, prolonged, and varied well in loudness—plus, smoothly changed in flow with other sounds. This suits the bill for calls and cries in general: analog. If this were the actual wake-up call, for instance, we could already see how it contains three of the five vowels, and analyzing the call would become easy. We could land *va, ve,* and *vo* with three different submeanings.

If this is right, it makes more sense that the brain would use vowels as the method of meaning change. This brings us back to the diagram. If one singled-out vowel sound, came to mean change the tense of the whole concept, it could become wired into the brain and used for that same tense change within other calls and cries. It would lead to an in-brain system, which I have made a diagram to represent. Only one exit and attachment allowed, except where an alteration of an alteration was needed, as in the Chinese verbs alteration with vowels. It would go back through the process again: be, bea, beautiful ... This has become our minds' algorithms.

I could find support for these conclusions if I were interested in putting in the effort and time. All one would need to do is correlate every *va, ve, vi, vo,* and *vu* with the meaning of the words' meanings, including the words that they appear in at the middle or end position, and then see if any of them fit with a concept more often than a coin toss would allow. I find the extensiveness of the task to be overwhelming and better suited to a professional analyst.

Now I have done the math, and it was not that painful, I hope. I have to have some faith that language happened this way. I say the same of the entire book I have presented. I have to believe that these aspects fit together well enough to work. If I am proven wrong, and I could be, I will accept the defeat and forget the whole matter. If the book is selling, I won't pull it from the shelves, though. It is easy to prove something can happen, but more difficult to prove it can't happen. Therefore, in closing this chapter, I will attempt to show why something that this thesis hints at as being impossible would not have happened. We need to have the concept first.

In a survey of 265 person marking systems, Cysouw (2001:72) argues that no language distinguishes a true first person plural—multiple speakers, as in a chorus—from the usual first person plural (speaker plus other nonspeakers), and likewise no language distinguishes a true second person plural (multiple addressees) from a pronoun denoting addressees plus possible non-addressees. This universal also demands theoretical explanation. (William Croft, *Typology and Universals*, 51)

I can't do it with this process either, due to complications in separation with concepts.

First person includes any descriptive word that can be said to include I: *I, we, me, mine, us, our,* and *myself* all hold true of *I* being included. This would be a natural concept as we know that we existed as a separate entity. *We* is also plural but contains the concept of a single *I* included. It could also be argued that the term for family includes *I* as a single unit. You can say I, which includes I; you can say me, which includes I; my wife, which includes I; or my children, which includes I. (These, by the way, we do see as examples in the literature.) It is possible that it even included all of one's tribe or clan and became separated out later. It is not hard to get the concept of I in any form.

Second person: you, your, and yours all hold true of I being excluded. I suppose that as soon as self was realized, we could form in our minds the concept of other self, "I" not included. With sound changes, I can work this out just fine with my analytical math.

Third person: he, she, they, their, them, and it (it is the neuter state). These too could also be divided out of the first person plural form: we. To single out one other person from a group of people, you would be making them an I, other than yourself, so he or she. The same with a portion of people: they, them. This too can become evolved from a single concept of "I" inclusive.

All three of these—first person, second person, and third person—have pronouns marked for singular, dual, and plural. In some languages, dual expresses precisely two (two objects or persons), such as both versus all, or either versus any, or twice versus any other higher number.

Sight plays a large role in language, as we can't name what we don't see, and sight is the window of revelation and knowledge. No one argues this fact. A true first person plural, then, would be we, which means more than one person, with me included, and we have this concept already. I take this to be "true first person plural (multiple addressees)." There needs to be evolutionary pressure to push for change. There would be pressure to push for either, separating we into I and you, or including I and you into we, as a normal means of relaying to whom is in reference. Both of these can be done analytically, using this math and alteration method. "Addresses" would be any persons who were there listening to what was being said.

I take "nonaddresses" to mean persons who were not present— or at the very least separate from the I concept of tribe or clan. If true, they may already have had names for nonmembers of their clans, and those would continue to be used. We sometimes say "worldwide" or all peoples and nations, even though we are talking about our own country. These fall under the concept of "others," which we have a word for. It could also mean additional, as in any other children born unto us: nonaddresses.

He also uses the word true in the statement here. I is true and we is also true, but other is vague and not of necessity true: other excludes I but not necessarily we. Complicated! We can be just you and I, or it can be you, I, and many others. To remove I from we, it could still have others; therefore, it's not true. It comes from a different concept altogether, so it does not go through my analytical math process the same way. I would expect not to have a true word for it. Admittedly, this is a poor explanation, but I am not trained well enough in language to fully understand what they *exactly* mean. Sorry!

It also hits home with the fact that we don't invent words with concepts unless we have the concept to invent with.

From here, we have some variety in altering concepts and sounds to choose from, and we can go in many directions. This will be the topic of the next chapter.

Chapter Twelve

Growing Words

But mere antiquity may often prevent our recognizing words, after all the complications which they have undergone; and we must remember that however far we carry back our analysis some ultimate elements or roots will remain which can be no further analyzed. For example, the word agathos was supposed by us to be a compound of agastos and thoos, and probably thoos may be further resolved. But if we take a word of which no further resolution seems attainable, we may fairly conclude that we have reached one of these original elements, and the truth of such a word must be tested by some new method.

—Benjamin Jowett
Introduction to Cratylus

Over the course of time, I have collected as many words with the V in them as I could find. I will ask the reader to write down all of the words she can think of that have a *v* in them—not just starting with the letter *v*, but also having it in the middle or end. You, as I was, will be hard pressed to come up with very many, and it has taken me a considerable length of time to collect all these words. I will only be working with a fraction of them, though. I need to show a high correlation of words using the letter *v* as having come from the same original source of meaning or total concept. This is the body of evidence that led me to stay with the letter *v* throughout the entire book. Just glimpse over the words if you would like, as the list is quite long but still incomplete.

Devious, divert, frivolous, divorce, cultivating, extensive, devoted, trivial, proven, nerves, revel, delving, derive, adventure, conversation, divulge, fervor, virtue, investigate, swivel, reveal, vigorous, vanquish, vertex, vortex, volition, vital, sieve, inversely, vertices, sever, several, vision, provision, division, vintage, averse, vertigo, navigation, avariciously, covet, servile, cultivated, visit, devolve, vigor, elevated, valor, previous, benevolence, invincible, avid, rave, Ravenna, subversion, diverse, evince, vast, savage, devise, vested, divested, vouchsafe, avarice, visage, rivals, slave, selves, contrive, alleviate, survey, evasion, invisible, intervened, wives, deviated, diversion, give, vary, very, vice, vulgar, vie, caravan, veil, feverity, travelers, availing, virago, vicious, aver, veneration, vigorous, virtues, have, seven, twelve, five, eleven, reserve, reverse, levity, prevailing, votaries, convenience, servants, valuable, vale, convents, believe, cover, devote, behave, village, devotee, above, vows, drove, absolve, vindication, grave, vanity, revelry, proclivity, provocation, cultivated, venal, bereaved, province, slovenliness, brave, advantage, observe, view, voluptuary, vivacity, Minerva, versant, sovereign, inviolably, coeval, victuals, convenience, disheveled, viands, victuals, marvel, vicinity, prove, solve, vanquish, vast …

Rather than continuing and working with pages of words, it is easier to work with ten or so words at one time. I will start with a base or root word of *vert*, defining it, altering it, and evolving it into the next ten whole word constructions—not literally. So from *v*, we can go from the huge concept of space/time into a smaller concept of a particular point in space/time, and words like vert appear, which can be put through the process again, giving rise to invert: change orientation; overt: to make clear; avert: turn aside; and divert: redirect or move away from that point in space/time.

We also get some dimensions, such as vertical: up and down; vertex: highest point; and vertigo: the dizziness from standing on the highest point. Well, I had to say something about vertigo! We could also push the envelope and go slightly higher here without saying too much. If we were to make the vertical represent a division of some sort, we could get to words like extravert: free from the vertical or outward; and introvert: inside the vertical or inward. I suppose we could, without too much of a stretch, even go to pervert: abnormal from the normal point of vertical, but that pushes into metaphor.

Now we can make just one slight change in a sound-cliché by changing one tilogoi and changing the concept slightly. From vert to vers gives us another run of words, and I will take them as far as I can go, until I have to change word-building strategies. Verse is mainly used to describe writing, but we will use it as a character change in the vertical concept still relating to space/time. If it were maplike thinking, using it as speech would now translate if from verse into conversation or talking about the seen environment. We had pervert above, and it automatically changes context when used in the form perversion: the *s* changes it. I will start with the closest and most applicable word, traverse: to cross, leading to navigate; inverse: the opposite; diverse: assorted or different; transverse: slanting or crossways. Now we hit the word universe: the whole of our containment. Then there's reverse: a change in direction to the opposite. The word visit entails traversing space/ time to get to another place.

At some point in time, there would have to be some means of expressing concepts that have not become innate in the genome, with their calls and cries representing them—that is to say, silent concepts. We wouldn't necessarily need these new concepts for survival, but we would have a feeling about them, or they could be concepts that now become manifested because we were learning to communicate better. We can define metaphor as relating an unknown concept, noninnate, into one that is innate, as a means of talking about unnamed concepts. Or we can define metaphor as relating a known concept, innate, which we have no sound for.

Then we can also go to analogy, parables, proverbs, and the likes as a means of relating our thoughts to something we are familiar with. In the more extreme cases, we tell complete stories in one form to relate them to a different concept that we have a hard time understanding. The Bible is full of such stories know as parables—para meaning beside, and I am unsure if the bles part relates to the same as fables, giving parallel (beside) fables or parables.

I lightly touched on metaphor in another chapter, but I will elaborate here because of its importance. I have not taken the time to do any researching on any sound or letter for any other concept from my list, except the sound/letter *v*. I made mention of *r* and *x* having some concept correlation in word construction in chapter 3, but I did not do anything beyond make idle comments, nor will I here. My main objective now is to show how we must use another means to talk about the world for lack of named concepts.

At the beginning of this chapter, I used the state of the concept implicated by the sound-word "V" in the position of vertical. The important thing is to remember position. "Position" becoming a new concept, or secondary concept, but not necessarily an innate one, or rather innate as part of a bigger one, allows it to change for other purposes. For space/time, we can get up-down, top-bottom, forward-backward, in-out, early-late, and left-right, plus it enables direction and a state of time: when. These are not all, of course, but they are enough to allow us to work.

The universe is a huge concept, for it is made up of galaxies, solar systems, and planets; not to mention ground, water, trees … Smaller concepts are still huge but more workable in the whole; to say a word is a smaller concept is misleading. Try to describe to yourself the concept of a tree that was taken out of the concept of a universe and see how big the small concept still is. The universe can be described as "big" but so can the tree.

From where I started, with the total-concept included into the one *vvvvv* sound, representing space/time as tilogoi (reminder that the singular of logos is logoi) and then separating the smaller concepts out of the larger total concept with vowel altering, it still leaves room for the new secondary concept to be large. This was part of my analytical math formula: $\{(ve) + (ri) + (fy)\} + \{(Xx1) - (X)\} + \{(X2) \times (x3)\} + \{(x1) + (x2) + (x3) \times (x4)\}$ = whatever sentence uttered. Notice that in the more complex version, I chose to use minus and multiply. I could have shown divide but did not. I have come to believe that this is the true nature of words: sounds are altered, added, subtracted, divided and multiplied, shuffled, and mixed to say whatever we need to say, exactly representing this mix of total concepts.

Re, for reverse, is placed before the *ve*. This order seems to be what I would expect to happen. If *ve* meant space/time, and *re* meant place—as I have worked *ve* and *re* into explanatory tools—

we would expect to see this for the sake of ordered grammar. In the case of reverse, by meaning we are saying change place of the space/time direction. Using *re* in other words causes them to take place again, as in redo or renew, or to bring back into the original place in space/time.

Veer means to turn, and it has the *ve* and the *er* I used earlier as examples, the *ve* representing some concept of space/time, and the *er* representing some concept of place. They are free to be used as metaphors, because both of them in and of themselves have huge concepts still attached to them. I also used the tilogoi N as a form of altering: the examples were or-nor, either-neither, show-shown. At the time, they were explanatory tools, and they still are. It might not be true of the next word I am going to transpose into a metaphor, but it fits so well that I can't help but be converted.

Let's use the two sound-altered tilogos that I just mentioned. That is the *ve*, the *er*, and the tilogoi N, which has not been sound altered yet. Let's say that the *ve* is a normal representation of your natural home in the valley. The mountains are high around you, but the sky is higher. From necessity, the mountains become the *er* as place, which equals higher. Together these sound-altered words become *veer*. Now the transforming N is added into the middle of these two sound-altered words, which have become the sound-cliché *veer*, and it changes it to the sound-cliché *vener*, which becomes the metaphor—stating the higher position of a person in relation to other people, better known as venerable.

Once this barrier was broken, any concept that did not have any sound attached to it could be described metaphorically at least. We would get more words like benevolence-malevolence, virtues, and sovereign, leading to the ability to describe love and feelings as up and down or good and bad metaphorically. From venerable, then, the concept change could be applied to good and evil and correlated with high and low.

Reverend is another term used to depict higher status; it seems to be too much of a strange coincidence, to me anyway, that we have both *re* and *ve* used in the word. Actually, *re* is used twice, and there is an *n* used. Of higher value or of higher authority would be the words I would use to describe reverend.

In both of these words, reverend and venerable, by losing the re and using ra, it goes to lower status instead of higher status. Ventral: lower part, from the Latin for belly. Ventricle: lower part of the heart chamber. What are the odds that this is some kind of random chance in operation here? Like one person winning the lottery many times over in her lifetime, it could be possible, in theory, but it never is.

In fact, the very word evil could be argued to mean the coming forth of ill: (evil = ev + il, or creation of ill). Adding *d* in front of evil gives us a persona of the evil coming, or devil. Evil also brings forth devious, and vicious, just to name two. Again, these are just tools, but when the tools work, there must be some reason.

I find that it also carries over into the territory of the word level in general. This leads us to words describing away from the level or leaven—raising agent—replaced by the word yeast. We can go from here with words like: elevated and alleviate, noticing that they both have the letter *v* in the middle of the word, as they are varied in concept.

I would like to step outside of the *v* for one moment, as I have read a counter to my thesis and find myself defending it before it is even released. I submitted this book for publication in May 2011, and I am making the recommended revisions. I have stalled them slightly, as I have found another book to read: *Reading in the Brain: The New Science of How We Read* by Stanislas Dehaene. Now it's July, and since I have used writing and reading as a building tool for language, I thought I should make sure the facts were correct.

As I defend my standing, keep in mind that the author used the words "essentially unrelated" when talking about "priming" (on page 23) in the following paraphrasing. Dehaene uses apart and apartment as unrelated and makes the statement that you will not be living apart in an apartment. In my own defense, if we use the word part rather than apart as a root sound-cliché as the starting of the morphing, it can be reconciled.

Part needs no introduction here, but *a* might. Asexual was used in the first chapter and defined, but I will remind the reader that it means one organism needed for reproduction, not two organisms, male and female. Adding *a* to words in some cases makes them singular of plural, for want of a better description here. *a* part becomes apart, with a slightly different use. A part is singular of two parts. Depart is for one party to leave the other parts of the party. Department is a place to store separable parts, much the same way a compartment is to store individual parts. Apartment might make use of the *a* in the same sense as asexual does. An asexual species has everything within its own genome to reproduce and does not require a mate. In the same spirit, an apartment has everything necessary for usage and survival in one partment. Or if you like, all of the separate parts needed to live in one place. Adjust your thinking and many more words follow.

I will include one more before I move on, hoping to leave you with a good sense of what I am writing about. It could become applied to the concept of sight for the very reason that we see all of space and need to describe what we see. On that note, we have vision, view, visible, invisible, provision, envision, visage (features) and division, from divide, which is the additional one we will examine. Dividing things up into smaller pieces, as with our total concepts, would be easer to work with and more natural. To divide them into their features would give rise to the sound-cliché visage, meaning features of the whole. Now division could stand in both places: dividing the world and seeing the various parts separately or features of the landscape. Some of these features have received names derived from the tilogos: vale, valley, and the place where we dwell: village.

Then we have the word volition, referring to the will—giving rise to the secondary concept of cause, effect, and intentional. It looks as if our list of twelve concepts has shrunk a little.

I could take almost all the ones on my short list above and make them fit into the schema.

> Intervened: to willfully stop something from happening.
> It could be a metaphor from entering a space between.
> Reveal: to uncover something or discover
> Swivel: to turn something around
> Survey: to look around or assess a situation
> Obvious: something in plain sight
> Oblivious: unnoticed or noncognizant of, unseen
> Devious: deceitful or purposely hidden (metaphor)
> Shiver: to move—shake—uncontrolled
> Vomit: to expel from the body
> Avail: bring about or result in
> Avalanche: overwhelmed or flooded by
> Avarice: excessive or insatiable
> Prove: to show in space/time, a happening and truth of
> the happening
> Solve: interpret and conclude the happening in an event
> Carve: to cut into space or remove parts thereof

Interestingly, we have viventi in Latin, meaning life; viva in French, meaning life; and living in English, dealing with life—all having the v in them.

If we look at some root-based words, we can see them transform into slightly different meanings also.

Animal, animus, animosity, minimal, anima, enmity,
Unanimous, anonymous, anonyms, ammoniums.

These all deal with the Greek meaning for soul. We have in English: soul, with soul, harsh soul, all souls, no souls, bad feelings, difference between souls, and the like. They all have the root base soul and alter it with add-on words. Add-on words have become known as prefixes or suffixes. When words were first being evolved, there would have been no such distinction. They would have been building word sentences to convey one whole meaning by adding other fitting meanings together.

When we look at what could be termed rootstock, even though not considered root words, we find strange coincidences taking place. I would consider *ould* to be rootstock, due to the properties of the stock not changing as other tilogoi are added to the sound-cliché. The stock *ould* is only slightly altered by adding W, C, or S to it. "Could" means that it is possible to *ould* whatever needs to be *oulded*. "Would" means it is your will to *ould* whatever needs to be *oulded*. Finally, "should" means that it ought to get done, whatever needs to be *oulded* in this case.

Suffixes are at the ends of words, and we have only a few in English. The few suffixes we do have change the states of the many words they are added to. We add *able, en, er, ful, ish, ize, less, ly,* and *ness* to already fully formed words and alter their meanings. These are actually permanent "words" we have in our vocabulary just for this purpose. I don't want the reader to get confused here. At first, we are building a complete language without any rules. All rules came later.

I have tried to show how concepts could have evolved into metaphor as words, but I have stopped at that. I will now attempt to show how and why it had to expand into larger metaphor and analogies, or parables.

When you have a small sampling of words to use, you can say a lot, as long as you are only using them to describe your small conceptual environment. You can place names on objects, which have a communicational value, to give or use as directions, much like in the "second story" I used, only in a cruder form. As soon as you have a realization that one of these sound-clichés has a metaphorical value, you can start combining them into sentences (a sentence within a sentence) and widen the metaphors to talk about larger structural complexities.

Instead of saying venerable, meaning that another is higher up in rank or position, one can now say things like this: He is more important to the tribe because he is the best hunter. At first, it might take the form of he venerable, best hunter. A tool again! The words used would come to be explainable by giving the reason why: they would have their meanings expressed by other words. In describing a saber-toothed tiger as more dangerous than a fox, say, venerable could then mean the best hunter, as an analogy showing why it should be revered more. This would take the concept and place it upon a different object or subject, allowing you to derive the same facts about it, relatively speaking. Gold is more venerable than stone, so we must crown the king in gold. This is the "different" analog I mentioned, as opposed to the "same" analog. This is still not what we would consider full-blown language, but it's an improvement. It will become more apparent in another chapter how the next level of communication came into being.

There must be another naming nature to our species that has somehow become innate or at least habitual—that is, our natural tendency to name things. It, from necessity, came later on in our history and is quite possibly the reason for our sudden appearance of language in the last ten thousand years or so.

It would be expedient to have names for every living thing and every nonliving thing. This in my unprofessional opinion would be just an *innate habit* or propensity to place names on things for the sake of being more specific or exact in our identification of the various parts of our world.

Chomsky has been critiqued for feeling that language syntactic structure is innate, but that evolution could not have produced it. That is what most of the stink is about. Pinker has shown that it could very well evolve by taking into consideration the sounds and voice box, our vocal appendages, to produce these sounds. In selection for these different sounds, our appendages have in fact evolved, even if only for more calls, cries, and other noises of communication. Syntax, on the other hand, does not really need to evolve, per se, because it rides on the back of ordered life: both for "syntax" and "beads on a string." You cannot have syntax or beads on a string if you don't have names or the ability to communicate concepts. I have dealt with concepts plenty and now must deal with our nature to name things.

Nouns are the proper names of things. Chickens are called chickens for a different reason than cows are called cows. Chickens could be called stones for all it really matters. "Hey, honey, we're having roasted stones for supper." As long as stones were what everyone called that delicious, edible bird, we would have no problems. For communication purposes, we really need to get into placing names on everything. Different names!

My youngest daughter Alicia, when she was three or so, used to call everything chicken. One day we were having hamburger, and as I went to put it on her plate, she said, "I don't like chicken." I told her it was not chicken but beef; she continued to insist that she did not like chicken. If it was beef, she called it chicken. If it was pork chops, she called it chicken. It seems that she confused the meat concept with chicken. In my mind, this means that we don't have an innate concept for meat and possibly only one for food or, more specifically, hunger in general. The categories of food and all other categories of meat are named and learned.

It is likely that when one is naming birds that the concept of both birds and chickens comes into play. They are both likely learned, as my daughter's misconception of "chicken" for "meat" shows. (She's better now, I think!) However, it does not need to be that they are without syntax when spoken. You say, for example, that a bird is a chicken, or a chicken is a bird. We could never name either one of them if we had not evolved voice, the concept of bird, the concept of different bird, and the nature to order them in voice. Either order does not matter, but when ordered with something else, it does matter. The more sounds one can make, the more names can be formed. First categories, then subcategories, and finally individual names. They can be learned and not innate, but animate and inanimate are very likely innate, or set to become innate, with the proper stimuli. However, we could say that it is innate for the brain to see things as they happen. It is just as possible that the brain could not see things as they happen. The cortex does store things in digital at random, so, out of order thinking, could occur. It would not be selected for.

You can make up any sentence you like and say it does not fit but is just made up. One word can be a sentence. Sara. The word is perfectly grammatically correct. So what does it mean within syntax. Without being there, almost nothing; you can only get out of it the name of a feminine soul. It needs to be taken within context; you have to be there. On the other hand, the word apple can become a fully understood sentence. Apple. It is ordered, within context, and understood with its full meaning.

This is because every apple is called apple, but not every feminine soul is called Sara. Names are placed on everything so we can automatically take them in context, as such, placing them into their world structure in the proper order. We know that apples grow on trees and then need to be picked, cleaned, and then eaten. Your brain can run this in reverse, of course: you can envision eating an apple and then think of picking a fresh one from a tree.

Apple is a learned word for the fruit, but food is known by the body—in one sense—innately and very well could have had a call associated with it. These are two different things and need to be treated as such. In order to name different foods different names and retain the meaning of them being food a rebracketing might have occurred. The rebracketing in this case would be to hold the meaning of food while dropping the word food. In the example below, the outside brackets hold the meaning of food and what that food is. The inside brackets just hold the name of the particular food. So as the actual name given to the specific food became known as a species of food, the word food could be removed within their context—food apple, food grape. [[food] apple] [[food] grape] would lead to a placeholder, losing food [[] apple] [[] grape] and would survive in the brain with the concept of food attached silently. Notice that these words, with the placeholders within the brain are ordered too. We could not evolve different names if we did not evolve different sounds to name them differently.

If I were then to do the same with sounds, we could see where naming comes into play. Using the same brackets [[Vvv] va], the concept of space/time would remain within the word as it changed into valley [[] valley], indicating a lower part of our space. Whatever concepts can be named from the calls—the topic of a previous chapter—they will be, and whatever names can't be named from calls will be invented, from whatever source is applicable. We shall see if there is any information to support this in the literature.

In her book *Naming Nature*, Yoon talks about two different figures: one has curves and roundness to it, and the other has many sharp points and jagged edges. The picture has this caption "Which of these shapes would you say was takete and which maluma?" She says that 95 percent of people choose the word takete as a name for the jagged edged picture and maluma for the more rounded picture. "Umwelt," is used to describe the feeling we intuitively use for naming things. With this in mind, she goes on to say the following:

> Somehow it's simultaneously obvious and impossible to explain, but that it is so crystal clear. And as with the pointy and the blobby picture, humans perceive the living world—big, gruff, growly, fuzzy things versus, say, little chittering, chirping things—in ways that likewise prescribe certain kinds of names as appropriate. (Carol Kaesuk Yoon, *Naming Nature*)

Yoon continues to describe the same kinds of things with the difference between bird names and fish names: 58 percent correlation.

> For as the undergraduates of Berkeley have shown, our umwelt, our sense of what the living world is and isn't, what it should and shouldn't be, is so well defined that we can feel out the birdiness versus the fishiness of names in a language we've never even heard of.

She goes on to talk about birds being named with the sounds they make and then turns to brain damage removing these properties of the brain to recognize innate things:

They hypothesized that humans have a preexisting functional entity in the mind, what psychologists term a "domain," in this case, built specifically for mentally processing the categories and names of living things. (Yoon, Ibid.)

We form domains within our brains, and these could be responsible for our propensity to name all things. I suggest these domains prompt naming but do not control the naming process. They might, for example, cause objects to receive appropriate names reflecting hardness or softness, but they have no real input for the sounds themselves, per se. The sounds in some cases would come from our innate base of cries, calls, or grunts, as something could be called mountain due directly to its height, which we have a sound concept for. Other cases would require just sucking it up and naming them. Some other cases would be derived from the different brain feelings about the object or subject being named: birdiness or fishiness, and softness or hardness, is somewhere in the brain and would work with the language control area. So in one sense, we have an innate nature to name things, but in another sense, we do not. Since we have language, we have a drive to speak and name, but language did not evolve for the purpose of naming.

Naming is a byproduct of communication, which the brain transposes onto the different domains from the actual real language areas of calls and cries, from where it originated. This transposition automatically names the things it can, with the concepts within its store. If the concept sound is not within its store, it must make up names.

I must discuss grammar a bit here, making make some corrections to the tense problem. Tenses would be, as secondary concepts, just as useful in forming words, but we must not confuse these with emotions. There are not only problems with tense changes, which the literature is infested with, but also sense changes. You almost can't read any book on language or knowledge that does not go into tense changes; it is the basis of the grammar argument. I have seen little or no sense change as far as I can remember. The problem of sense change is just as great as tense change, though.

When she was around three years old, my oldest daughter Tiffany, now the new mother, heard her mother using the word "embarrass" and questioned her as to what it meant. Later on that night, I went into her room to read her a story and she was half-naked, getting her pajamas on. She covered herself up some and said, "I am so embarrassing." We teased her and said, "We know, but we love you anyway."

She knew, without any schooling, that embarrass had to be changed in *sense* somehow, but did not know how to change that sense, or what to change it to. Neither did you when you were her age, and you had to be taught the proper way to express these changes, so stop picking on her. The most common example I have seen used is that of "goed" instead of "went" for tense change. The same logic must apply to a sense change too. I suggest that the emotion of embarrassment was triggered with the word once she learned what the word meant: the word/concept connection. The state of the concept could be altered, and an attempt was made, albeit incorrectly.

The sense of embarrassment is an emotion. It can be altered from a different person's perspective. Adding the "ed" to embarrass does not change "time" or the tense of the word. It changes the person or state of emotion. He embarrassed me. She is embarrassing to me. I have embarrassed myself. She embarrassed me not only places it in past tense but also imposes the emotion of embarrass from another to one's own self. This is not tense change. You might be embarrassed if you were to caught naked in your living room by an unexpected guest. You say, "I am embarrassed," but you mean now and not past tense of the word by adding "ed." We use the same adaptations, though, which is interesting in itself. We use "ing" and "ed," which are "words" used for tense or time alteration analog with sense. I will attempt to easily explain why this is so when I create our language origins in this chapter. We must first look at another problem.

From my own children, I will include some more examples, which are dear to my heart. When she was a small child, we had family over to visit. As family goes, we often get into the teasing mode, and that day they were heavily into teasing me. I don't remember what I was being teased about, but it was done in a light manner, not a heated conversation. Tiffany, listening to them tease me, took offense, and at the age of maybe three or four, she jumped up in anger and said, "That's my daddy," as if they should leave me alone, and then she came to me to be picked up and cuddled.

Even though children do not speak perfectly articulate language, they seem to be quite able to understand everything spoken and more, knowing what it means, at least in concept form. She called me "my daddy" as an extension of herself. They were harassing me, and it needed to stop. She intervened and came to my rescue. All of these actions were concepts and actions needed for survival and passed down from our ancestors. She learned rapidly how these words were applied to different concepts, both innate ones and named ones. All this was possible because of the ability of the brain to analyze, name, and organize things into sound-symbols for communicating the world structure in the proper order. She learned that the name of this little girl, which was her essence, was Tiffany. The name Tiffany is not an innate concept, albeit a loved one; however, girl is, or might be, an innate concept representing the female part of our two sexes species.

At about the same age, Alicia wanted breakfast right after getting up one morning. I asked her what she wanted to eat, and her reply was simply the word "toast," rather than saying, "I would like some toast, please." Manners, like language are taught. I then asked her what she wanted on her toast, and she replied, "B jelly." I asked her if she meant jam. "No! B jelly!" After a few moments of scratching my head, I informed her that she would have to show me what she meant. I picked her up and opened the cupboard door, and she pointed to a bottle with a picture of a bee on it. Honey! There was nothing the matter with her. She knew exactly what she wanted. I, on the other hand, did have the problem: my speech was too refined to understand her. Imagine "honey" instead of "bee jelly," which is what it was to her. We, in our infinite wisdom, placed the name "honey" on her beloved "bee jelly."

At some point, foreign concepts would start to take place. We would be forced to innately create new calls and cries and to enter them into our repertoire and put them through the same analytical process. This would not be possible, and if it were, it would take too long for selection—to work on them, to keep up with the demands. Words would have to become very diverse in order to keep up. I will delay this semiproblem to a better place of discussion.

Chapter Thirteen

Dissecting the World

Each Volvox is at liberty within its own envelope; but it projects protoplasmic extensions which pass through its cuticle and place it in communication with its neighbor. It is probable that these protoplasmic filaments act like so many telegraphic threads to establish a network of communication among all the individuals of the same colony; it is necessary, in fact, that these diminutive organisms be in communication with each other in order that their flagella may move in unison and that the entire colony may act as a unit and in obedience to a single impulse.

—Alfred Binet
The Psychic Life Of Micro-Organisms

This quote shows two things—division and unity—and I could think of no better quote to begin this chapter. If I were forced to use only one quote in this book and had to get rid of the rest, this one would be my choice to keep.

It requires some form of communication to have a colony of cells work as a whole. It is the same within our bodies and brains. It represents the form of communication going on inside the brain but also the form of communication going on outside the brain. That is, communication to every other member of the colony so the colony can act as a whole. As an extra bonus, it shows how far the mind has come in its analyzing of the world.

I will get back to art, symbols, and writing toward the end of the book because we are looking for language origins and not the origin of knowledge as such.

I understand that William James defined knowledge as the naming of things, but I think a more accurate description is available to us. Communicating to others the knowledge we acquire requires it to be named both internally—before the brain can dissect anything, it must have the same information in different areas—and externally.

Why different areas? Placeholders, at the minimum. Try to dissect any one object without having it held in the brain at least twice. If the "wiring" is redundant, so is the information it contains. As soon as you went to divide the concept of that particular object in half, the object would have disappeared and you would be left with half. Half of what? The object is gone! You need redundancy, which has taken the place in the brain of parallel paths for nervation. The naming of things requires a certain amount of cognition to be present, a base, before one can start the process of naming, and I think that properly, knowledge is the consciousness that things are being named (conscious knowledge): a starting point for the tree of knowledge. "A tree to be desired to make one wise," the difference being that wisdom is knowing what best to do with the knowledge you have, or a truer conscious process, actually becoming a niche of another kind. The wisdom niche!

I would argue that there were two language steps or three, with wisdom and naming a byproduct of the last. Symbolic knowledge is unique to humans, as scientist say, the same as logical thought and planning the future, to name a few, as far as we know. Because logical thought and planning for the future arose, they must have wired or structured the brain to allow for the same language process as for the thought process. That's right—wired the brain, not the other way around. The brain circuitry did not arise out of selection and "choose" to wire red. Red, on the other hand, chose to wire into a neuron as a representation of a survival advantage. The same thing happens with sound concepts. That is, they wire the brain, and we bisect sounds and separate out the individual concepts with sound alteration. The same would apply to separating out the rest of the world along with it. With man, it coincides with language, and I believe they share the same process.

I have argued that one brain increase not pressured for by use would allow the space needed to accomplish this. When you start to alter things around you, needs arise. The need for wisdom, as defined by my definition, the need for higher communications, and the need for a higher conscious plane, however slow a process, would be completely possible if the hardware were already in place, which I have tried to show.

I used a computer template starting with the structure of 01001011 hardwired, representing our basic calls and cries, innate within the brain. I advanced to DOS commands and then Windows to control these DOS commands more easily, by just clicking on them. Now all we need is the mouse to click on the Windows and let it be called the finger of attention, which we call "I," or the soul. The more RAM you have, the faster the thinking process is, compared to hard drive space, which accounts for more memory.

Wisdom, or at least the drive to gain it, would be the push needed to go from a lower-level language to a higher-level language or, actually, articulate speech. What are words but the combining of concepts or the naming of arbitrary things? From that point forward, not all words would have to be conceptual, or literal, just the names of things, which is handled by the memory. Not everyone would have to be on the same naming plane, especially in a larger community like Babylon:

> And the whole earth was of one language and of one speech ... and the Lord said, behold, the people is one, and they have all one language; and this they begin to do; and now *nothing will be restrained from them*, which they have *imagined* to do. (Gen. 11:1, 6; emphasis mine)

Going from level one language to level two or three and calling them different things would certainly confound their tongues. In some cases, it would create the air of a "sudden appearance" of language. They set before themselves to build a tower to the heavens, which would create problems requiring solving. A need to name technology or industrious knowledge is now present yet is another changed niche, going from a niche of language acquisition to a niche of language and wisdom acquisition. It also could have been localized, explaining the different language and vocabulary problems on the other continents. If the worldwide split was Babylon and these descendants went to all the other continents, as was supposed, we would expect to see a continued search for knowledge, and the Americas would have been trying to prove the world was round and met Columbus at the halfway point, complete with their guns and crosses. They shaped a different niche for themselves as their needs dictated.

Differences among languages, like differences among species, are the effects of three processes acting over long spans of time. One process is variation—mutation, in the case of species; linguistic innovation, in the case of languages. The second is heredity, so that descendants resemble their progenitors in these variations—genetic inheritance, in the case of species; the ability to learn, in the case of languages. The third is isolation—by geography, breeding season, or reproductive anatomy, in the case of species; by migration or social barriers, in the case of languages. (Steven Pinker, *The Language Instinct*)

I suspect that there were a few splits, and one general one was around Eurasia, leading to our own languages. One split before this was when other ancestors left Africa and spread to the other continents. As industrious nature would drive for a higher language facility, we would expect to see a more complex language where industry is highest.

This leads to the conclusion that once the system was in place for language to evolve, it could have done so independently on other isolated continents. At any rate, we see these separations of clans as they migrate onto the other continents retarded in their industry. This retardation of industry is possibly from the retention of the old way of life, because there was no, or at least less, evolutionary pressure for change, unlike Europe and Asia. It would only take one group of peoples to push themselves harder than other groups of the same species of people to drive for learning. Then they would spread their learning within closer communities and learn from others. This is what we see in the world histories. It is time to leave the different tongues of language created by the different "keys" of separating the concepts into different digital sounds, i.e., ve meaning in Latin the same as ev in Hebrew, and apply the same process to learning in general.

The only reason for this avenue of thought, which I could have omitted altogether, is to show how intricately intertwined language and knowledge are. Expanded knowledge forces language to expand as names are required for communicating the new knowledge. This gives us a bird's eye view of the reality of it. The more knowledgeable peoples in the past had the better vocabularies. To this end, I will explore some possible observations on nature—the only thing we have to learn from—which could have led to some of our words, understanding, and gray thinking throughout time.

I have not mentioned curiosity in any chapter so far, and I must rectify this immediately. Most animals that I have observed have displayed some form, more or less acute, of curiosity. Dogs, when seeing something or hearing something strange for the first time, turn their heads in a funny pattern as if trying to understand what the stimuli is. Monkeys and apes are known to be curious. Curiosity is just one more ingredient multiplied in man, making us human.

I will use a few stories to show how this curiosity-driven knowledge could have dawned on us, but first I will give another reason for our ability to learn. There is plenty of speculation and discussion on language evolving from our interaction and our social natures. We are a species that heavily depends on closeness of contact, closeness of our intimate group. It is how we learn from one another. Alas, it is how language was able to come into realization. Dissecting sounds into their various parts and separating out the different sub-concepts would never have happened without this closeness of ours on so many levels. We can tell what others are thinking or feeling with minimum effort because we have another ability to communicate besides articulate speech. If our words did not mean something on an innate level, then they would just be meaningless sounds.

If we have this ability to understand one another on all these levels, then we have the ability to understand each other when examining for content. If tilogos the sound-word had the same concept that your feeling of knowing had, we would take it as true. This would be our knowledge. Your *vvvvv* had the concept of space/time. Think of the fact that for years we thought the earth was the center of the universe and the sun and stars moved around our flat planet. Oops! The earth was not considered a planet. This was the thought even before Aristotle, and it lasted until the enlightenment, even though a few before Copernicus had suspected it moved. The same held true with the world being flat and not spherical. A lot of wrong information, which was thought to be correct information, had to be sorted out. I will go back to an earlier time, before these were questions, but I need to mention something first.

If one dwells on the amount of time and effort that goes into figuring systems out by their complex observations, with the understanding that not all things lead to survival, then one must ask why. Copernicus spent the better part of his life studying the skies and determined that the earth also moves. This was not in any case a survival advantage, especially to his immediate predecessors. We can only conclude that this truth seeking is a by-product of analytical process generated by the brain.

I have been working on this language issue for many years now, and it will not give me a survival advantage over my competition for life. The only reason I keep giving myself for the search is that of finding out the truth. We have become truth seekers.

With all this in place, specifically the ability to analytically transpose calls and cries into articulate language, it would drive the same ability to analytically transpose our surroundings into our use and control. Both would grow together and evolve into a search for industrious capabilities. Everything would become a question needing an answer. Thus we have interrogative and indicative.

There are a few views on how agriculture got started. One view is that as hunter-gatherers, mostly female, harvested plant seed for food and discarded the seeds upon some becoming spoiled, which is equivalent to accidentally planting them where she dwelt. I might remind you that if no notice was ever taken, it would never have led to farming. It would just be more places to gather. "Notice" happens to be a key factor and I will work with that. As speculated by others, if for some reason a hunter-gatherer happened to be looking at prey through the grasses and "noticed" that she was in a bed of edible plants looking at seeds, the food part, in different stages of growth, observations could be made. I will call these observations bisecting the world. Just as one total sound concept could be bisected into a different part of a smaller concept leading to language, the same would happen to the world. The ability is now set to transfer the world into another nature.

This seed she recognized as food is now there in front of her at different stages of development. She sees that there is a seed on the ground, just like the seed in the plant. One of the seeds is just starting to open up and sprout out. Another is a little bit further along in its growing and has a small root just starting to enter the ground. A few more are rooted, and a small set of leaves are in view. Then there is one that is grown enough to resemble the plant that she eats from, except it has no seeds yet. Since the placental complexity has been overcome and we have the attention driven ability to analyze, it would seem reasonable for this hunter-gatherer to analyze that this food came from this plant. The plant also comes from the food; they are one and the same.

Now I don't quite think that it would become instant farming on her part. It might have started out as grabbing an extra handful of the seeds and planting them closer to home. They might possibly be forgotten about until the next season, when she went to eat the seeds as food and then remembered planting them there. More batches could have been planted to provide easy access to quick food. Most of the meals would still have come from hunting and gathering. In the meantime, more could have been planted, and she could have made more observations on the growing process. It would never take off, however, until it became an advantage to have the plants close by and in larger numbers.

With each new planting, there would need to be a new dawning of the knowledge of another kind. You can plant your food closer to where you dwell: this would be a second dawning. This by no means entitles the concept to take off en-mass. Just because one notices that these, say, wheat plants, were "plantable" from the food source itself, the seed, does not mean that it would automatically cross into the entire plant kingdom.

Fruit, for instance, would have the seeds inside the fruit, and the fruit is not what gets planted—it's the seeds. A third dawning would have to take place before this could happen. Maybe an ancient discarded some spoiled fruit and then remembered doing so when she saw a fruit plant growing there the following year. She might now be inclined to see why these trees were growing where she discarded the fruit. A member of this ancient clan might have then taken some fruit and opened it for a closer examination to see why it would grow into a tree. This would be our new analytical properties at work here.

If all foods fell into the concept of food in general as a wide concept of eating, analytically, food would start to be separated into what part of the plant does the growing of the fruit. This would be the analyzing of the world starting to take shape. Even this first fruit plant experience might not be enough to start them farming. She—mainly woman gathered and men hunted—might plant more berry plants, but the concept of farming need not occur to her. The same situation as with the above-mentioned grain plants, which did not lead to farming. At some point it would dawn on her that she now had some grain and fruit growing closer and in larger quantities. She would come to know that these plantings were done at her own hand, and that she could do more of them. This would be another dawning.

The last dawning that would need to take place would be that if these few grains and plants grew from the seeds, then maybe other plants did as well. They would then start to analyze more grains and plants and enter into the territory of trees. Puzzled by some things not having seeds, or at least the appearance of not having them aboveground, they might start to investigate belowground. Transplanting would possibly evolve from this, but so would the drive of wanting to know how the plants grow: another dawning. All these things rely on one thing: the ability to analyze.

By necessity, each new step would be a new dawning of knowledge about the world we live in. This is taking complete concepts and analyzing them into smaller concepts, the same as I claim happened to words. With knowledge, some of these newly minted concepts can be manipulated and put to other uses as other needs arise, which is what I call wisdom.

There are myths, albeit few, that are written just to tell one when the best times are to plant and harvest. The Greeks had Hesiod writing about the *Works and Days*, *Theogony*, and *The Shield of Heracles*. Just because you yourself have discovered something does not mean that it will survive with your genes; the opposite is in fact true: it will die with you, which makes memes so important. To be sure, some of these myths were related as myth for the transfer of knowledge. Some of the characters in these myths were the ancestors of discovery or invention and became known as the gods who created them, or the sons of the gods who were sent for that purpose. At least they were passed by myth on to the next generation, so they did not have to learn everything afresh.

Wine from the grape was a complete accident, as I have been told, and it has become widely known. They have been making wine now for thousands of years. There are records dating back eight thousand years. If you leave grapes with the skins open, the natural yeast on the skins will work it into wine. If it turned to vinegar, it was still usable as a seasoning for food, and not much was thought about it.

The Mesopotamian culture had hieroglyphs giving instructions on how to make wine. You don't put new wine into old wine skins, as Jesus pointed out. They burst. A lot was known about making wine, but nothing was known about why it became wine. They would place silver, which acts as a bacterial inhibitor, into the wine mix to stop it from going bad until alcohol built up enough to take over—but they did not know why. It was only in the mid-nineteenth century that people learned about germs.

Germs are the known source of fermentation in wine and vinegar. It did not stop them from making wine and finding ways to prevent it from becoming putrid while in the barrels. They'd keep them in the sun for a season to kill off everything in the barrel, even though they did not know they were killing bacteria or they might have preferred to call the bacteria small animals instead. Of course, this procedure did not always work, and batches of wine were destroyed. I use wine here not for its invention but for its word value.

For any climbing or trailing plant, Latin uses the word *vinea* in the larger sense of the word vine. Their narrower sense of the word is grapevine, or *vitis* in Latin. It includes any and everything relating to the grape vine. I will expand on this because it shows the need for a conceptual change. This one word was used in the Bible for anything related to grapes.

This is where some religions believe that Jesus was referring to grape juice and not wine (alcohol) when he instituted the blessing of Holy Eucharist. They believe it is sinful to drink any alcohol at all, so it must be grape juice. There is no more proof for this than there is that it was alcohol. So *vitis* would be grape, grape juice, vin or wine, vine, and vineyard. When it turns to another substance, it is known as vinegar, which is also spelled with vine. Maybe the ivy thing I mentioned before has some merit to it after all. My point is that this leaves much unclear. Names for the fruit, separate from the vine, separate from the juice, and separate from the wine would be needed for clarity.

This actually makes a good example for the other reason that they are spelled with *vi*. It pertains to spreading out or climbing up, and we are, after all, looking for language origins.

The example of wine does not have as much dissecting and analyzing to it, but I decided to use it for the language benefit and also the analogy benefit. It is known almost universally that gossip is spread and referred to as hearing it through the grapevine. The connotation is that word spreads like the vine of the grape, the same as workers spread gossip in their toil! As a metaphor, it has become a sign of age, not only in wine but in automobiles and many other uses. We recognize the word vintage as meaning old—but better for it. One more example and I'll move on to the next topic.

Grafting was not just thought of one day and tried. Grafting goes back a long way in the history of man. It was around literally before Christ, as the apostle Paul, I believe, used it in one of his epistles as an analogy to graft yourself onto Christ. It is thought to have been invented in China around 2000 BC, and it is technically called inosculation or natural grafting. It then spread to Eurasia.

In grafting, we cut the trunk of one tree and install the trunk of another tree at the cut. As a natural process of healing, the new tree will take its nourishment from the root system of the rooted stock base. It soon heals onto it and grows as a complete unit. In fact, you can take two or three branches of different trees and grow them onto one rootstock. For instance, you can have an apple branch, a peach branch, and a plum branch all from the same tree. By the way, they do bear true to the branch and not the root base. The only qualifying facture is that they are related enough, species-wise, to take. Some trees won't graft onto others.

Mistletoe has the property of growing its roots into the bark and wood of other trees. It is what they call parasitic. It does not grow directly into the ground but gets its sustenance directly from the host. In grafting, the roots of one tree do not grow into another. This would slowly become obvious to anyone trying it.

Grafting would have to have been learned from nature somehow. It can be readily observed that when branches of one tree lay across another tree, they graft themselves together at the point where they are touching. What would it take to figure out what was happening here? Attention and curiosity. With attention, curiosity, and analytical properties of the digital brain, one would be able to figure out that branches could be grown onto other trees.

Maybe at first both were planted and the branches were purposely made to touch. Then they were separate and grown to see which survived and produced which fruit. At any rate, it did happen. If 100 percent of the time you could get plant X to grow on plant Y but never get plant Z to grow on plant Y, it would soon become known that it can only be done with some plants. Experimenting will find all the matches for you. Why not apply this new knowledge to hybrid plants now? No concept would have been in place for either of these ideas. Since the concept was not innate, complete with sound, it would have to receive an appropriate name. The name for this concept of grafting could have become all the added together names for the process, i.e., to grow one tree onto another.

I hasten to add that I did not look up any detailed history on grafting, and there is probably another story that tells more closely the truth. I only wrote it after this fashion because of the analytical properties it shows in the process. Remember, I need tools to work with, the same as I did with words.

Here is where the naming part comes into it. The stories of the grapes and grafting have two contrasted words sources. Grape vines use an already existing concept to name them: spreading out or climbing. Grafting probably means to grow onto another, which would have been different concepts added together—the traditional thought process on making up words. If you can name what you are doing, it can be taught better to others. This topic will be covered better in another chapter.

I don't remember the name of the show now, but there was a nature show on television not long ago where some great hunter traveled the world and hunted down animals for study. On one show, he went looking for wild hyenas. At one village, the elders of the village sat at the village edge and fed the wild hyenas fresh meat. They claimed that it kept the hyenas from attacking the village. The same process has been suggested for the taming of the wolf, which led to the unconscious selection for the different breeds of dogs. Dogs would be of great survival advantage because of their keen hearing and will too defend. The tamest selected for and bred until they became dogs. It is also said that we self-selected for the tamest of our own species, if you can call our history tamed.

Animal husbandry probably came into being as result of trapped animals, as was hypothetically brought forth. If many were trapped, what was needed for your tribe's survival would be taken, the rest left. It is just one more step to conclude from that dawning in concept that if you had some sheep contained, they could be slowly consumed and would not need to be hunted. As they gave birth to their young, another dawning would take place; you could grow them, and in the process, they would become tamed also. The speculation is that this is what happened to sheep, goats, and other heard animals. Hunting would have had to come into being first.

There is evidence that we began by eating the carcasses of dead animals left over from the kills of other predators. Teeth marks left in bones reveal this. Older sources of bone had human teeth marks on top of animal teeth marks. Newer bone sources have our teeth marks first and the other predators second, as they finished our scraps. Watching other animals and studying them would eventually lead us to know their tactics for hunting. We could then analyze these tactics and try to duplicate some of them ourselves. Wolves surround their prey. Other predators, when being followed, circle around and come up behind their followers: the hunter becomes the hunted.

The tracking of animals would need to be learned and would be a great way of catching them if you knew how they worked. With few numbers of clan members, the pressure would be high to keep a watchful eye out for predators. Anytime a predator was spotted, it would be advantageous to watch it persistently to avoid it catching one of the few members of the tribe. In watching its hunting moves, one could easily learn the strategy and counter it effectively or, better, put the same strategy to work for oneself. All these examples rely on the ability to pay attention for longer periods while at the same time picking apart every aspect of nature. We are still focusing on language here, and I can't help but think of a common analogy: know your enemies. This one has evolved into wisdom: keep your friends close and your enemies closer. Before my theory on language will work, concepts must come into being, that they may become analyzed and named.

I try to use different examples than other authors, but it is difficult to be original all the time. Richard Dawkins, in *Climbing Mount Improbable*, used his computer program called The Blind

Watchmaker, from the name of his earlier book, and altered it to design spider webs. I will get to webs in general, but for now, I want to use this example of one spider in particular:

> A bolas (or bola) is a weapon originally invented by native South Americans and still used by gauchos for hunting (for example) rheas, the large flightless birds of the pampas. It consists of a weight, such as a pair of balls or stones, on the end of a rope. It is slung towards the prey with the purpose of entangling its legs and bringing it down. The young Charles Darwin experimented with the bolas while on horseback and managed to catch his own horse—to the amusement of the gauchos though not, presumably, of the horse. The bolas spider's prey are always male moths of the family Noctuidae, and for a reason. Noctuid female moths lure their mates from a distance by releasing a unique perfume. The bolas spider lures males to their deaths by synthesizing a closely similar perfume. The "bolas" is a weighty bob on the end of a single thread of silk, which the spider holds in one "hand." It waves the bolas around until it entangles a moth, then hauls it in. (Richard Dawkins, *Climbing Mount Improbable*)

He goes on to analyze the complexity of the "bolas," which is very interesting but does not concern us here—except to point out our analyzing abilities in more detail.

I am sure Richard Dawkins has thought of the same thing, that the bolas was copied from the spider, but he is writing for another purpose, that of web design. The reason for using such a long quote is that I needed to show the connection of the bolas weapon of the gauchos and the bolas weapon of the spider itself. This is where I want to focus attention.

If the gauchos "invented" the bolas, it was probably from seeing the spiders do it. Suppose that one day a gaucho sees a spider that looks as if it is waving a string. Curiosity kicks in, so he watches. He observes that this is how the bolas spider catches its prey. He would not need to know the perfume part at all; this would come centuries later. So what? Does this mean that he can go out straight away and do the same? First he would need to break down the individual parts of the bolas that the spider uses. He would need to know that it uses one end in its "hand." It made a string and had some sort of weight bound into the other end. I doubt very much that gauchos could make strings from their bodies. The string would need to be studied carefully. This string is actually web, and they did not have microscopes to study the construction of them.

Keeping this in his mind, in, say, hidden areas while the brain worked on it would leave an opening. One day while doing something else, he notices a fine vine hanging in the woods, and it reminds him of the "web string," which at this point had no name. The hidden area reports that this could work as the web string. He somehow wraps a stone around it for weight and uses it as a foot entanglement. This foot entanglement would have had to have been thought about also, but I won't go that far.

This bolas does work some of the time, but it breaks a lot. Bigger vines are tried, but they don't work very well because they are too thick to tie properly. He ties two smaller ones together, and it works better, but they become entangled with use and need to be remade every time he uses it. Someone examines the entanglements, and it dawns on him that these entanglements might be the answer to the problem. He entangles a few of these vines together himself, perfecting them into a woven rope.

The tribe now has an imperfect rope, which he gets the job of making for the rest of the tribe. It would, by the analytical properties of the brain, at some point dawn on him what he has actually succeeded in doing. You can, after all, be doing something for a long period before it dawns on you. Now this "inventor" could go back over this in his mind and discover the answers to solving the problems. Use smaller vines and entangle them. Bigger ones are too bulky and hard to work with. Answer: use something smaller again.

I am sure that something of this sort could have happened on the European continent too. There are spiders there, and they also make webs, but no bolas. Using the same base example, only in Africa, though, we would still be in the same position to advance it.

The grasses, or at least the stalks, are strong, and when worked enough, they can become very pliable and soft. The discoverer can entangle or weave them into the first smaller, stronger man-made rope, yet another dawning: smaller but more of them used. Now they could use smaller ropes called thread, which required stripping and weaving the finer peaces of stripped straw back together. With more weaving, an older concept by now, materials or cloth could be made. Even today, we wear woven grasses and cotton woven into thread, which have a fire retardant sprayed in them.

It has not fallen below my radar that if anything is at all true of Genesis, they sewed fig leaves together and covered their nakedness. Skins as clothing came later. The Maring people of New Guinea, the last isolated people to be discovered, and in the twentieth century, have cloth made of fine woven plant fibers. See Roy A. Rappaport's *Ritual and Religion*. He mentions it in passing, while describing their warring rituals. I made the assumption myself, based on this author's words, that the Maring people were not taught the art of making cloth after they were discovered. As a scientific basis for some word origin and evolution of words, I have included appendix I, based on Rappaport's book.

While on the topic of spiders, I may as well add this. Once these spider strings were invented, they could be used to duplicate other spiders' tactics. If one noticed that the standard web of a spider was used to catch flies, a spider's hunting tactic or strategy could be duplicated to advantage. He already had his own spider string or rope invented; he might take the analogy a step further and build a web (better known as a net) of his own so he can catch birds. It is only a small step to go from a bird net to fishing net or vice versa. A more probable insight would be for one to notice that spiders lay their eggs in special webs that house the babies. If you have ever seen a web full of small spiders attached to your house, note that these are their babies. It could be conceived that this would be an eye opener to the fact that it contains many spiders and something similar could contain other smaller animals like birds and fish.

If one were to watch the little spider as it toiled building its web, that person would notice that the spider bound small ropes across large openings and then joined them together with smaller spaces in between. With each new string the spider placed, the gaps became smaller and smaller, until the spider could walk across to the other side of its web.

It would only take someone to say to himself, *I can build a web to cross between the two sides of this great gulf.* So he could intently watch everything the spider did and try to do the same. Problem after problem would be solved by watching the spider work. Within a few days, he could manage to join the two sides of a great gulf and then work at filling in the smaller sections.

Finally, man could succeed in crossing the great gulf with his family. This would be a nice explanation for why we still have rope bridges to this very day. Unfortunately, I can't say this is for sure the case. It is just a so-so story, as they say. In fact, these are all just so-so stories, but they do show possibilities.

Meanwhile, they work out names for what they are doing as they are doing it. They use the analogy of what the spider does to describe the process of what they are doing and name the spider, the web, and their invention all the same name: bolas. The new concepts of bolas and rope were discovered, and they were not innate concepts. The new concepts would have been the driving factor in both language and wisdom. New altered sounds would have needed to have evolved through analogy or metaphor to name these things, which would have become our new habit and niche.

Another observation is that a plant that holds water could have been the idea behind a vessel that carries water. The orchard is an example. These plants have pitcher-shaped flowers, if you will, and they hold water for another purpose altogether. I won't go into the details of what the water is used for but will use it as a tool to get another tool: our own pitchers. It would be of great survival advantage to bring a water supply with you, or to the village.

If one of our distant surviving ancestors were to notice that these plants had pitchers to hold water, he might have thought to invent his own. I won't go into detail as much, but all it would take to convert this into a possibility was for him to notice that bigger leaves held water after rains. They could bend these bigger leaves into or close to the same shape as a pitcher plant and carry water to their dwellings instead of always having to go to the water.

Now add to this the fact that some bees and wasp build their nest out of earth and in container shapes. As these dawnings would have occurred to our forefathers, yet more concepts would be born. They could also make containers out of mud. Problem, though! Water would get them wet, and they would fall apart. Throw them out into the hot sun and forget about them. Now, weeks later, after being baked in the hot sun, it begins to rain. Several days after the rain stopped, someone noticed that they held the water and did not fall apart. This poses a question that can't be answered quite yet, so it is stored in the hidden areas of the brain.

Time passes, and as one of these ancient people sits in the sun, he begins to realize that the sun is very hot. He notices also that some of the bare ground around him has minor cracks from drying out, and these cracks resemble the broken pieces of their dirt pots, which also baked in the sun. The ones that held their shape did not crack but held water. It dawns on him that this is the very reason they hold water. What else do they have that dries things out and heats them up? Fire—and now pottery is born. Wisdom is not having knowledge as much as knowing what to do with it once you have it.

The next topic will be on housing. Every animal lives somewhere, and to call them all houses would be a little silly. As mentioned, some bees and wasps build their houses out of earth or mud. The bowerbird builds extravagant housing that looks so big and structured that seeing them would make one think that man made them. Weaverbirds build woven structures around tree branches, making it difficult for predators to get into them. Some animals build dens underground, and these are also well defended. Beavers might have the ultimate home when it comes to defending it from predators. What? We lived in caves away from our food sources in most cases. In order for farming to become a great advantage, we needed to be protected in the open fields needed to grow crops. Once more, we are back where I started.

To notice a nest built of twigs and the safety or, more to the point, relative safety it provided would be a survival advantage for man to have a similar one. Or for that matter, one built of clay. Man would soon discover that clay did not stay up on roofs without defying gravity. Two things are already known here. One, when clay is baked hard, it is waterproof, so build it from clay and let the sun bake it. Two: woven sticks and twigs make good coverings to keep weather out and camouflage. Build the roof out of sticks and cover then with layers of leaves.

Defying gravity does present a big problem, and it too can be overcome. Lifting heavy stone into place to build these huge monuments throughout the earth would require greater analytical thinking. The earth is riddled with examples of how animals build structures and at great heights. Even the lowly spider web could have been the example needed to climb to high places. Build a ladder based on the design of a web. At any rate, the farming communities would never have come into being before we learned to dwell safely in the open fields we used for growing.

Of course, this is just idle speculation in my overactive brain, but many creatures build huge structures for their relative size. When we learn to observe nature, by applying attention, we can produce the same effects I have suggested on applying attention to calls, cries, grunts, and sighs. Thus new concepts would come into being, named and altered by word and our analytical ability. If you can analyze structures made by other animals for their content, then you can analyze calls and cries for their content. Soon nothing would be withheld from us.

I have not gone too deeply into heavier matters, but it is not necessary to in showing how our brains have evolved into seeking the truth. Once the first few barriers were broken and they became an advantage to us, a new niche would have come into being. This niche would be one of wisdom but also, and more importantly, one of seeking the truth. We would look for the real ways in which nature works, learn how they become conscious to us, and name the acquired information. We would always use it to our advantage. We would never stop looking; it would become a compulsion. Where there was once black and white, we would see only gray and strive to make a better understanding of this gray.

I have often heard that we were fully conscious beings, or became fully conscious beings, when Adam ate from the forbidden fruit, which was not likely an apple. I have both reservations and cautions. I agree that we are conscious, but fully, not so much. Fully suggests that we know everything and are full. I suggest that we will only be fully conscious when we know everything—no, when we know that we know everything.

Before I get into the last chapter of my book, a quick summary of the process, but not in full detail, would be in order. Complete with biological and physiological suggestions, I have attempted to reconcile a single phoneme as a starting point of a complete concept, being innate. I have called them tilogos, or sound-words, and transformed them into sound-clichés, becoming root words available to be recombined, leading to our current word language. If, by my lineal explanation, phonemes, evolving from calls and cries, became innate or innately ready to trigger the representation of complete concepts, e.g., vision: sight, saw, seen, look, glimpsed, and the like, in one sound, in one part of the brain, half the problem would be solved. Another part of the brain could become able to separate the concepts and then recombine them (mix their meanings), along with the sound changes required for words to grow, but only words with literal meanings at first.

With such tools as "yolk sac to placenta" and "analytical math," I have tried to show that it is possible to go from wide concept to specific concept in 140 sounds or fewer. Then, as invention grew (wisdom), so would the need to start naming things irrelevant to meaning—a niche of language and wisdom—and both words with meaning and casual words would grow into our current digital vocabulary, bringing with them our yet-to-be-reached full potential consciousness.

There are two natures at work here. One is innate as a complete total concept, for which I have used space/time as my main example, but there are more. We derive from space/time such words as from, here, there, if, as, height, width, and the many more needed to communicate the secondary concepts contained in space/time. We have a second basis for communication, that is, for naming things. We place names on noninnate total concept objects such as apple, cow, rock, and the many more examples I have used—such as naming birds after their sounds.

The reason that man has learned to speak or become industrious is due to his analytical abilities alone. If we had not learned to analyze or literally dissect our world, we would still be animals. The driving force for both language and wisdom is the same driving force and occurred at the same time in our nature.

Once it occurred, say, in Adam and Eve, and they started bisecting calls and cries to each other, each understanding what the other meant, it could be passed on—taught—to their offspring. More importantly, it could be learned easily because of the innate basis from whence it sprung. It would be easy enough for just two or three persons, but not one person, to discover that you can communicate more precisely by sound alteration as you point to or make gestures of things you interact with. Utilizing mirror neurons, and the like-mindedness produced by interaction with fellow members of our species would ensure fidelity of meaning. Vowel alteration, accompanying different areas of the object as pointed to, would be repeated with the same vowel alteration and understood to mean the same *v* concept, but a different portion or secondary meaning *va* or *ve*. By taking turns naming and understanding by repeating them communication in the form of conversation would come into being.

Another outcome is that our observations of the world are equally important here. Seeing the world differently by many different persons pushes for different observations being made. In whole subjects or objects, other people are likely to make different discoveries than someone else might make. Seeing the same things slightly different by babies is in fact what leads to different personalities or interests in life. Identical twins could live under identical conditions and still see different things in a different way, and these differences would hold sway to their interest as adults. All this is possible because babies are born with so many extra neurons. With so many things being observed completely differently, or slightly differently, many gray areas would appear. As with anything gray, we would want to know what of it is right and what of it is wrong; questioning nature would ensue, and truth would always be looked for and held dear. God saw diversity and said it is good; it is, then, the end of boredom.

As culture grows, we need to depend on ourselves less and less for survival. Specialization can and does occur and is directly attributed to niche change. If one changes one's niche slightly, then the changed niche forces the same form of species to change again to adapt to the change better. This also leaves places within the brain open to having their neurons stolen, or recycled for other uses, per Stanislas Dehaene's theory. In short, not everyone needs to be a duplicate hunter-gatherer. Other employments are now open to specialization. There is no need now to speculate that any stolen brain space would place a damping effect on our species. As some might lose the ability to fight, they would supply our food, and others would specialize in fighting to protect our food. Yet others would specialize in building our homes and towns. This is known as community and culture, the two main drives in developing both wisdom and language.

Chapter Fourteen

Learning to Speak

With birds the voice serves to express various emotions,
such as distress, fear, anger, triumph, or mere happiness.
It is apparently sometimes used to excite terror, as in the
case of the hissing noise made by some nestlings-birds.

— Charles Darwin
The Descent of Man

This is the last chapter on language, and we must now start all over again from the beginning. First I must destroy any and all conceptions that language was invented by some smart humanoid. Then, as hard as it is to believe, I will prove that language was invented by some smart humanoid in the guise of discovery.

It would be too complicated to design a language. In fact, you need to have language to create, design, or invent language. If design and invent are excluded as possible, then we are left with discovered. Since Chomsky came up with the innateness of grammar, there has been much written on the evolving of language. Chomsky was the first to observe innateness of any kind, and we own him at least that honor. True, I have tried to show that the ordering of the world was natural and language followed on the back of this nature.

Why couldn't we have just made up words and invented language? Would it not amount to the same thing? Let's examine the problem of language invention. Some men and women are working on inventing new languages. I will not, nor cannot, comment on their work, but I can point out one great truth: they have an already existing language to start with. You can buy books on word problems, which have cryptograms in them. They use a different letter of the alphabet to replace the proper letter, and you need to guess which letter is replaced by which. For example, the letter *a* might be used instead of the letter *w*. So the word "work" might be spelled "adzq," and you need to figure out what that word is. Military coding and decoding was on the same basis—sometimes you needed a number for a starting place before beginning to decipher. Start deciphering at the sixth letter, for example. Many different ploys were used.

Again, we have what is called Morse code, which is not top secret but has permanent noises—dots or slashes—combined to represent the different letters. You can tap out the sounds of letters electrically. Bottom line, it still used the standard alphabet. We will take one more. Braille has been invented to aid the blind in seeing the written word by dots raised on paper. Again, they use a standard alphabet. From these examples, we get the picture loud and clear: we can't invent language without having language to invent it with.

You can't invent a word in the wild and expect it to be understood by anyone. The clash is that without language, you can't explain what the word means. Body language and gestures would undoubtedly help, you say? Sure, to a small degree only, if at all. The problem here is knowledge that you are actually naming anything or even inventing language. In addition, it requires that the connection be made between the sound and the concept—and then remembered long term by all involved.

True to form, it could happen that some animal uttered the word snake and it stuck that it was the name of that other dangerous animal. Wouldn't this parallel a call or cry? I firmly believe that I have a better explanation in the first chapter on calls and cries becoming innate with concept. These noises would be carried over through long lines of divergence and not need to be invented at all. It would take too long to invent calls and cries under the guise of words. It took hundreds of thousands of years to go from one poor type of spearhead to another poor type of spearhead to finally an iron one. There is more here than invention.

It does not stop at the complications of inventing names but also includes the complications of creating a system of articulation. In a crude point form, I shall look at them before moving on.

~ Articulation is the speaking in phonemes, one after the other, adding them into words.
~ The 140 sounds produced are not enough to cover all needed concepts *directly*. Call a stone the sound *g*, and from that, everyone is supposed to know what you mean? You go through the village and name 140 things … and then what?
~ We would have had to have all these concepts in order to be able to be intelligent enough to invent language in the first place.
~ You can't call it invented if you don't do it all in one stroke of the pen. It would mean that you basically need our refined vocal system in place before it can happen: the 140 sounds. By the way, English uses only 40 of the 140 sounds in speech. What would drive for the selection of those sounds if they were not needed for communication of some sort?

Not even if language were to be designed by a deity would he make so many sounds if they were not intended for speech. I can't see past the dilemmas to find design or invention. The only way to invent a language is to have a language in which to invent it. However, calls and cries are a language in their own right, so we must start with this base.

Sure, you are probably thinking that this articulation argument is nuts because no one ever truly suggested that the sounds of the letters of the alphabet actually had meaning to begin with. I will lkosgr vuunerz gaui biaeeouiac yt hqbbb iax d ic vvqwm. With those final words, we continue.

In the quote from *Fingerprints of the Gods*, they found an algorithm to transcribe other languages. I have also produced an algorithm naturally with digital sound. It is also automatic: as soon as you add two of these sounds together, they automatically shorten and become phonemes digitally. No selection for shorter sounds is required. A second method would be a stop short, better discussed in a moment.

In case you are wondering, this is not a real invention of language. Yes, it does need to be initiated by more than one of our ancestors, but it does not need to be designed by them, so no design, no invention. Discovery of a way to separate larger concepts into smaller ones by vowel alteration would be a better description. It was discovered that altering a concept, by altering the represented sound of the concept, was possible and became a learned, taught behavior or was invented by discovery.

In my opinion, they are two different processes, and the one built upon the other. Any evidence I have seen from any material I have read seems to point to this fact. Otherwise, as I have pointed out, you could throw letters on a piece of paper, calling them whatever you want, and it would be a word with meaning. The concept for space/time could very well have come into existence through the method I have proposed. It would be passed on to every subsequent generation from antiquity in total concept form along with the sound, call or cry attachment. This would be the case due to the origins coming from calls and cries, which would be innate.

Without great detail, I already went over how coming up with enough calls and cries would be a problem for selection. The thousands of words used to write this book could not possibly have occurred by the route of calls and cries being selected for. Natural selection would have to create word additions, concept understood, one word at a time. Then these new words would need to be added to a small vocabulary until we have the hundreds of thousands of words we have today. It simply would have taken too long. I might here add that the creation theorists are constrained by the same problems. God would have had to have created the concept-to-sound innate base within Adam and Eve's genome for the learning ability to be passed on. Also, it would need to be built into their phenotype so that they immediately had the ability to articulate with meaning. Not that this would be impossible for a god. In fact, I believe that the only problem with language is that you need to have a concept-to-sound base.

The historical evidence is pro sudden appearance of language and does not support long selection processes. Several times now, I have read accounts of language stating that language seemed to have taken off at some point in time, ranging from the last ten to fifty thousand years. Apart from other theories, my thesis has the ability to answer this question. Some of this chapter will be a summary, but much of it will also be new and explain how and why it happened this way.

No case was ever known of a child being able to read without being taught, even though the parents had exercised their faculties in this direction all their lives.

Children do not even learn to speak untaught, although not only their parents, but countless generations of ancestors, have exercised and perfected the brain and vocal organs by learning and speaking a language. (August Weismann, *Essays upon Heredity and Kindred Biological Problems, vol. 2*)

It is true that speaking needs to be taught. This isn't really a problem for my theory, though. In experiments of our cruel past, babies were separated and raised without any form of communication at all, and they did not learn to talk. However, in one experiment, they did learn to make the sound of a sheep that was nearby. This was not an accurate or controlled experiment. No one recorded the other sounds that they very well could have made: crying from pain, grunts or moans, sighs, or any other noises that could have been innate. However, I don't suggest that we do the experiment over again under more controlled conditions.

Here we seem to have some bridges to cross. Language is learned, but innate? I have written on the problems of brain size and suggest that learning articulate sounds instead of the calls and cries would lead to replacement of the calls and cries. That explanation, at least to me, seemed sound enough. It did not answer how they arose in the first place.

I will use the notion of learning a bit later, but for now, I will focus on the cognition of our Adam and Eve. I will first entertain the notion of a stop short—halting the sound or call before it is complete—and see how far it will take us. Before I state anything, remember that syllables don't have to mean anything in, or even have to occur in, a call. If a call were to be several syllables long, or the equivalent of several syllables long, only smoother in form—analog—it would always be the same. It would always start with the same sound and end with the same sound. The way the brain works, and I have indirectly dealt with this—the diagram I used for word recognition earlier—the start of the call would already be forming this concept as it was being produced. In other words, the first part of the call's sound would trigger the whole concept, or at least part of it. A stop short at any point in history could produce an "I get it" moment.

We see that it very well could have produced some of our digital short sounds. In addition to the main thesis of the book, placing two sounds together automatically produces the other sounds as shortened and altered, giving us two good areas to work with.

While out hunting one day, Adam says to Eve, "G," instead of the usual call: "Ggggrooouffffnghhhss." (If you don't like my call, make up your own.) Eve stops dead in her tracks, avoiding the bite of a deadly serpent—no pun intended. From the first sound in the call, the concept of freeze in your tracks is manifested in the minds of both Adam and Eve. "'Plosive' consonants," according to Dehaene from *Reading in the Brain*, "are produced by suddenly stopping the air flow in the vocal tract." Why wouldn't they be?

From this we get back to Adam and Eve and discover that it works with everything. Their minds are very much in sync; refer back to the four brains of love mentioned in a previous chapter. That is where I asked how many people it would take to realize language—and how well they would have to know each other. It really is only one more "I get it" moment, and it very likely did happen this way. She understood Adam from a stop short and respected the "rule of the call," whatever that rule was, and the first articulation of a consonant was born. Further, he understood that she understood. Understand? Now we have mutual understanding, and it would take little, I think, to realize that all our calls, cries, and other noises could be, at minimum, shortened. Remember here my exercise on "getting it" and what all it entailed.

It is conceivable that they worked slowly toward altering the sound with vowels to communicate the different secondary concepts and produced a few hundred root bases to which would become the standard. Correct me if I am wrong, but is this not discovered and further invented by the dawning of the discovery? As long as you have an innate meaning-based sound, call, or cry—your language—you are free to invent cryptosounds with it. This satisfies our placenta template quite nicely. It answers the sudden rise of language. It fits well with the niche change theory.

Adam and Eve now have the ability to use these calls and cries in a different manner. On their own, through *understanding the cognition of the sounds*, they can now manipulate other calls and cries knowingly. They can also teach their offspring as they develop new sound-words, or tilogos, eventually adding these tilogos together into sound-clichés. Phonemes would take the place in the innate brain concept area of the calls and cries they displaced. This was the whole reason I went into babies' brains having to grow for longer periods of time, to become less dependant children, which opens a possible change in brain wiring to replace the innate wiring. If Adam and Eve were to be the first to employ articulation after this manner, then their offspring would learn the phonemes and syllables, complete with the innate concepts. This answers the problem of children never learning to speak without being taught.

In *Reading in the Brain*, Stanislas Dehaene sums up Annette Karmiloff-Smith's theory as follows:

> A fraction of the child's brain, including the prefrontal cortex, learns to redescribe, in an explicit and abstract form, the older implicit knowledge that is buried within specialized modules. The acquisition of the alphabetic principle provides a nice example of internal redescription.

At birth, infants already possess, albeit implicitly, some knowledge of phonemes. It is only after explicit learning of the alphabet that this buried knowledge is consciously extracted and becomes full-fledged phonemic awareness—the ability to consciously represent and manipulate phonemes. In this domain, mental synthesis, conscious representation, and cultural invention clearly go hand in hand.

To perfect the process requires a means to that perfection. I believe we have some great examples in the literature. Cave paintings were around for a very long time. It could never be proven that they only arose after language, or before language—just for the reason that no one had defined language. I think I should be clear on this point. It is assumed that a protolanguage was the start of it all. No one has yet made any firm definition of "proto." Calls, cries, and hand gestures, plus some made-up words of around two hundred, are commonly suggested. No one says how many of what type, or when these would be considered a protolanguage. With my theory, I don't need to, as noise communication would be naturally there and only needing a slight push to evolve into articulation.

Now I return to the cave paintings. They might be the first attempts at writing. It fits somewhat, as they are analogous, as in "same," which I discussed in some detail earlier. If you were to break sounds down into my idea of tilogos and sound-clichés, it would be of great advantage if you could show in analog, via pictures, what these new sounds applied to specifically. I don't hold that this was "the" start of it all but only suggest that it was an extra aid or boost.

Starting back at cave paintings, it would be very beneficial if we had some means of communicating better. To draw a picture would allow us to see what we are gathered for. They say that some of these caves were the place where the men used to gather and plan their hunting campaigns. In *The Seven Daughters of Eve*, Bryan Sykes has some inventive stories that he uses to express this. I will call it a type of school, for my purposes.

If you were to teach your younger tribe members how to hunt an antelope, for instance, you could "show" in picture form where to best strike it for the kill. Let's look at this for a moment. In analog form, a picture is drawn. Remembering the puzzle analogy, it is now possible to digitalize the picture, while at the same time digitalize the calls or cries, or alter the now digitalized new sounds or consonants. This would eventually lead to naming the parts of the animal.

To be clear here, it would not cause it to happen. It would allow it to happen, by pushing for a different sound to describe the different parts of the body. It could, for the same reason, carry over into describing the front area of the beast as opposed to the rear area of the beast. You would need to be able to say, "Get in front of it and make it change its direction and head for us, the trap." This would help account for the Wernicke's area I wrote about earlier, which is believed to be an action-to-word area of the brain. Using an English example here to differentiate *re* (from *re*ar), or ro (from *fro*nt), say, would be advantageous.

Without citation, most of the literature on cave paintings has at best concluded them to be places of ceremony ritual, rites to becoming a man, or a caveman actually dancing around a fire demonstrating how to kill whatever animal was painted on the cave walls. Why not simply conclude school? Worth a mention before going on is that there were not only pictures but also lines or dots. I have no suggestion yet. Having our Adam and Eve teaching their descendants what they have learned, within the safety of a cave, makes much more sense to me.

Brought to my attention from the book mentioned earlier, *Reading in the Brain*, where I said I might need to defend my ideas later (I don't), there were also hands painted. These hands, as he supposes, not unlike myself, were signs of some kind. They were commonly thought to be missing fingers. Dehaene assumes for sign language of some sort, but I go further and add some kind of sound to them as well. Sorry, no suggestions on the sounds. This leaves us open for building our language, both verbally and in written form, discussed better below. Dehaene does an excellent job on written language and reading, and it should be interesting to you if you follow the language argument at all. All this language and writing also impose a problem to be examined first.

Inspired by the neuroscientific research of Richard Sperry, Edwards taught that the "verbal," "logical," and "analytical" left hemisphere perceives in ways that actually interfere with drawing and tends to overpower the right hemisphere, which is better at drawing. (Norman Doidge, MD, *The Brain That Changes Itself*, 281)

This might seem to counter my theory of analyzing "art" into language, but it really is not. As I must defend these kinds of counterstatements, I might as well bring them up myself. If we take these caves to be classrooms, and the art, once it has been drawn, as permanent, the whole of our analytical abilities need not be in conflict with drawing the art at all. There does not need to be any conflict between these two brain areas or hemispheres in either of the two cases: drawing them or analyzing them. It also does not reconcile the problem of writing when scrutinized under my microscope. Have you ever seen the hieroglyphics of Egypt, or other places like South and Central America? They are for the most part pictures! They evolved into symbols and then letters, which are in reality just different pictures from a different source. The Chinese still use pictures for words, which we call characters or symbols. They differ only in that they have become symbols representing concepts of language, which is actually, as I have explained, dealt with in the left hemisphere, the Wernicke's area. There is no real or imagined reason that drawing symbols as pictures could not become wired under an analytical force, drawing from one brain area and wiring them into a separate brain area if the pressure is great enough. There is also no real or imagined reason that the first "picture" area has to modify itself in any way to accommodate the process. It only has to mix into another area, taking inputs from art—to art they would be outputs and not affect the setup it has—and inputs from language, making them symbolic in another area of the brain.

If we then take the difference in written communication and liken it unto how language changed, we see that it would fit conclusions well enough. Whole pictures would be as whole, complete concepts. Pictures become transformed into hieroglyphics, which have vague concepts enough to add into crude sentence structure. Then, as language proceeds, letters are invented to claim concept of these sounds, replacing the more vague symbols. In doing so, it would make words as writable as they are speakable for the most clear and specific meaning possible, as opposed to the vagueness of hieroglyphics. In this analyzing process, the symbols would become part of communication, separate from drawing, and any drawing for pleasure without communication factor would still "interfere" with these above-mentioned abilities: analytical, logical, and verbal. The same author has in the same book his own counter equating to what I have just written.

This theory provides an elegant bridge between localizationist emphasis on things tending to happen in certain typical localizations, and the neuroplasticians' emphasis on the brain's ability to restructure itself.

What it implies is that people learning a new skill can recruit *operators* devoted to other activities, vastly increasing their processing power, provided they can create a *roadblock* between the operator they need and its usual function. (Norman Doidge, MD, *The Brain That Changes Itself*, 212, emphasis mine)

There is no real problem, then, to get writing from art as long as it is roadblocked, and I believe the roadblock to be our attention, analyzing the art and language at the same time.

The hieroglyphics in Egypt, South America, and Australia use some pictures as well as symbols to "speak" in writing. Clay cuneiform is found around Mesopotamia, and they use symbols as words and numbers. Actually, they used the same or close to the same symbol placed in different groupings and orientations. I will remind the reader that we use Roman letters in English and most other languages today. The Chinese stuck with symbols. The Greeks used symbols for letters, but to us they look like symbols only because we are used to looking at our symbols, which we call letters. In reality, they are symbols too.

When we look at the template of going from cave painting, to symbols, to letters, it reminds me of the process that language has undergone, if my thesis is close to the right answer. In comparison, we use the Arabic number system almost worldwide as the best system of counting; the Chinese still have their own number system. For us, Roman letters and Arabic numbers became our systems because they were easy. Roman numerals were hard to use. Actually, the Arabic number system is originally from India. I'll get back to the writing issue later, as I want to touch on the brain relationship here.

This would be directly related to faith comes by hearing, and knowledge comes by seeing. When you see something for yourself, you know it to be true. When someone tells you something you haven't seen, you need to believe that person; this is faith. If you read something, you get both knowledge and faith at work, but it only leads to faith and not necessarily knowledge; it could be true or false. A picture is a bit different, as it is not a symbol used to relate something. As you see the words written, your brain actually sounds the words out and your brain actually *hears them*, through your eyes. The letter symbols are actually sounds to the brain. As faith comes through hearing, it leads to believing what you read and not knowing with certainty what you read. It places a kind of conflict where one should not be. On the other hand, you are more likely to know what you hear if enough people are saying the same things or writing the same things.

I don't want to deal with the higher processes and be that exact, as I am only looking for speech, not brain studies. If you hands are writing these symbols as your voice is commanding, then it makes sense that your brain area in charge of rationalizing would need to be developed into the writing role. You need to learn the shapes and analyze each part of the symbol to make high-fidelity symbols match the sounds every time.

That said, we can hypothetically account for the fact that we "hear" words when we read. It accounts nicely for the Wernicke's area part of the brain. It makes sense of knowledge coming through the eyes and believing coming through the ears. Plus the fact that because of sight, what is written is revealed to us at the same time, albeit at lesser levels. This is known as revelations. What is revelation but the dawning of what you see becoming knowledge?

I mentioned above that pictures are different. They are different in that they pose a reality, thus knowledge. A picture would be close enough to a real object. Now, for the first time, this real object would become a unique concept, and a name placed upon it would benefit every student of the cave.

> Attaching words to these concepts, of course, allows one to share one's hard-won discoveries and insights about the world with the less experienced or the less observant. Figuring out which word to attach to which concept is the *gavagai* problem, and if infants started out with concepts corresponding to the kinds of meanings that languages use, the problem is partly solved. (Steven Pinker, *The Language Instinct*)

Now with the ability to analyze words and the world for separate concepts, we could take what we do know and use these as tools. I will shortly use a parable from the Bible as an example, as it is a good source for parables.

Metaphor was the only way to communicate anything, above the naturally occurring sound complete concepts. These had to start small by going into metaphors, then into complete stories in the forms of parable, analogy, proverbs, and such, which are all the same in one sense. They are used to compare one concept with another in more or less detail. As I covered some material on metaphors in an earlier chapter, I will not bore you with it here. I will only make the observation that metaphor can be expanded on.

First I will give you this example of an analogy. I used the computer system of the automobile as a template for the explanation of the brain functioning. I did not mention it there, but it is easier to talk about separate modules if they are in fact separate. The home computers cannot be talked about without extensive knowledge and lots of writing. The modules are already separate in the automobile and named, so it makes things easier to explain. I now call it an analogy, while biting my tongue, instead of template.

The analogy on computers was a complicated one, and we need to start smaller, like to describe in our ancestors' terms—before counting arose—number. If I wanted to communicate that I saw a greater number of sheep to my clan, I could use whatever communication I had for sheep and state that they were in quantity, like the handful of pebbles I just picked up: many. I'd be using the "many" pebbles as an analogy for "many" sheep. This gives rise to the saying "They were as numerous as the sands of the sea." At least until language or, in this case, math can catch up and name them billions or trillions. Now for the parable:

> For the kingdom of heaven is like unto a man that is an householder, which went out early in the morning to hire labourers into his vineyard. And when he had agreed with the labourers for a penny a day, he sent them into his vineyard. And he went out about the third hour, and saw others standing idle in the market place, and said unto them; go ye also into the vineyard, and whatsoever is right I will give you. And they went their way. Again about the sixth and ninth hour, and did likewise. And about the eleventh hour he went out, and found others standing idle, and said unto them, why stand ye here all the day idle? They say unto him, because no man hath hired us. He saith unto them, go ye also into the vineyard; and whatsoever is right, that shall ye receive. So when even was come, the lord of the vineyard saith unto his steward, call the labourers, and give them their hire, beginning with the last unto the first. And when they came that were hired about the eleventh hour, they received every man a penny. But when the first came, they supposed that they

should have received more; and they likewise received every man a penny. (Matt. 20:1–10)

I will stop the quote here, although there is more to it. This is all I need of the parable to explain the use of parables. Every man who had to earn a living would have known all about vineyards. Any man who ever worked for another would have known all about wages. Many would have been familiar with the concept that if you only work a part day, you only receive a part day's salary. Fine, so far. It is now used to express a concept about heaven: "For the kingdom of heaven is like." The wages or salary is eternal life. Every man who partakes of heaven gets the same wages: eternal life. You can't divide eternal life into part-eternal life. You either get the full thing or not at all. It does not matter at what point you partake of heaven; you can only receive eternal life, nothing more, nothing less. When eternal life is a concept and it is hard to explain, you use a parable or parallel example to explain it for you. The parable is used to communicate something you do not understand or conceive, using something that is commonplace. If you were to cut a penny in half today, for a half day's wages, the penny would be worthless.

Why would I go through the effort of writing both a parable and an analogy when they are the same? I will point out the major difference. An analogy is the strict use of using one example to explain another example. A parable is actually telling a story that relates the two different examples. To turn my analogy into a parable, I would have had to start it out like this: There was once a man who wanted to design a better mode of transportation ... A story or myth would possibly be easier to remember and pass along.

The main thing we need to remember here is that concepts are best explained as other more familiar concepts are used to explain them. If we had another concept at the beginning, a homology, and realized that we could use another innate sample to overlay upon this homology, already known sounds would be used for the same purpose—to describe the ways it is similar to a preexisting concept. This would make them analogies fit for yet more overlays onto other homologies, analogies, and even different concepts altogether.

At any rate, the examples I have used are both large ones. The first parables, fables, or other methods of metaphor most certainly would have started out smaller than these. At some point, language would have become kick-started into full sentences, leading to stories. I suggest that this starting point was the dissection of complete concept, innate with a sound-word, becoming both sound altered and conceptually altered, eventually leading to what I have termed as a sound-cliché: speaking in digital form. This would be our language niche.

It takes a few steps to get there, though, and I will examine only a few random ones:

> Of special interest in this connection is the relationship between *context* and its content. A phoneme exists as such only in combination with other phonemes which make up a word. The word is the *context* of the phoneme. But the word only exists as such—only has "meaning"—in the larger context of the utterance, which again has meaning only in a relationship. (Gregory Bateson, *Steps to an Ecology of Mind*)

To take something in context is to say that you need witness the situation, understand the situation, and be able to remove any one part of the situation for separate examination as it relates to the whole, reassembling it back to its whole. This is the only way to get the whole meaning, the separate meaning, and relate it back to the whole meaning. This puts pressure on language, but more importantly, the mutual understanding of that language.

I will use some terms with some explanation because of the importance of them. I believe that turn-constructional unit (TCU), or *turn-taking*, might have arisen in the first place because of the need to guarantee that the same concepts were interacted upon. Turn-taking is where one person stops talking and the next person starts talking, with cues given for when it is appropriate for the other person to speak. When we need to make certain that another person has the exact same concept for the word used—in context, of course—we make him repeat it. I have shown in my analytics that we sound alter words. If we want the same secondary concept to be derived, we must gesture, show, or whatever other method suits the situation, while sounding the proper form of alteration. The other person must also repeat the sounds with the gestures ... There would be a natural time lapse of a fraction of a second, which would become the cue to repeat. Learning to dissect calls and cries into sound-words, then into sound-clichés, would require turn taking as a basis for understanding the changes taking place. It would not have to be innate.

> Fox argues that "it is not just that a particular language is deployed to fulfill the needs of turn-taking; rather that language is almost certainly shaped by turn-taking needs." (*The Interactional Instinct*, Namhee Lee et al.)

These only show that they are necessary for getting the complete thoughts of others and not really a driving force for the selection of language's innate structure. If anything, it shows that language arose as the best form of communicating knowledge or the dissection of knowledge. If we needed to wait until the full idea being constructed was complete before acknowledging it, we would never know if we understood what was being said. By Adam repeating Eve, or Eve repeating Adam before moving on to the next aspect of the conversation taking place, turn-taking would supply the needed cognitive time. It also gives us time to ask a question for clarity and add our own observations to what is being analyzed. This, in short, only ensures that we are on the same page.

We now see that as learning improved, our Adam and Eve, out of habit, would continue to pause, making sure that each one knew that the other one knew. Written like this, we can see the seeds of knowing that you know what I know, and I know that you know, in the highest form possible. Some authors make a case that most primates have the base of knowing that others know. I only suggest the seeds for the highest form, not its beginnings.

Another area I will address will be rebracketing, as mentioned in *The Interactional Instinct*. The authors use the example of *orange* being derived from [a [narangi]] becoming [an [orange]] through reinterpretation.

They also acknowledge that words change from mishearing the sounds, and words change from using them in different context. I do not have to deny either of these conditions, as I can accept any changes to or by cultural interaction without denying this. I can assert that these too are there from learning.

Mishearing I can do nothing with; it is what it is. Words changing their meanings from using them in different context I have actually dealt with already. I will elaborate a little. Using metaphor in relating a thought, allows a single sound or phoneme to represent that thought or concept. Then by adding one more sound to an existing sound, or altering the existing sound into another sound, would let that metaphor change concepts. Compare it to sentences by adding words. Thus, words would change from using them in different context naturally. I can allow for sounds to change for their better sounding effect, or I can allow for the effect of rebracketing combining words differently.

I have already used rebracketing in another chapter, showing how one complete concept would hold along with the secondary concept and then become silent [food [apple]], if you remember, having the food part become silent. Slightly different, you say? True, but after all, we do have to have a basis for the evolution of language to happen. This is the purpose of this chapter.

Another example is something that I have not mentioned yet. All sound based calls and cries would have an innate base, but what of concepts with no sounds? The word foot is innately known to all who possess one, and to the best of my knowledge, it has no sound—unless you squeak when you walk. This forms an avenue for names placed after the fact, to be chosen originally by concept of what it does. By example, foot might be named for what it does: stand. However:

> As for wheel, proto-Indo-European is thought to have had a word *kwel, meaning to turn or twist, of which *kwekwlos is assumed to be a duplication. But it could be that proto-Indo-European had no word for wheel, and what happened was that its daughter languages each independently used their inherited *kwel/turn words to form their own words for wheel. (Nicholas Wade; *Before the Dawn*; each asterisk indicates a reconstructed word)

This is quite a different innate process from getting a name for turn in the first place. A wheel could never have become an innate concept. Nor could past evolve into a concept of time. Time evolving into past is the only way to get a tense change and have it learned: at least in placing a name on them. On the other hand, everyone knows what it means to turn, which is an innate concept even if not a named one. First the innate concept would become named, then the name transferred to the wheel. Speaking it correctly would get it hardwired into the brain in proper form, or an altered sound concept.

I really make only two claims here. First, a sound comes to represent a complete concept, and these first level sounds—calls and cries, are innate. Second, the new altered sounds are not completely innate, but only secondarily innate with the new altered sound containing the altered concept, and must be learned as separated. Then they can be placed upon appropriate objects or subjects.

Placing names on objects makes them communicable. Placing the concept name on an object gets us a wheel. Placing an imitated sound on a bird—chickadee—gives it a name for communication purposes, just as placing the name honey on bee jelly does. I might point out that it is so much easier to communicate subjects and objects if they are named. I also pointed out that many feelings and concepts are understood without actually having the names of them as part of your vocabulary. Naming things does have a value: we could even argue that it's a survival value. As discussed already, if we are in fact poor at primal survival, then our communication in the form of language would need to become our stronghold on the world. We can make more sounds than any other animal and, by extension, have more innate concepts than any other animals.

Next up, I will lightly consider divergence of languages as a recap only, starting with tenses, which Chomsky pointed out. These different tenses could have become slightly different sound alterations in many brains even within the smaller clans and common community. As we dealt mostly with space/time, conveying it with the tilogoi *v*, I will give an example of two different end results meaning the exact same thing. *Ve* and *ov* could have the same meaning: both ways of saying *past*, for example. The curvy French girl next door might invite your English ass for dinner. She would understand the *v* portions of the word, as would you at first, but she would have a different tense, or sense of it. As words grew larger, they could have led to two different languages as they diverged. Or they could have battled as to which one would become the surviving meme. I favor the programmed key concept mentioned earlier. The seats positions were programmed to the individual drivers' keys. Why would different languages be any different here?

Wow, I seem to have gone astray here, but we need to rehearse these notions and proceed with the whole of language. I have suggested that stop shorts were replacing calls and cries, and were understood to be replacing them. Cave art might have been classrooms for learning at these first origins of articulation. Concept names became secondary concept names slightly altered, then in some form placed upon subjects and objects. I think, personally anyway, that language can only *evolve* so much, innately, and any higher refinements would have come about from another source or process. The "second story" I used in the grammar chapter on proper order would be as refined as language would ever have needed to get in order to be a survival value.

Henri Bergson said, "The eye sees only what the mind is prepared to comprehend," and we sometimes overlook important facts. "Is You Is Or Is You Ain't My Baby" was the title of a popular Louis Jordan song in our not-all-that-distant past, the 1940s. I must be missing something in evolving language. Everyone can understand this and knows exactly what he was saying: Are you or are you not my sweetheart? It does not need to evolve past this poor grammar to be understood. I honestly believe that a better sounding form had as much to do with language evolving as communication had. We must admit to mishearing the proper sounds also. I have read comments on better sounding ways of articulating a word—euphonia gratia—changing the sound of the word, but not the meaning. That could be one answer for words changing, but applying the same reasoning to sentences changing works just as well.

There is a great example within writing itself. You need to think more and formulate better what you are saying when you write it down than when you are just speaking to someone. I believe this for two reasons: one, you can go back and fill in the missing data when someone doesn't understand your *spoken utterance*; two, you also see what is being said when you write.

This made me think about a problem I could not solve with the high level of grammar we have currently acquired. That is to say, we speak smooth, complete sentences, with most of the details included within the sentence. It has become known that Socrates hated writing and thought it would ruin their passing on the myths by proper word of mouth. On the other hand, Plato, Socrates's student, did make full use of writing. All older forms of writing were slightly vague or crude in form; think of hieroglyphics. Going from art, to letting hieroglyphic symbols represent concepts, down to alphabetic symbols is for sure an evolution of mass proportions. Why not let language ride on this back?

When you are speaking, it does not really matter whether or not you get the perfect point across; as with continued effort and speech, you can fill in the missing information. In a novel, the author can make any character say anything in any way he or she chooses. Because this book is not a novel, I must be as accurate as I can be in one sentence, then move on to the next. In fact, this Microsoft word that I am using flags me with green underlines whenever I have fragmented sentences, thank God. The longest part of writing this book is getting them to be "not green" anymore. Red either! This is the price you pay for two-finger typing.

A novel might have a character saying, for instance, "I got one too—I mean, a banana, that is—back at the store. He went to the store, and I went with him, my friend, that is, and got the banana. He went to the store for batteries, and I got my banana when he went." We would see by this that the character might be a little confused, but I have no doubts that this just might have been the way language was performed in the beginning, only a little cruder. It would have been much easier to say, "My friend went to the store to get some batteries, and I went with him and bought a banana at the same time."

I know I promised no math, but I count forty-seven words in the first statement and only twenty-three words in the second statement. The second statement was a lot more clearly stated (and no green underlines). Could the invention of writing have pushed language to take its better form? If for no other reason, it would take longer to write your properly conceived sentences, as you would not be able to make corrections as easily, forcing the clarifications required in getting the proper point across to be done before commitment to paper. Writing would become quite complicated and would lead to a writing system that remedied the problem. Take the time to better formulate your thoughts and write them down with fewer words in clearer form.

Writing very much needs to be taught and is not at all innate, as I have so many times read or heard. When children are taught to write, they also learn how to speak properly as part of the process. I for one wonder if this is just a strange coincidence or if it is how all these "rules" came about in the first place. Remember what I said about language and grammar becoming only so innate? For the life of me, I could not see any need for language to become perfected on its own. (Define perfection, after all.) The minimum we need to say to get a point across and what we now say with education are two different processes. We only really need word order to be innate, not smooth continuum. The old symbols of drawings and hieroglyphics would have also served this same purpose, in a more vague way.

Plato indeed got it part right. He claimed that the state made new words as needed. I suspect proper words were taught by and passed along by the words discoverers, those who made the words, as these words arose in our ancient societies. The words were then added to and altered in meaning as they arose. Maybe the elders who taught in the caves creating these new words became part of Plato's thinking, relayed through myth.

The innate bases whence it sprung was from all our innate capacities, combining into one dawning. That is, we could separate things to talk about them. The brain is digital in all vertebrate; most mammals have speech of some sort: calls or cries. Chimps learn to use tools as an extension of themselves. It is only with man's extra layer of soul, as it were, that dissecting or analyzing was realized. When the tools are all present for other purposes, it only takes a selective push to force potential into reality. One unused brain increase, caused by one gene mutation, was the suggestion I had made.

Forever after, every time man did something he would not only be dissecting but also naming whatever he was dissecting. Applying the same natural process to both speaking and learning how everything around us worked, then applying both to our advantage, would raise us to the top of the animal kingdom.

Most of the ideas throughout this book are not original with me, but I find that they mix well with the general thesis of my work. In some cases, I have left the ideas to hold their own meanings, and in other cases, I have altered the ideas to my own purpose. I am not an expert in any of these fields, and I could be mistaken in some areas. In other areas, I am sure the facts are right. As for my own ideas, I continue to try and find support for them. We have self-selected not only for wisdom but also for the truth of knowledge to be sought out.

As an afterthought, I was thinking about symbols (sounds), and it dawned on me that I should check out going from speaking symbols to writing symbols. I thought about that wonderful—and now overworked—letter *v*. I used it as a starting point: time, out of, into, and the like. I also realize what a perfect shaped letter it is for the time concept/space concept. As a symbol, it is used to show the concepts of lesser than or greater than, by lying on its side one way (<) or the other (>). It starts with nothing at the bottom and expands as it rises. It is used in the tree of life, as a branching method, becoming a *y*, and I could think of no better symbol to use in its stead.

Appendix I

In talking about evolving words from single sources, there does seem to be a hint of it happening when examining the myths. These are discussed in the scientific literature. It makes a good source for words also, so I will include it as an appendix.

In Ritual and Religion in the Making of Humanity, Roy A. Rappaport, while speaking about myths, mentions some growing of concepts, which come from a single source and evolve into many concepts. One of these cases fit with words so well, as I have been using them, that is, so I will use the example here.

Christ is not, in this conception, simply the word, but the living word, and *Memra* is not merely word, but *utterance*—breathed word. It is of interest to note here that the nuer word for God, *Kwoth*, derives from the word breath, as do Latinate spirit (from *spirate*, to breathe) and the Greek form *pneuma.* The Hebrew *Ruah Elohim*, the primordial wind that sweeps the formless waste in the first lines of Genesis, may be rendered as the breath as well as the wind of God, and *Ruah* carries the meaning of spirit as well as breath and wind. It was, moreover, *Ruah* that God breathed into the earth (*Adamah*) that was to become man (*Adam*) and finally the first particular man, Adam.

He goes on to mention more peoples who have the basis of creation founded on the wind or breath:

We may recall here that for the Navajo it is not word or language or thought that finally orders the world. It is utterance or speech. Now speech in the Navajo view itself partakes of substance as well as form, for the Navajo take air to be a substance.

I will elaborate somewhat. At the very least, air can be felt, so we can understand that it exists. When someone blows on you, you can feel it as wind. We can't live without breathing, so it seems a natural "knowledge" that air equals life, which would also come to be called, in some cases, spirit. The use of one word, or that word slightly altered in form, would come to mean all of the above.

The problem has always been, where did the original word come from in the first place? My answer is that the general word "wind," in its different language specific forms, is made up of a complete meaning of the separate phonemes added together in the first instance. We say wind or breathe because we have different words to choose from today, but originally they did not. The word could literally mean this: W = air, I = move, N = with, D = force. When I say literally, I don't mean the word wind, but that wind's original word form, which we may never know, is to be taken literally. Wind is only a current word used here, as I don't know the original word form.

On this account, we find that it would now fit all the categories. Wind moves about the air with force; your lungs move the air about with force; and the prime mover (spirit) moves your body about with force.

If words evolved as I have suggested, then this would become a natural occurrence, with many concepts and words throughout many different languages on all continents. It would also explain the reduction in letters—properly, phonemes—in words like *Adamah*, meaning breathed into earth, giving rise to *Adam*, meaning breathed into species, and this finally ending with Adam, the actual bona fide name of the first man.

More to the point, almost all myths use some form of wind moving upon the waters as a creation story: all time and space are supposed to have come about by this procedure. Time and space were well used in my examples, so I won't dwell further here. What is interesting is that they have it backwards. Time and space cause wind. It does not take much to see that wind moves the clouds, smoke from fires, dust from the ground, and makes waves on water. It's a creation force. How many conclusions—secondary concepts—could be drawn from the blowing of the wind? I don't think you would need ten innate concepts to start with: time and space are enormous and can or do account for the bulk of our knowledge—and, I think, words as well.

The English word "time" derives its meaning from the Indo-European root *di*, "to divide," and I must conclude that if we are to refer to any point in a continuum, that continuum must be divided. Almost every culture has their own word for year. Some cultures use the word for rice, which is planted and harvested twice a year, to stand for the time period, making them six-month cycles or six-month years to us. However, the real point here is that all people have some form of time, be it "punctual" or "durational." I have also come to believe that this first set of words derived for time or place was in fact derived from a common "call" innate to our species.

Finally, from above, wind as a prime mover would have, in our ancestors' minds, the power to cause time and space to move or become created. Just look at the relationship here and it seems inevitable to have happened this way: cause and effect, derived from time/space.

Appendix II

I have done the best that I can to explain my thesis, and even as I have been writing this book, I've tried to keep current. I was not kidding when I referred to *The Other Brain* as a new read. Also, while writing, I could not resist *Reading in the Brain* when I saw it. I noticed that Steven Pinker has another book out on language, and I have not even had time to buy it. The reason is that I am currently trying to finish another book I just bought: *Descartes' Error*, by Antonio Damasio.

I swore to myself that I would have these revisions of the manuscript off to the publisher before or on 11/11/11, as a nice number to remember. I am on page 162 of 267 pages. Since it is now November 10 and the corrections are made and ready to go, I don't have any more time to incorporate additional material. I have already used one quote from Damasio's book while making my revisions, but that was just a supportive quote. The information on page 162 of *Descartes' Error* is very close to what I have used in my book for another purpose. I would have too many alterations to do to incorporate the work of Damasio. I will therefore take the quote from where I just stopped reading and add commentary after.

This sense of precise cause-and-effect may arise from activity in convergence zones that perform a mutual brokerage between body signals and signals about the entity causing the emotion. Convergence zones operate as "third-party" brokers by means of the reciprocal feedforward and feedback connections they maintain with their sources of input. The players in my proposed arrangement are an explicit representation of the *causative entity*; an explicit representation of the *current body state*; and a *third-party representation*. In other words, the brain activity that signals a certain entity and transiently forms a topographically organized representation in early somatosensory cortices; and a representation, located in a convergence zone, that receives signals from those first two sites of brain activity, by feedforward neural connections. This third-party representation preserves the order of the onset of brain activity, and in addition maintains activity and attentional focus by means of feedback connections to the sites of brain activity. Signals among the three players lock the ensemble in relatively synchronous activity, for a brief period. In all likelihood, this process requires cortical and subcortical structures, namely those in the thalamus. (*Descartes' Error*, Antonio Damasio).

You will note here that Damasio's theory is in the same spirit I have used in my analytics when separating the sounds and concepts into a third-party persona, complete with a sound and meaning change. I could ignore it completely, but it does show that I was not too far off of the mark. I need to find as much proof as I can to support my theory, and this is support. Here, Damasio is referring to emotions and how they are interrupted by the brain. He, unlike me, does this for a living, and I am glad I found a similar if not identical resolve for a problem of a different kind. As noted in the text, I did place an insert within the main text as evidence for another topic.

This manuscript will definitely be sent out on my November 11 self-imposed deadline, but I will not have completed reading Damasio's work. It may upset the publisher a bit, but if I find more support before this goes to print, I may be adding another appendix or two.

Incidentally, Damasio, in the same book, does an excellent job discussing Phineas Gage and the soul in the first few chapters.

Endnotes

Chapter One: The Baldwin effect has both pros and cons argued well in *Evolution and Learning: The Baldwin Effect Reconsidered*; several authors, edited by Bruce H. Weber and David J. Depew

How the Mind Works by Steven Pinker is also worth the read in understanding how important having innate knowledge is, and how it is believed to be done with shapes under the two scenarios I commented on. I did not do it justice.

The sounds of many insects (tanana) and birds are well described and worth the read in *The Naturalist on the River Amazons*, by Henry Walter Bates.

Chapter Three: Cognates, as well as a genetic time frame for the appearance of language, are discussed in *Before the Dawn* by Nicholas Wade. He also discusses the other genes that are believed to make language possible.

I also had a few more runs on words that I could have used but neglected to. If you don't get what is being implied with a few dozen examples, more will not make a difference.

The Third Chimpanzee: Jared Diamond has a lot of content on languages changing around the world and through time.

Chapter Four: The information on the computer systems of vehicles can be found in more detail on the Internet, freely accessed to anyone. Just type in "GM high-speed LAN" and pick a site. Official GM site is only accessed via password. (LAN may be familiar to most readers because other companies use its technology.)

One can only go so deeply into a topic that many people will not understand. I therefore did not delve too deeply into electrical car systems—just enough for the reader to hopefully understand the concept of separate modules communicating on a single wire for the purpose of less "noise" in the systems, but still sharing data throughout the entire system.

Chapter Five: I could not figure any other biological way to explain the need to change strategies for forming different objectives. The change needed to go from yolk sac to placenta, in my mind, was the same needed to go from calls in analog to digital in speech. It fit both a need and a method to handle this complexity.

Chapter Six: Both *The Other Brain* by R. Douglas Fields and *The Mind and the Brain* by Jeffrey M. Schwartz give excellent details on the working of the brain in intricate detail. They were indispensable to my thinking and rethinking

Phineas Gage has information on one of the most documented case studies on brain damage; visit the following website: www.deakin.edu.au/hbs/GAGEPAGE

Too many aspects go into making a mind or a soul, and I had to choose the ones that I thought best.

Chapter Seven: *Mirroring People* by Marco Iacoboni gives a wonderful explanation on the actual processes the brain uses to form mirroring. I only needed to show disconnect for the purposes of words and did not go into detail, but I refer the reader to his book.

Emotional intelligence is well explained in *On Being Certain* by Robert A. Burton, who shows how, from within, we make our beliefs real but not necessarily true. He explains well the feeling of knowing and hidden areas, for those interested in reading up on the subject.

Chapter Ten: I honestly never thought of how many concepts you would need until I read *Adam's Tongue*. I don't want the reader to think that the concepts I discussed are in any way ipso facto. There is a danger to stating these as fact, which is why none were stated in *Adam's Tongue*: the author knew better. I have taken the chance and might live to regret it. That said, of all of the concepts I did list, I am certain that time and space was one of those must-have concepts that would be on anyone's list. Before this list was brought to my attention, I'd worked in my mind with only the concept of time/space as being the most important one for survival: where and when. Try to make your own list and see what difficulty it poses.

Chapter Twelve: Biblical Hebrew was not written with vowels like YHVH, which is either pronounced Jehovah or Yahweh. This does not mean that the ancient Hebrews did not speak with vowels, use them for stop short, or otherwise include them. They just did not write with them. It also could be that some true words were without vowels and the consonants were stop short in their own right. I was more interested in showing poor communication, with one word representing two or three senses and the need to evolve another word for the other sense.

Note also that YHVH means either "I am that I am" or, better interpreted, "I am that am." If in this case the two *H*s meant "am," depicting place in time, now, continuum; and the *V* meant "that," again, out of time or place; it would leave the *Y* to mean "I," time-and-place-now-time-and-place and would become "I am that I am," depicting eternal.

Chapter Thirteen: *Biomimicry* by Janine M. Benyus has many accounts of copying nature in all aspects and among animals themselves. There is a chapter on healing, finding cures like a chimp. If you venture to read the book, keep in mind how many individual efforts and how much accumulative knowledge went into finding all the answers to how nature works. In the book are examples of other animals also learning from nature.

It is hard without having any idea where our knowledge of things came from originally. Many examples that are current to our collective knowledge could have been used. No one really knows the true story of where it all started because lots would have had to have been discovered before it finally dawned on an individual to pass these things along. Sorry, but no record means making your own, as hard as that is to do.

www.ingramcontent.com/pod-product-compliance
Lightning Source LLC
Chambersburg PA
CBHW031233090426
42742CB00007B/179

* 9 7 8 0 9 9 2 1 5 9 4 0 5 *